PENGUIN BOOKS

AND ANOTHER THING . . .

Jeremy Clarkson began his writing career on the *Rotherham Advertiser*.
Since then he has written for the *Sun*, the *Sunday Times*, the *Rochdale
Observer*, the *Wolverhampton Express and Star*, all of the Associated Kent
Newspapers, and *Lincolnshire Life*. Today he is the tallest person
working in British television.

Jeremy Clarkson's other books are *Clarkson's Hot 100*, *Clarkson on
Cars*, *Motorworld*, *Planet Dagenham*, *The World According to Clarkson*
and *I Know You Got Soul*.

And Another Thing . . .

*The World According to Clarkson
Volume Two*

JEREMY CLARKSON

PENGUIN BOOKS

PENGUIN BOOKS

Published by the Penguin Group
Penguin Books Ltd, 80 Strand, London WC2R 0RL, England
Penguin Group (USA) Inc., 375 Hudson Street, New York, New York 10014, USA
Penguin Group (Canada), 90 Eglinton Avenue East, Suite 700, Toronto, Ontario, Canada M4P 2Y3
(a division of Pearson Penguin Canada Inc.)
Penguin Ireland, 25 St Stephen's Green, Dublin 2, Ireland (a division of Penguin Books Ltd)
Penguin Group (Australia), 250 Camberwell Road, Camberwell, Victoria 3124, Australia
(a division of Pearson Australia Group Pty Ltd)
Penguin Books India Pvt Ltd, 11 Community Centre, Panchsheel Park, New Delhi – 110 017, India
Penguin Group (NZ), 67 Apollo Drive, Rosedale, North Shore 0632, New Zealand
(a division of Pearson New Zealand Ltd)
Penguin Books (South Africa) (Pty) Ltd, 24 Sturdee Avenue, Rosebank, Johannesburg 2196, South Africa

Penguin Books Ltd, Registered Offices: 80 Strand, London WC2R 0RL, England

www.penguin.com

First published by Michael Joseph 2006
Published in Penguin Books 2007

4

Copyright © Jeremy Clarkson, 2006
All rights reserved.

The moral right of the author has been asserted

The contents of this book previously appeared in Jeremy Clarkson's *Sunday Times* columns.

Set by Rowland Phototypesetting Ltd, Bury St Edmunds, Suffolk
Printed in England by Clays Ltd, St Ives plc

ISBN: 978-0-141-02860-6

To Andy Wilman

The contents of this book first appeared in Jeremy Clarkson's *Sunday Times* column. Read more about the world according to Clarkson every week in the *Sunday Times*

Contents

I'm a nobody, my jet-set credit card tells me so

I suppose all of us were out and about before Christmas, pummelling our credit cards to within an inch of their lives. So, some time in the next week or so, we can expect a sour-faced government minister to come on television to explain that we are now borrowing more than we're saving and that it has all got to stop.

In the mid-1970s, shortly after credit cards first emerged, we owed £32 million.

Now we've managed to get ourselves into debt to the tune of £50 billion, which works out at about £1,140 for every adult in the land.

As a result, the economy is teetering on the brink of collapse and little old ladies are having to sell their cats for medical experiments. And children are being lured into prostitution and up chimneys. It's all too awful for words.

But there's a darker side to credit cards. A sinister underbelly that is rarely talked about. I'm talking about the misery of not having the right one.

We've all been there. Dinner is over, the bill has arrived and everyone is chucking their plastic on to the saucer. It's a sea of platinum and gold. One chap has produced something with a Wells Fargo stagecoach on the front. Another has come up with an HM Government procurement card, just like James Bond would have.

And then it's your turn. And all you've got is your green NatWest Switch card.

Socially speaking, you are about to die. Or are you?

A couple of years ago I read an interview with some chap who'd got a fistful of cards in his pocket and claimed that the more shiny examples, specifically the much-coveted black American Express, gave him 'certain privileges'.

Obviously, I had to have one. So I lied about my salary, handed over 650 bleeding quid, and there it was, in a leatherette box, presented like a fine Tiffany earring. My very own passport to the high life.

A few weeks later I was flying economy class to some godforsaken hell hole – I forget where – and found myself sitting in one of those oyster bars at Heathrow, fielding questions from men in nylon trousers about Volkswagen diesels. After a while I remembered the black 'key' in my wallet and recalled a bit in the booklet that said it opened the door to airline lounges around the world.

So, I plodded over to the club class lounge with my cattle class boarding ticket.

'I'm afraid not,' said the woman cheerfully.

'Aha,' I countered, 'but I have a black American Express card which affords me certain privileges.'

It didn't. So I went back to the diesel men at the oyster bar.

A month after that I was checking in at Blakes Hotel in Amsterdam when, again, I remembered the card and thought: 'I wonder if this will get me a room upgrade.'

Joy of joys, it did. All I had to do was check into one of the emperor suites at £1 trillion a night and I would be automatically upgraded to a maharajah suite, with the enlarged minibar, at no extra cost. So, off to the economy broom cupboard I went.

As the months went by, I kept producing the jet-set, jet-black Amex and the result was pretty much always the same. 'Non.' . . . 'Nein.' And in provincial Britain: 'What the f★★★'s that?'

Actually, I'm being unfair. It wasn't only provincial Britain that was mystified.

Pretty well everywhere east of New York and west of Los Angeles doesn't take Amex, no matter what colour the card is. Some say this is because Amex charges too much.

Others because the Americans are infidel dogs.

Eventually, I found a fellow customer and asked what she saw in it. 'Oh,' she said, tossing a mane of pricey hair backwards, 'it's marvellous. Only the other day I needed 24 variegates and my local florist didn't have them in stock. So I called the Amex helpline number and they got them for me.'

Great. But I have never ever felt a need to fill the house with variegates. More worryingly, I seldom have the courage to produce the black plastic on those rare occasions when I find myself dining in a restaurant that accepts it. Because what message would I be giving out?

When you produce a black Amex, what you are saying is that you earn £1 million a year. Is the waiter really going to be impressed? And what about your friends? They either earn a million too, in which case so what, or they don't, in which case they won't be your friends for much longer.

Having a black Amex is not like having a big house. That's useful. And it's not like having a big car. That's more comfortable than a smaller one. The card exists, solely, to impress. It has no other function.

If I were the sort of person who had clients, then maybe this would be useful. But a word of warning on that front. I lied about my salary to get one, so who's to say that the sweating golfer who whipped one out over dinner last night didn't lie, too. A. A. Gill has one, for God's sake.

As a result, I shall be getting rid of it. This will help Britain's economy in a small way. But more importantly, it will do wonders for my self-esteem.

Sunday 11 January 2004

Oops: how I dropped the US air force right in it

Given the American military's dreadful reputation for so-called friendly fire incidents, many people will not have been surprised last week when it was revealed that one of its F-15 jets had dropped a bomb on Yorkshire.

I wasn't surprised either, but for a different reason. You see, a few years ago, when I was flying an F-15, I inadvertently dropped a bomb on North Carolina.

I was making one of those *Killer Death Extreme Machine* programmes which called for me to go very fast in a selection of different vehicles. So it was obvious I should hitch a ride in the fastest and toughest of America's airborne armoury. The Strike Eagle. The unshootdownable F-15E.

What you saw on the television was me flying it, and then me being sick. What you didn't see – for reasons of time, you understand – was me trying to drop a laser-guided bomb on the ranges at Kitty Hawk.

Now, you've all seen the news footage of such weapons being fired through the letter boxes of various baby-milk factories, so you know how they're supposed to work. The man in the back of the plane – that would be me – lines up the camera on the target and releases the bomb, which goes to wherever the cross hairs are pointing.

These cameras have a phenomenal range. The distance they can 'see' is classified but I noticed the range dial went up to 160 miles. That means the plane which bombed Yorkshire could have been over Sussex at the time.

On my first run, the pilot, Gris 'Maverick' Grimwald, said he'd come in low and fast, jinking wildly as though we were under attack from surface-to-air missiles.

In the back seat, I tuned one of the three screens to give me a picture from the plane's belly-mounted camera, which you then steer by moving a toggle on top of the joystick.

I'd had two days of training and figured it would be like playing on a PlayStation. And so it is. But can you imagine what it would be like trying to operate a Play-Station while inside a tumble dryer? Because that's what it's like trying to operate a remote-control camera in an F-15. More realistically, have your children tried to play on their Game Boys while being driven in the back of a car? And that's at 60 mph in a vaguely straight line.

Grimwald was doing, ooh, about 600 mph no more than a few hundred feet off the deck, and to make matters worse he was flinging the plane from side to side so that one second the screen showed the faraway Appalachian Mountains and then the next, fields screaming past in a hyperspace fast forward blur.

By the time I'd finished being sick, we were over the sea doing a six-G turn to get back to the starting point again. 'This time,' said Maverick (or 'Bastard', as I liked to call him), 'I'll make it easier. We'll go a little higher, a little slower and I'll be less violent.'

It didn't help. I saw the river where they filmed *Deliverance*, I saw the swamp that bogged down Jude Law in *Cold Mountain* and then I noticed the waterfall behind which Daniel Day-Lewis had hidden in *The Last of the Mohicans*. And then we were over the sea again and I was bringing up some cake that I'd eaten on my ninth birthday.

Bastard was not pleased. 'Did you know,' he said, 'that each time we do one of these runs we're costing the American taxpayer $7,000 in fuel?'

Do you know what? I don't care about the American taxpayer. So there was no way I could summon up a tear from the back seat of a jet that was, at the time, pointing straight at the sun. We were 90 degrees nose high, climbing vertically at a rate that you simply wouldn't believe.

Let me put it this way. The lift in the BT Tower is fast. It gives you a 'funny tummy' as it climbs 600 feet in 30 seconds. So imagine what it's like in an F-15 that climbed 17,000 feet in 11 seconds. This was a cosmic zoom, made real.

It's the F-15's party piece. Because there's so much thrust from its two Pratt & Whitney turbofans, it can not only do 2½ times the speed of sound and carry 9,000 lb more than a Eurofighter, but it can also accelerate vertically.

We'd gone high for the third run so I'd have plenty of time to locate the target with the camera, release the bomb and then hold the cross hairs in place as it fell to earth. Easy peasy, lemon squeezy.

And yet somehow I still managed to make a hash of it. Frantically I swivelled the camera around but could see nothing resembling a target, so I thought: 'I know. I'll drop the bomb anyway, because by the time it reaches the ground from this height I'm bound to have the cross hairs in place.'

I didn't. Bastard felt the plane twitch as I pressed the release button and said: 'You have the target?'

'Yes,' I replied, swivelling the camera some more.

But I didn't, and to this day I have no idea where that bomb went. It certainly didn't hit the target. I'm not even certain it hit North Carolina.

So who knows? Maybe the bombing of Yorkshire wasn't incompetence. Maybe it was payback.

Sunday 18 January 2004

Sorry, Hans, brassy Brits rule the beaches now

When package holidays began, all of a sudden we could experience life at close quarters with people from other nations. We thought the Germans were the most ridiculous people on the beach.

As Monty Python pointed out years ago, they pinched the sun beds and barged into the queues and frightened the children. And if you weren't at the buffet spot-on seven, Fritz had wolfed all the sausages.

But with the advent of the Boeing 747 came the long-haul holiday and we realised that the Germans were country mice compared with the Americans. No shorts were too large, no thong was too small.

What's more, Hank does not like to sit on the beach and read a book. He likes to shout and play volleyball. When the Yanks are around, it's like being on holiday in a primary school playground.

For years the Americans were in a class of their own, but then the Berlin Wall fell down and, as a result, from the Indian Ocean through the Middle East and the Mediterranean to the Caribbean, Boris and Katya were making all the running.

In many ways the Russians are like the Americans. They're either far too fat or far too beautiful. There's no middle ground. And again, like Uncle Sam, no part of the body is immune from man-made enhancement. The

Americans go for surf-white teeth; the Russians for alarming special forces tattoos. And neither seems to see anything wrong with breast enlargement. I saw one Russian woman on the beach in Barbados the other day who had the body of a walnut and a chest that put Antigua in the shade.

However, where the Russians move into an easy lead is beach attire. For the men it's the traditional Speedo, while the women seem to get their fashion pointers from internet porn sites. I haven't yet seen anyone strutting down the beach in stockings and suspenders but it's only a matter of time.

Today, though, a new contender has come along and blown the old favourites into the seaweed. The title of Most Stupid People on the Beach has gone in 2004 . . . to Britain.

We were designed to make Spitfires and Beagles. We're supposed to be in a shed, in gloves, inventing stuff. We therefore do not look good on a beach. We're piggy white and if you expose us to the sun, we turn into Battenburg cake.

We're designed for bracing walks along the front in Scarborough and wet camping holidays in Scotland. But our newly discovered wealth means we can now go to the tropics. Because it's new money, we really have no idea what to do with it.

Women are the worst offenders. On the beach they have a swimsuit, a watch and a pair of sunglasses. Not much, in other words, to show other holidaymakers that they are 'considerably richer than yow'.

It doesn't stop them trying. Obviously they don't go

for the American thong or the Russian nipple tassels, but bikinis are held together with ludicrous gold clasps, sunglasses have absurd hinges which look as if they've come from a maharajah's front door and as for the watches, they're more like carriage clocks with straps.

At lunchtime things get worse because now there's an excuse to cover up. So out comes the T-shirt telling everyone that you've been somewhere else and the bejewelled sarong.

I had to ask my wife where on earth these women buy their clothes, and she knew straight away. Dress shops. Specifically, dress shops in provincial towns that have been bought by husbands to stop their wives sleeping with the binmen.

So where do the dress shops get their stock from? She was stumped. Not Armani, that's for sure, or any designer anyone outside Leicester has ever heard of.

You've never seen chintz like it. And whatever happened to the simple flip-flop? Now it cannot be considered footwear unless it has a flower on it and some high heels.

Then we get to the question of these women's teenage daughters, who strut around with the word 'Sex' on their bikini bottoms. Or 'Peachy'. This is unnerving. Try to read a book about steamships of the nineteenth century when you've got a 15-year-old advertising her backside nine inches from your face. It's especially unnerving for the Russians in their tight, revealing Speedos.

Something must be done, so I've come up with a plan. When you're in a shop buying an outfit for your holiday, apply this simple test: have you ever seen Victoria

Beckham in anything remotely similar? If the answer is yes, put it back on the peg.

If this doesn't work, the government must step in. Again, I have an idea. Airports already have the technology to screen luggage for nail scissors and tweezers, so surely it can't be that hard to look for, and then confiscate, gold slingback shoes, overly complicated sunglasses and any swimsuit with adornments.

I don't mind what provincial British women wear in their own homes. But abroad they're not just letting themselves and their families down − they're letting the country down, too, and that has to stop.

And men: the Burberry baseball cap. No. All right? Just no.

Sunday 25 January 2004

Learn to kill a chicken, or you'll get no supper

When children from St George's middle school in Norfolk went into the playground at break-time recently, a shoot at the nearby Sandringham estate had just begun and as a result it was raining dead and wounded pheasants.

This was a perfect opportunity for the teachers. The children could have been marshalled and shown how the birds should be plucked. 'Right, now gather round, everyone. You, Johnny – put the pheasant on its back and stand on its outstretched wings. Now pull the legs firmly . . .'

It would have been a marvellous illustration of how animals get from their natural habitat into a lovely casserole.

Sadly, this didn't happen. Instead, the teachers ran around wringing their hands.

The children all cried. And letters were sent to the estate managers at Sandringham asking that birds are not shot while the children are outside. This way, the little munchkins will continue to believe that burgers grow on trees and that Coca-Cola comes from natural springs in Wyoming.

After the incident, a woman in the *Daily Mail* said that she objected to organised shoots because the birds are bred specifically for slaughter. So how do you think bacon happens? Few people keep pigs for fun, you know.

I am becoming increasingly depressed at the way we're

trying to insulate ourselves from the reality of the food chain and the wonders of the natural world.

Last week a 55-foot sperm whale that had beached itself in Taiwan was being transported on a lorry when it exploded in Tainan city. Passers-by, buildings and cars were drenched by 50 tons of blood, goo and blubber. It can't have been a pretty sight. And doubtless there will now be some kind of legislation banning biologists from taking dead whales through a built-up area.

Why? When an animal dies, or a human for that matter, the stomach fills with methane gas. Sometimes the pressure becomes so great that the carcass goes off like a bomb.

I'd like to think this explosive power could in some way be harnessed. I don't want to get lavatorial, but the cows in New Zealand produce 900,000 tons of methane every year. It's one of those little facts that I keep in my head for emergencies such as this.

Anyway, it would be nice to think that we could get milk from their udders, meat from their legs and electricity from their bottoms. But I know that in this day and age people would be reluctant to switch on the lights at home if they thought that the power was coming from Daisy's farts.

We are seeing this kind of nonsense on the current series of *I'm a Celebrity . . . Get Me Out of Here!* The contestants, with their man-made lifestyles – and in some cases their man-made breasts – are absolutely incapable of dealing with the jungle wildlife. Do they really believe that the producers would let them put their heads in a tank full of properly dangerous spiders and snakes? Of course not.

So if they're not worried about being eaten or dying in screaming agony, what's the problem? It's not just creepy-crawlies that get them running around squealing, either. On Thursday the team were presented with a dead chicken for their supper.

'Eugh. I'm not eating that,' cried Kerry, predictably. Fine. Leave it out in the sun and let it explode.

The same thing happened recently on the American show *Survivor*. The starving contestants were given some chickens but couldn't bring themselves to kill and pluck them. They're chickens, for God's sake. And chickens are basically vegetables. We're talking here about a bird which is so daft, it can operate normally with no head. Anyway, while they were deliberating about what should be done, the birds were eaten by a couple of monitor lizards.

I remember watching a report about Malta on some televisual travel show. We'd seen the harbour, heard about the tedious local customs and were moving on to the indigenous food. 'They eat rabbits!' cried the presenter with the sort of tone I might have used if I'd found out that they eat each other.

For a moment I was baffled. They eat them whole and raw? They eat them alive? No. They kill them, skin them and put them in a pot with some onions, just like we do. And yet this woman, bright enough to be given a job in television, was astonished.

I honestly don't understand this. Out there in the real world, away from the twenty-first-century supermarket/freezer/microwave chain of catering, there are insects which eat their partners after sex, there are turkey vultures that will vomit on you when threatened, there are cats that kill for fun. And there are leopard seals that play aquatic tennis, using penguins as the ball.

So in the big scheme of things, shooting a pheasant in the face or attaching a Friesian to the national grid really isn't all that bad.

Of course, if you don't want to be a party to the killing or the exploitation, that's fine. Be a vegetarian. But if you're going to eat meat, don't stand on tiptoe and shriek when you find out how the cow became a McMeal.

Sunday 1 February 2004

To win a war, first you need a location scout

Hollywood's powerful film and television workers' union has called for cinemagoers to boycott *Cold Mountain* because this all-American Civil War story was 'stolen' by the British and filmed in Romania.

Brit director Anthony Minghella has hit back, saying that he shot the movie in Transylvania because these days North Carolina, the actual location of *Cold Mountain*, is 'too full of golf courses'.

This isn't true. North Carolina is a spectacular place with many smoky mountains, frothy rivers and spooky forests. It was the setting for *Deliverance* which, like *Cold Mountain*, needed huge vistas to give a sense of scale. But I don't recall catching a glimpse of Tiger Woods wandering through shot as Ned Beatty was being asked to squeal like a piggy.

North Carolina was also used as an epic backdrop for *The Last of the Mohicans*, and again Daniel Day-Lewis did not have to worry about the French, the Huron and being hit on the head by one of Colin Montgomerie's tricky little chip shots.

Nevertheless, Minghella insists that he went to Romania because the Carpathian Mountains more ac-curately reflect America in the 1860s. It's hard to argue with that. Certainly the 1,200 extras he hired for the battle scenes were more realistic. None that I could see was to be found fighting with a pistol in one hand and a £3.99 McMeal in the other.

However, I suspect that the real reason why Minghella went to Romania rather than America is money. It's reckoned that, because of the cost of living and the minimal fees charged by all those extras, he saved about £16 million. Seems like plain common sense to me, but that hasn't stopped the Americans crying foul over the location, the Australian lead actress, the British lead actor and Ray Winstone's amazing Deep South (London) accent.

This is rich. In fact, it couldn't be richer if they weighed down the argument with five gallons of double cream and two hundredweight of butter. What about *Pearl Harbor* in which Ben Affleck managed, single-handedly, to win the Battle of Britain? I know Tony Blair once made a post-9/11 speech thanking the Americans for standing side by side with us during the Blitz, but then he doesn't know the difference between a .22 air pistol and a Trident nuclear missile.

In reality, there were some Americans who came over here to help in the early days of the war — 244 of them to be precise. But don't think they came in a state of righteousness. Most were wannabe fly boys and adventurers who came because they had been turned down by the USAAF for being blind or daft, and they felt that the battered RAF wouldn't be so picky.

We are, of course, grateful to them, even though the day after the Japanese attacked Hawaii, just about all of them went home, taking their Spitfires with them and leaving us with the bill for their training. This point, I feel, wasn't accurately made in the Affleck film, but that didn't stop me buying the DVD.

Then you have *Shaving Ryan's Privates* in which the American army won the war despite the British making a complete hash of things, and *A Bridge Too Far*, in which Ryan O'Neal failed to storm though Arnhem thanks to the incompetence of Sean Connery.

Oh, and let's not forget *U-571*, where Matthew Mc-Conaughey bravely stole an Enigma decoding machine, thus clearing the way for Steven Spielberg to take his Band of Brothers through Belgiumshire.

And why was Steve McQueen wearing his home clothes in *The Great Escape*? What branch of the services allows you to face the enemy in a pair of chinos, a baseball jacket and a T-shirt?

Then there's Vietnam. Not once, according to Holly-wood, did the Americans lose a battle. So how they lost the war is a mystery. This, I suspect, is the main reason why Hollywood didn't make *Cold Mountain*. Who's the bad guy when both sides are, er . . . American?

It's a good job Britain still had a proper film industry when Second World War films were all the rage. Other-wise we'd have had Captain Chuck Gibson bombing the Mohne Dam with Brad and Tod in tow. And what kind of a name is Barnes Wallace? We'll call him Clint Thrust.

Hollywood's record with the truth is simply abysmal, which isn't so bad if you treat the cinema as a place of entertainment. But in America the multiplex is just about the only place where anybody learns any history. After *Black Hawk Down* the audience left the theatre with a sense that America had been in Somalia fighting the humanitarian fight. Not simply trying to depose a warlord who didn't like the idea of US oil companies stealing all the oil.

This, surely, should worry the Hollywood film and television workers far more than where a movie was shot. In *Saving Private Ryan* the French beaches were Irish. In *Full Metal Jacket*, Vietnam was the London Docklands, and in boxing Lennox Lewis was British.

Who cares? I certainly didn't mind where *Cold Mountain* had been filmed or how much the extras had been paid. I just thought it was one of the longest films I'd ever seen. Good, though.

Sunday 8 February 2004

Fear of fat can seriously damage your health

Scientists revealed recently that a child born in 2030 will live five years longer than a child born yesterday. So by the middle of this century there will be more people drawing a pension than people going to work.

This will have a catastrophic effect on the economy because simple arithmetic shows there won't be enough money in the kitty to keep all these old people in hips and cat food.

So what on earth are we going to do? Make people save more so they're self-sufficient in their old age? Get everyone to have more babies? Or ship in thousands of healthy young immigrants who can run around actually doing some work? A tricky decision.

But then last week along came a report saying we won't be living so long after all. Thanks to the efforts of McCain with its oven-ready chips and McDonald's with its McMeals, we're all going to explode by the time we're 62.

Now you'd have expected the government to greet the news with a sigh of relief.

But not a bit of it. John Reid, the health secretary, said a big debate was needed to challenge the problem of obesity.

So what's going on here? One minute we're told that we're all going to live to be 126 and that we'll have to eat each other to survive. Then we're told that actually it'd be best if we ate nothing at all.

At first I suspected this might have something to do with cool Britannia. Tony likes his art galleries and funky bridges and frankly he doesn't want the place cluttered up with a load of fat ankles and prolapsed stomachs.

Then I thought it was another bit of me-too-ism with Dubya. 'Hey, George. We've got fat people as well.'

But then a man in a suit went on the television to say the government really ought to tax oven-ready chips, and suddenly it all became clear. They tax us when we move and tax us when we park. They tax us when we earn money and tax us when we spend it. They tax everything we put in our lungs and now they want to tax everything we put in our stomachs.

Well, I have some observations. First of all, the American idea of obesity is far removed from our own. They have people who have moved beyond the point where fat is a problem or a joke and into the realms where it becomes revolting. We do not.

I've checked, and in Britain I'd be officially obese if I weighed 18 stone. But 18 stone when you're 6 foot 5 inches isn't even on nodding terms with what the sceptics call fat: 18 stone would, in fact, make me Martin Johnson.

Last year, when *Top Gear* was running, life was so hectic that in one week I remember eating supper on a Thursday night, thinking: 'God. I haven't had a bite of anything since Sunday lunchtime.' There just hadn't been the time and, as a result, in just a few months I lost more than two stone.

Now *Top Gear*'s not on air, I can kick around the house in loose robes all day, looking in the fridge every 20 minutes for cold sausages and filling in the gaps by tucking into Jaffa Cakes and Penguin biscuits. I'm relaxed and happy and I've put on a stone.

So which is the healthier option? Stressy and thin or fat and happy? I'm not a doctor but I know what the answer is.

Plus, think what this fat phobia will do to children. None of mine is what you'd call a waif and I'm genuinely scared that thanks to the nonsense being peddled by these health-obsessed Nazis, they're going to start throwing up their lunch in the bike sheds.

Perhaps then John Reid could admit that Norman Tebbit was right all those years ago and that we really should get on our bikes. Or maybe he might like to think about subsidising food that is good for us, rather than taxing food that isn't.

Better still, he might like to address the real cause of misery and stress in this country today. A few years ago I took out an endowment mortgage of £75,000.

There was no mention in the sales patter that the investment company might lose my money, but that's what it's done. Last week I got a letter saying that there will not be enough to pay off the mortgage and that I'd better do something about it if I want to keep my house.

That's why I don't have a pension. It would be a complete and utter waste of time because you're entrusting your money to a bunch of suits who are too stupid to get a job in banking or estate agency.

Look at their offices in the City. Big gleaming towers of glass and steel. Who's paying for them? We are. And it's the same with their soothing advertisements on the television.

You want my advice? Spend your spare cash on chips and chocolate because that way you'll die the day you stop work with a smile on your face.

And being carted off in an enormous coffin at 62 is better than lingering on for 40 more years, hoping for a handout from the next batch of immigrants the government has shipped in to keep the country's average age below 400.

Sunday 15 February 2004

Scotch – stop skiing and return to your sheds

For a while now, things have been going badly for Scotland. The shiny new parliament building is 10 times over budget and already three years late. The economy is stuttering, and all's not well under the kilt either because the birth rate is almost elephantine.

Last week things got worse. The Welsh beat them at rugby and then again at football, and now we hear that the Glenshee Chairlift Company has lost £1 million in the past two years and must sell its two Highland ski resorts.

Apparently, global warming is to blame. In the olden days, the Scotch people got some respite from the weather every winter because the ceaseless rain turned to snow, which was at least pretty. But now it just rains all the time.

Good. I never really saw the point of skiing in Scotland. The tourist board says in its bumf that heading north of the border with your planks is a 'really good way for novices to try out the sport before committing to a high-cost holiday elsewhere in the world'.

Really? I would imagine that anyone who tried skiing for the first time in the Cairngorms would come away from the experience with frostbite, hypothermia, iced-up hair and a passionate resolve to give up the sport for good. Learning to ski in Scotland is a bit like learning to scuba-dive in a quarry. You get the basics, but not the point.

Of course, I don't much care for the act of skiing itself. As I've said before, I never understand why people ski down a slope to a bar and then go on a lift so they can ski down the same slope again. That's like walking to the pub on a Sunday, then going home and walking to the pub again. Madness. I ski to a bar and then go inside for a drink.

This part of a skiing holiday I like very much. The crystal skies, the jaggedy mountains, that pin-sharp air and all those pretty girls in salopettes. It's a fun-filled blizzard of primary colours and you get a tan.

Even the Val d'Isère doctor's surgery – where I go, having fallen off my skis on the way back from the bar – is full of wondrous new injuries. I once saw a bloke in there who had a ski pole sticking out of his eye.

And then in the evenings you can drink wine until it's coming out of your ears, knowing that the mountain crispness will zap your hangover in the morning. Lovely.

This, however, is not how I imagine a skiing holiday in the Highlands might pan out. I'm not sure anyone would get much satisfaction from executing a nice parallel turn on sheet heather. So, Scotland has to rely entirely on its après-ski activities and, er . . . Well, quite.

Sure, Val d'Isère is full of people called Bunty and Rupert who throw bread rolls at you and enjoy debagging one another, which can be wearisome.

But what do you have for company in Glenshee? A family of weird beards from Tipton and a pint of McEwan's. Skiing is supposed to be sophisticated, and Scotland just isn't.

Of course, you might say that Scotland is only 500 miles away and is therefore easier to get to than Val d'Isère, but actually both are an hour or so away by plane. Yes, it's easier to drive to Scotland but you should be aware that if there is any snow on the hills, it will have blocked the roads. So you won't get there anyway.

If you do make it, you'll certainly find good access to the top of the mountains, thanks to the new Cairngorm funicular railway, which seems to have cost the taxpayer nearly as much as the Scottish parliament. And now isn't really needed because, according to *The Economist*, the number of McPasses sold since the 1980s has halved.

The Glenshee Chairlift Company does believe a buyer can be found for its two resorts, but unless they can find someone who has the business acumen of an otter, I wouldn't hold your breath. With cheap air fares and no sign of a recession, France and even Colorado are always going to be less wet.

This might be sad news for those who worked there but it's good news for the rest of the world because John Logie Baird was Scottish. Alexander Graham Bell was Scottish. Alexander Fleming was Scottish. James Watt was Scottish. Charles Macintosh was Scottish. John Dunlop was Scottish. Scottish people invented everything: the kaleidoscope, paint pigment, carpet cleaners, the US Navy, adhesive postage stamps, hypodermic needles, anaesthetics, golf, paraffin, radar, hollow pipe drainage, breech-loading rifles. This list is simply endless.

Plainly, the Scotch were put on the earth to invent stuff. And for the past hundred years or so they have been sidetracked by this ridiculous flirtation with skiing, and getting their chairs back from Westminster Abbey. They took over every trade union and ballsed them all up, and now they're making a pretty good fist of wrecking Westminster too.

Pack it in, the lot of you, and get back to your garden sheds with your spanners and your microscopes.

George Bush said recently he wants to go to Mars. So how about one of you forgets about winter sports for a while and builds him a spaceship.

Sunday 22 February 2004

My son thinks I'm gay, and it can only get worse

It was a perfect scene. My boy and me walking back across the fields from his Sunday morning game of rugby. The sky was bright. Lunch was in the Aga. And all was well with the world.

'Daddy,' he said, pointing at our new garden shed. 'There are people in India who live in houses that are smaller than that.'

'Huh,' I joshed. 'Never mind India. The first flat I owned in London was smaller than that. And even then I couldn't afford it on my own, so I lived there with another boy.'

There wasn't even a pause while his seven-year-old brain processed this information. He just came straight out and said, in the vernacular of youth: 'So were you, like, gay when you were younger?'

A few days later, the subject came up again. Some homosexual people were on the television news complaining about George W. Bush's views on same-sex weddings, and I thought: am I going mad?

Of course you can't have same-sex weddings. It undermines the whole point of marriage, the concept that two people form a stable unit in which children can be conceived and raised. Arguing that homosexuals should be allowed to marry is as silly as arguing that I should be allowed to play for Manchester United.

I was born with the ball skills of an emperor penguin, so I can't play football.

Andrew Lloyd Webber was born with a face like a melted wellington, so he can't be a model. And if you're born with a predilection for members of the same genital group, you can't get married. Get over it.

And yet, actually, it's me that will have to get over it because soon my children's generation will be in charge and they see nothing odd about boys marrying their boyfriends. My son, as we know, thinks his dad used to be gay, and that's fine with him.

It's not just homosexuality. Any item from the news leaves me feeling bewildered and alienated, a stranger on my own planet. A government employee who passed secret emails to her mates isn't to be prosecuted. Marks & Spencer has opened a Lifestore, America won't intervene in Haiti because it's an election year. Posh doesn't want hair like Jordan. It's all just too incredible.

The trouble is that I'm 43 and therefore past my dead-by date. I was designed to live until I was 40, and now it's only central heating and Mr Sheen furniture polish that's keeping me out of the crematorium.

So now we've got the young bloods raring to go, but they're permanently at odds with the wrinklies who are still around, not really wanting anything to change. I have a name for this. Prince Charles Syndrome. He wants to get cracking with his vision of Britain but his mum's still in charge, being cautious and opening day-care centres for the handicapped.

This is a problem. All over San Francisco there are lots of vibrant young men and women who think it's perfectly acceptable for homosexuals to adopt babies. They think that having two dads or two mums would in no way skew the child's view of life. But they're being held back by an old guy in Washington.

Here, young people who only watch Buffy and Dec want to abolish the licence fee but find themselves at odds with old people who wonder what they'd do without John Humphrys in the morning and *Antiques Roadshow* on a Sunday afternoon.

If I were dead, the children would listen to Chris Moyles over breakfast and there would be peace. But since I'm not, the radio is in the bin and there is war.

A lot of people are asking whether Christians and Muslims can co-exist in our shrinking world. But I'm more worried about the cocktail of young and old. Of course, it's bad enough for me at 43, but what must it be like for my mum, who's pushing 70? There can't be a single thing in her life that makes any sense at all.

We took her to a pantomime at Christmas and even that, so far as she was concerned, might as well have been performed in Klingon. 'Why,' she wondered as we came out, 'don't they do all the old songs?' The same reason, I suppose, that M&S has Indonesian knick-knacks among the bananas and bras.

Here we have someone who can't watch American television programmes because 'I can't understand what they're on about', and yet she's living on the same planet at the same time as her grandchildren, who've watched so much Australian soap they go up at the end of sentences.

She takes them out for supper and all they do is sit in the restaurant with their big twenty-first-century thumbs playing on their Game Boys. This must be horrible for her generation, but it's going to be worse for ours because we'll live longer and the pace of change will get even faster.

You think it's bad now, but imagine what will happen when your kids are in charge.

Gay vicars, internet reality TV from your next-door neighbours', public inquiries every time anyone dies, satellite speed traps, thinking computers, cloned dogs, foxes on the parish council, Polish on the curriculum, holidays on Mars. The world is their oyster. But for the rest of us it'll be a pearl-free barrel of bilge.

Sunday 29 February 2004

Sorry, but the public apology is a Big Lie

To demonstrate the toughness of a Toyota pick-up truck for a television programme, I found a tree and then crashed into it.

Unfortunately, when the film was shown an eagle-eyed viewer thought the horse chestnut looked just like one in his village, so he toddled across the road and, sure enough, there were smears of red paint on the trunk. Naturally he reported the matter to the parish council, which wrote a letter of complaint.

As a result I was summoned to the office of a BBC bigwig, where I spent half an hour looking at my shoes, saying, 'I dunno sir,' and, 'It was only a tree.' I also argued that if it were a parish council tree, this meant that it was public property and therefore I was entitled to drive into it.

But it was no good, and a letter was sent back to the parish council offering an unreserved apology and guaranteeing that in future *Top Gear* would try to drive through the village without crashing into anything.

I wasn't really sorry and I'm still not sorry. I only agreed to say I was because then the situation would die down and we could go to another village and crash into something else.

Ever since Clint Eastwood ordered those gunmen to apologise to his mule in *A Fistful of Dollars*, there's been a sense that saying sorry to make everything all right has been a bit of a joke. If the baddies had apologised, the film would have ended immediately. But they didn't, so there was a lot of shooting and, in Clint's case at least, plenty of squinting too.

But then along came Tony Blair, who, after the Hutton Inquiry, said that all he had ever wanted was for the BBC to apologise to his mule, Campbell. As a result of that, apologising has become a global obsession. Spurs players were recently castigated, not for losing a match but for not saying sorry that they'd lost.

I am afraid that His Tonyness's attempts to appear as big-hearted as Eastwood may have set a dangerous precedent. What's to stop Saddam Hussein apologising to his captors for all the genocide: 'I don't know what came over me. I really am most dreadfully sorry. Can I go now?'

No, really. In Pakistan a man responsible for selling nuclear secrets to Libya and North Korea has escaped prosecution by begging on television for the nation's forgiveness. Oh well, that's all right.

We occasionally see apologies in newspapers when they've said – oh, I don't know – that Jordan has 17 A-levels and a degree in nanotechnology from Harvard. But it'll be in a typeface so small that it's not visible to the naked eye, it'll be on page 38, next to a distracting shower advertisement, and it'll have been written only because some hotshot lawyer was standing over the writer with a gun in one hand and a writ in the other.

Saying sorry because you've been forced to means you're not sorry at all. An apology has to be real to heal. As G. K. Chesterton said: 'A stiff apology is a second insult.'

Justin Timbertrousers apologised after baring Janet Jackson's breast live on American television. But was he really sorry? Bill Clinton apologised after his game of hide the cigar became public – but only because he'd been caught.

And now that Jimmy Hill lookalike who's running for president has apologised for saying all Sikhs are terrorists. But John Kerry is a politician, so actually he didn't apologise at all. He said he was sorry if his remarks had been misunderstood, which is the same as saying 'I'm sorry that you're all too stupid to understand what I'm on about.'

As a word, 'sorry' is a useful get-out-of-jail-free card when you're having an argument with your wife and there's only 10 minutes before your favourite television programme starts: 'Yes, I know I've dropped coal in your hollandaise sauce. I am a useless husband on every level and I'm sorry. Now can I watch *24*?'

Sorry works when you tread on someone's toe, or if a child accidentally burps after drinking too much Coca-Cola. Sorry is for minor indiscretions like being a bit late. When you need to squeeze past someone at the cinema to reach your seat, you say sorry because it's another way of saying excuse me. And excuse me just won't do if you've done something big: 'I've just shot your husband in the middle of his face. I do hope you'll excuse me.'

Of course, to bring a bit of gravitas to the moment of humiliation and to dispel the illusion that they've done nothing more than spill water on someone's trousers, people who make public statements today have learnt to adopt a serious face and say that they are making an 'unreserved' apology.

But when you saw Lord Ryder making his 'unreserved' apology on behalf of the BBC to St Tony and the half-horse half-donkey Alastair, weren't you reminded, just a little, of John Cleese dangling, upside down, from that loft apartment window in *A Fish Called Wanda*, apologising to the psychotic ex-CIA man played by Kevin Kline?

Elton John once said that sorry seems the hardest word. But that's not true. A brave man, a man with a spine and some iron in his blood, would say: 'I don't accept your apology and I want you larched.'

Sunday 7 March 2004

Calling your kid Noah or Coke – how wet is that?

Lots of my fortysomething friends seem to be taking a leaf out of the Blairs' book on birth control and squeezing out a last-minute baby.

There are two things you must remember when someone rings to say they've just produced an offspring. First, and for no obvious reason, you must ask how much it weighs, and second, you must try not to drop the phone when they tell you what name they've chosen. 'Chardonnay?' you have to say in measured tones. 'How very, ummmm, oaky.'

The annual list of most popular names shows that the Bible is still a source of inspiration for most, and that the two names at No. 1 are the super-traditional Jack and Emily. But look beneath the top 10 and it's a maelstrom of lunacy where working-class children are named after Australian pop stars and footballers' wives. And the middle classes are no better, going for increasingly ludicrous handles. I mean, what kind of a name is Araminta?

We grew up laughing at Frank Zappa for calling his daughter Moon Unit, but today we're naming our kids after remote Himalayan villages and exotic cheeses.

People have always named their children to reflect their aspirations – that's why Ruby and Opal were so popular in the nineteenth century, and it's why my poor old mum was named after Shirley Temple. I suppose it's also why so many people coming from the Caribbean in the 1950s called their boy kids Winston.

This is no bad thing, being named after a prime minister or an actress your parents admired. But in America people aspire to goods and services, and that's resulted in a surge in popularity for names such as Armani, Timberland, L'Oreal and Celica, which is a type of Toyota. One poor sod last year was called Del Monte.

At this point, I was about to launch into yet another attack on the Americans who regularly choose a child's name by picking letters out of a Scrabble bag. But I've just remembered that over here Harvey Smith called his horse Sanyo Music Centre, so let's move on.

Before naming a child Diet Coke or Josh Stick, it's important to remember that the name you choose will have a huge impact on how the poor thing's life will turn out.

When Mr and Mrs Gauntlet christened their son Victor, he was going to be the chairman of Aston Martin, and so it turned out to be. If Mr and Mrs Arkwright call their son Stan, he's going to be a plumber. Mike Pemberton, on the other hand, is going to be a pilot and Brooklyn in all probability will be a bridge.

One of my friends was deeply concerned about this. He originally wanted to call his new boy-child Jack, because he said Jack Wilman sounded like a rogue CIA agent and he liked the idea of his son being endlessly lowered from helicopters into nuclear submarines. 'Ah yes,' I pointed out, 'but I can also see "Jack Wilman" written down the side of a van.'

This isn't necessarily a bad thing. If it's written in squirly script and the van is full of home-made crusty-bread potted-meat sandwiches, that's fine. But Jack Wilman? That's the sort of van that would have ladders on the roof. So he's gone for Noah, which means the boy will almost certainly grow up to be gay.

To make matters more complicated, a survey out last week suggests teenagers are a lot more conservative than we might think. They're in favour of the monarchy, long prison sentences and patriotism, so this would lead us to believe they'd be against having silly names such as Rawlplug.

But my oldest daughter disagrees. On a really, really drunken night, my wife and I seriously thought about calling her Boadicea, but the following day over the Nurofen we went for Emily. And now she's livid about it, riding around the garden with knives on her bicycle wheels, saying we were dull and unimaginative.

I am dull and unimaginative because when I was little two of my tortoises, Sullivan and Bubble, died. That left me with Gilbert and Squeak, which made me a laughing stock and gave me a profound respect for a sensible naming policy.

This is why I admire the Icelandic system so much. Up there, your surname is your father's Christian name with either 'son' or 'dottir' tagged on the end. So Prince Charles would be Charles Philipson and Nigella Lawson would be Nigella Nigelsdottir.

It's not a policy supported by feminists, but it has worked for centuries and they don't want to see it being abused by people who suddenly get it into their heads that their son ought to be called Snowmobile. Because then his daughter, if he were similarly inclined, might well end up being called Fifi Trixibelle Peaches Snowmobiledottir.

That would be ludicrous, so the government has drawn up a list of approved names from which you must choose.

If we had such a system here, we could use it to maintain the beauty of traditional English names. There'd be no Tiger Lily and no Anastasia. Mr and Mrs Beckham would have been told to stop being so stupid. And my children would have been called Roy, Brenda and Enid.

Sunday 14 March 2004

Put Piers on a plinth, he deserves immortality

For 150 years, people have been arguing about what or who should be immortalised on the empty plinth in London's Trafalgar Square. And then last week came the news that we're to get a statue of a disabled and pregnant woman called Alison Lapper.

My first reaction was: why not the Flying Scotsman? It's for sale at the moment for just £2 million and would be ideal, since it fits in with Ken Livingstone's much publicised love for public transport and genuinely reflects Britain's glorious engineering achievements of yesteryear.

The trouble is that whatever you choose will be used as a pigeon perch and then vandalised. And it would be a shame to see the lovely old engine treated this way – so how about my next brainwave? If it's to be a bird bog and a magnet for drunks and yobs intent on ruining it, then why not put a statue of Piers Morgan up there?

You may have heard that at the British Press Awards last week I strolled over to Piers, the editor of the *Daily Mirror*, and punched him in the middle of his face.

That, however, is only partly true. I also punched him on the jaw and on his cheek.

Why? Well, he seems to think that if someone appears on television it is all right to publish photographs of them kissing girls goodnight and appearing on the beach while fat.

I disagree.

Which is why I haven't and won't spoil his fledgling career on the box by revealing details of his complicated private life.

This disagreement has been running for some time. It all started when I refused to jump ship and write for the *Mirror*, saying I'd rather write operating manuals for car stereos, and the feud became public on the last Concorde flight, when I emptied a glass of water into his lap.

So when everyone noticed we were both at the press awards, an air of expectancy fell on the room like a big itchy blanket. In recent years this do has become a back-slapping festival of bonhomie and fine wines, and everyone felt that here, at last, was a chance to go back to the old days of fisticuffs and abuse. Journalists behaving like journalists and not businessmen.

Nobody came over and said, 'Piers says you stink,' but there was a playground mood nevertheless.

The problem was, I'd never hit anyone before. I may not have the intellect of Stephen Fry but the reason I don't have his nose is that I have enough nous to know that if I punch somebody they will punch me right back.

Besides, fighting is so undignified. Who can forget John Prescott, his face all screwed up, as he lashed out at the protester in the run-up to the last general election? And then there was Jimmy Nail, who invited A. A. Gill outside for a spot of pugilism last year. You just wanted to say: 'Oh, don't be silly.'

The first time Piers and I came close, he was talking the talk of the terraces, saying that I might be big but I'd go down like a sack of potatoes.

Sadly, I don't speak 'football' and by the time I'd worked out what he was on about, the editor of the *News of the World* had stepped in and was asking us to break it up.

I honestly can't remember what it was that finally triggered the action. One minute we were trading insults and the next I felt the hot surge of adrenalin and punched him.

At this point the *Sun*'s diminutive motoring correspondent waded into the arena, addressing nobody in particular with a menacing: 'I'm warning you. I'm from Newcastle.'

Off to my left, a fat man in a white tux and with a huge Cuban cigar was drawling, 'Finish it. Outside. Finish it,' over and over again.

And then there was the brother of a former famous editor of the *Sun*, rushing hither and thither as thought he had inadvertently trodden on 6 million volts. In other words, every single man in there was suddenly seven years old.

It's funny. Over the next couple of days women asked with a look of disdain why I hit him. Men, on the other hand, asked with barely disguised glee where I hit him.

Piers fell into the man camp magnificently. Much as I don't like him, I have to hand him full credit for saying after the third punch: 'Is that all you've got?'

Later, he explained he'd had worse drubbings from his three-year-old son.

And me? Well, I seem to have broken one of my fingers. It's bright blue, won't move and looks like a burst sausage. How can this be? Bruce Willis finished off a whole skyscraper full of baddies without so much as tearing his vest, whereas I hit one middle-aged bloke and came away broken.

I'd like to say this is because I'm weak and fragile and unskilled in the ways of the ruffian. But actually I suspect it has more to do with the strength of Mr Morgan.

That's why it's such a good idea to immortalise him with a statue in Trafalgar Square.

You can insult it, throw things at it, get birds to foul it and punch it from now to the end of time. But it'll always emerge completely undamaged.

Sunday 21 March 2004

Hurricane Hank pulls a fast one on the scramjet

So Nasa has smashed the speed record for plane flight. In a test last weekend, an unmanned 'scramjet' was dropped from the belly of a B-52 bomber and reached a speed of Mach 7, or almost 5,000 mph.

Pundits are talking about planes that could get from London to Sydney in two hours and from Paris to New York in 30 minutes. So well done, America, for making it work and God bless Mr Bush.

Except for one small thing. Two years ago a British scramjet quietly, and with no fuss, reached similar speeds over the Australian outback. Yup, like everything else, scramjets are one of ours.

For 40 years scramjets have been the holy grail for the world of aviation. Unlike in a normal jet, air comes into the front of the engine, is mixed with hydrogen, ignited and then hurled out of the back. There are no moving parts, no harmful exhaust gases and, best of all, the faster you go, the faster it goes.

Theoretically, they have a limitless top speed.

The British version was developed by an operation called QinetiQ which, over the years, has come up with stuff like microwave radar, carbon fibre and liquid crystal displays.

Today, in their unheated pre-war prefabs, with nicotine-yellow walls and damp concrete stairwells, men with colossal brains and plastic shoes are working on power systems for America's new joint strike fighter and a huge sail that harvests fog. (It's based on a sub-Saharan beetle, the stenocara, which collects moisture from the night air on its back and then has a handy water supply through the day.)

Do you remember reading recently about the milli-metric scanning device that can see through clothes? It was designed for airport security, but there was much tittering about other applications. Either way, that was one of theirs, too, so I should imagine that a simple little thing like a scramjet gave them no problems at all. They probably did it in a coffee break.

The big question, however, is why they didn't make more of a fuss when the test was successful. Is this a return to the days of the jet engine and the hovercraft, yet another example of British inventiveness being thwarted by British corporate and governmental apathy?

No. No fuss was made because, contrary to what you've been told by the over-excited Americans, you will never go to Australia or anywhere on a scramjet.

'Anyone who tells you different is in an election year,' one expert said last week.

Here's why. First, the hydrogen needed for a 12,000-mile trip to Sydney – and hydrogen is light, remember – would weigh more than the plane it was fuelling.

Next, scramjets start to work only when the plane is doing Mach 5 (3,810 mph). And how, pray, are you supposed to reach that kind of speed?

The Nasa plane in last weekend's test was taken to an altitude of 40,000 feet by the B-52, where it was dropped.

A rocket then took it up to 90,000 feet and Mach 7. At this point the scramjet took over and yes, there was minimal acceleration, but it was out of fuel in just 11 seconds.

You may recall the British Hotol project from the late 1980s. This, it was said, would use scramjets and rockets. Brilliant. Sydney would be just 45 minutes away.

But not even Britain's boffins could figure out how it would get off the ground in the first place.

I don't want to sound like a doom-monger, but think about it. You have a 15-minute bus ride from the car park to the terminal, a half-hour queue for check-in, another half-hour being laughed at by security staff as they 'look' through your clothes, and then an hour's walk to the gate.

Here you'll board a bomber that will take an hour or so to reach the right altitude, before you are loaded into a rocket which shoots you up into space. You then career back down again in scramjet mode, landing in Australia at about 14 million mph. Where you'll be eaten by a crocodile.

'Scramjets will never happen,' one expert said. I told him never was a big word, but he was adamant: 'Not just not in your lifetime. Never.'

Nasa has to smile sweetly when people talk about getting to the moon in 30 minutes because they have to whip up the imagination of Hank from Minnesota. They know that, with no bucks, there's no Buck Rogers.

The British team members, along with their Australian partners, never made a big deal of their success because they knew it would work only on cruise missiles and tank shells. I'm afraid that we're still stuck on our Airbuses and jumbos, lumbering through the ozone layer at a miserable 500 mph.

Don't despair, though. While the Americans are busy congratulating themselves for their 11-second leap into the record books, the boffins at QinetiQ have moved on to the next stage: a plane that will cruise at Mach 5. It's called the sustained hypersonic flight experiment, it uses the proven ramjet from a Sea Dart missile and the first model, they say, will be airborne in 18 months' time.

Expect to read about it in about five years when the Americans make it work too.

Sunday 4 April 2004

Health and safety and the death of television

At the Last Supper Jesus washed his disciples' feet, and for 2,000 years Christians have followed suit, going to church at Easter so the vicar can move among them with a wet towel.

This week, however, at the Maundy Thursday celebration in Sheffield Cathedral, the Revd Jack Nicholls had to use a different towel for each member of the congregation in case he passed on a bout of athlete's foot. Welcome, everybody, to the mad and dangerous world of the Health and Safety Executive.

This is a world where army training courses in the Brecon Beacons must now be fitted with handrails in case the soldiers fall over and where baby walkers are banned in case the toddler topples into the fire.

I need to be careful at this point. The Health and Safety wallahs are a touchy bunch, saying they do important work such as stopping nuclear power stations from exploding. Almost certainly they would say, if Jesus came back to Earth tomorrow and washed two people's feet with the same towel, that they wouldn't prosecute him.

Unless one of them had leprosy, of course, in which case they'd have no alternative. And no, Mr Christ, we won't take into consideration the fact that you have in the past brought people back from the dead. Also, can you stop walking on water, because that's just stupid.

I don't deny that the Health and Safety Executive stops children from going up chimneys, but mostly what it does is infect the nation with a sense that 'being safe' is more important than being happy. They even argue that 'health and safety is the cornerstone of a civilised society'. But this couldn't be more wrong.

Health and Safety is the cancer of a civilised society, a huge, ungainly, malignant, pulsating wart.

In the past, companies used to live in fear of the trade unions, who would walk in through the front door and usher every worker they found out through the back.

We thought the Arthur Scargills and Jimmy Knapps had been killed off by Margaret Thatcher; but no. They have simply metamorphosed into the Health and Safety Executive, and now they're back, sticking their trouble-making noses into every single aspect of every single thing we do.

Only last week it was revealed that in the past three years 15 people have been killed on a single stretch of road in Wiltshire. One road safety campaigner greeted the news by saying, 'It's the same as a jumbo jet crashing every year.'

I'm sorry, matey, but if you do the maths it just isn't.

Today, companies can get a government bribe of up to £100,000 if they employ workers' safety advisers. But don't be tempted, because these idiots will argue that your office carpets are more perilous than a terrorist bomb.

No, really. We're told that 95 per cent of major slips at work result in broken bones. (Is that so?) And that somebody falls over in this country every three minutes, which, they argue, incurs an incalculable human cost.

No it doesn't. The human cost of the Holocaust was incalculable, whereas I fell down the stairs only yesterday and it cost nothing. There's more, too. Just last week the lift doors at the BBC's White City building closed on my knee and wouldn't open again. And the bruise I received was completely free.

Still, the HSE says that simple cost-effective steps can be taken to ensure that nobody trips. Spillages, they say, must be managed, suitable footwear should be fitted, effective matting systems must be used, offices must be redesigned and workers must be retrained. Cost-effective? How can it be when the staff do nothing all day except work to stay upright?

Health and safety is now so out of control that I find it nearly impossible to do my job. Certainly the series I made a few years ago called *Extreme Machines* simply couldn't be produced today.

Back then, we gave the sound recordist a heart attack when we asked him to abseil off an oil tanker at 3 a.m. in the middle of a Cape of Good Hope storm. We put the cameraman in such a position that he fell off a 1,000-bhp swamp buggy in Florida and then, after we got the mud out of his lungs, we wedged him in a two-seat Spitfire that ran out of fuel at 5,000 feet.

I climbed into drag-racing snowmobiles and fighter jets without a moment's thought. Yes, it was dangerous, but it was fun. We knew the risks and we took them because a) it was a laugh, and b) hopefully it made great telly.

Nowadays, though, producers must fill in a hazard assessment form before they go on a shoot. They have to show that they've thought about all the safety implications

and if there's a breach, they – not the BBC – are liable.
Result: they won't take any risks at all.

On *Top Gear*, we refer to the Health and Safety people
as the PPD. The Programme Prevention Department.

Sunday 11 April 2004

Getting totally wrecked at sea isn't a crime

Oh no. The government has begun a four-month consultation period to see if weekend sailors pottering about on the Solent or the Norfolk Broads should be stopped and breathalysed.

Now, I can see that it might be difficult to drive a tank while under the influence of heroin. And I understand that Huw Edwards would find it tricky to read the Autocue if he were off his face on acid. But sailing a boat, on the sea, after a few wines? I'm sorry, but that doesn't sound hard at all.

Sure, there was the case of the drunken Icelandic trawlerman who crashed into a British couple's yacht, causing damage that cost £25,000 to put right. A year later he sailed over to apologise and, having drunk some wine on the voyage, crashed into their boat again.

I think that's quite funny, but of course those of a busybodying disposition won't.

And then they will point to the recent case of a captain who smashed his dredger into the pier at Hythe, having downed six pints of lager. The Methodist Mariners will also mention 'drunken yobs' on jet skis terrorising swimmers.

All very worthy, I'm sure, but unfortunately the consultation paper also implies that ordinary sailors will be entangled in the legislation. And that would be a shame.

Only the other day I went for a small sail. We set off at the obligatory 45 degrees, an angle at which it's impossible to drink, as your glass keeps falling off the table. And anyway, every time you fancy a swig, the captain decides to 'go about' or 'gybe' and you have to rush around pulling the wrong rope.

Still, at lunchtime, we parked, broke out the rum punches (it was Barbados) and spent the afternoon getting plastered in the sunshine. Is this not what sailing's all about?

Certainly, Olivier de Kersauson, the eminent French yachtsman, thinks that's what the British do. He took me out on his huge trimaran a couple of years ago and explained why all the big races and records are won and broken by French and American people these days.

It's a far cry from 1759, when our navy pounced on the French fleet as it attempted to break the blockade. In the ensuing battle off Quiberon, Britannia really did rule the waves.

But not any more, and de Kersauson thinks he knows why. 'These days, you British all sit around in your yacht clubs, in your silly blazers, drinking gin and tonics. No one actually goes out there and sails,' he said.

So, new drink-drive limits for sailors may put us back on the map vis-à-vis the Jules Verne Trophy, but there must be more to it than that.

What, though? It's not as if Britain is out of step with the rest of the world. So far, only Finland has placed alcohol restrictions on sailors but no one has been arrested yet because the police can't think how the law might be enforced.

We'd have a similar problem here. It would, inevitably, be the job of the Hampshire police to cruise around on the Solent, but I feel sure that senior officers could find better things for the force to do than harass Colonel Bufton Tufton for taking a sherry on his Fairline Targa 48.

Furthermore, who would be deemed responsible? Certainly, if I were to be apprehended by the River Filth while weaving out of Cowes harbour, I'd say my completely sober five-year-old daughter was in charge. Then I'd invite them to go away and catch some burglars.

There are a quarter of a million shipwrecks off the coast of Britain, and almost all of them were caused by one of four things: incompetence, bad weather, the French, or the Germans. Banning alcohol from the high seas to save lives is therefore pointless.

Perhaps it was dreamt up because the infernal health-and-safety, fresh-air, vegetarian Nazis are running out of ways to make our lives miserable on land. But why is it being seriously considered?

To get an answer, we need to think about the potential punishment. You cannot remove a sailor's licence if he's found to be drunk because he doesn't have one.

And you cannot realistically send Bufton Tufton to jail for sailing while under the influence of Harvey's Bristol Cream.

The only realistic punishment is a fine and there you have the appeal for Tony's slack-jawed sidekick in No. 11. Explain that drinking and sailing must be outlawed 'to save children's lives' and watch the money come rolling in. It's the speed-camera syndrome. Tell us that speed kills, then 'tax' us when we're caught proving it doesn't.

That said, I would be enormously peeved if I were the winchman on a rescue helicopter, dangling on a rope in atrocious weather trying to save the skipper of an upturned yacht who kept saying 'You're my best mate,' and, 'I f★★★★★★ love you.'

There is a way round this one, though. Rescued sailors who turn out to be drunk should be made to pay for the cost of plucking them to safety. This way, the fine would serve a purpose and there'd be no need for pricey police patrols.

What's more, the freedom of the open seas would still be a blessed relief for those who, like me, increasingly believe we're no longer living in a free country.

Sunday 18 April 2004

We used to work to live, then we gave up living

There is no doubt that, economically speaking, the country's in rude good health at the moment. We have lower unemployment than most other major industrialised nations, we have among the highest house prices in the world, we are drowning in venture capital, and we are all fat.

When pushed, many experts credit Gordon Brown for the endless parade of good news stories, thanking the good Lord that we have his canny, cunning, dour, Presbyterian, wily, Scottish hand on the tiller.

Rubbish. Britain's metamorphosis from lame duck to golden goose has nothing to do with Brown and everything to do with your eating habits at lunchtime.

In the olden days, people used to go to the canteen on the dot of one to unwind with mates over a plate of something big in pastry. Now everyone gets their lunch from the Grab 'n' Go shop.

Do they have Grab 'n' Go shops in Italy? I rather think not. Over there, they're still downing a couple of bottles of wine at lunchtime, and then sleeping it off until six.

If we do go out for lunch in Britain, it's only an excuse to get some more work done. And so is dinner, and so, increasingly, is breakfast. In fact, we're running out of meals over which we can do deals. Soon, people will be buying and selling products over a midnight feast.

And who drinks at lunchtime any more? The other day, in a Notting Hill restaurant, where people were planning TV shows and new ad campaigns, I ordered a glass of wine, and a deathly hush descended.

'I could never drink wine in the day,' said my horrified guest. 'I'd never get anything done in the afternoon.'

And there you have it. Back in the early 1980s you worried about your performance at work because you knew that if you were kicked out, you'd be jobless until the end of time.

But now people worry about their performance at work because, unlike the continentals, we no longer work to live.

We live to work, and you can't function properly with a glass of Chablis swilling around your arterial route map.

Ten years ago you knocked off at 5.30, irrespective of what you happened to be doing at the time. Shops went in for half-day closing. You always took your holidays, and if you felt a bit peaky you went to bed for a month.

Oh, how times have changed. Now, when the guys on *Top Gear* call a car firm in the sticks at 7 p.m. and get a message saying, 'I'm sorry, the office is closed for the day,' they slam the phone down and spend the rest of the evening muttering about what they call 'provincial sloppiness'.

People go to work, having been savaged by Bengal tigers. If you catch ebola, you must get the deal done before your liver liquefies. And half-day closing? Now, you can buy arugula at 3 a.m. seven days a week.

Today, and this has nothing to do with Mr Brown or his warmongering boss, the entire British workforce suffers not from absenteeism but presenteeism. When I began in local newspaper journalism, it was 1978 and the country was a complete shambles. Dead rats, big piles of rubbish and a limited choice of crisp; salt, vinegar, or neither. And I was happy to contribute to the general feeling of malaise by working a 3½-day week.

No really, we were out of the door on a Thursday lunchtime when the paper went to bed, and we didn't start again until Monday.

If the news editor wanted me to cover a parish council meeting in the evening, I'd spend the whole day harrumphing and lobbying my union representative to get me time off in lieu. Now, I work seven days a week, every week.

And how did Gordon Brown effect this change? Well, it's hard to say really, since he was on paternity leave at the time.

How can this make the country strong and prosperous, for crying out loud? A dad's role in the birth of a child is to ensure the infant has the right number of fingers and toes, then get back to work. If we all took a week off to mop up baby sick and do night feeds, we'd be back to 1978 in a jiffy.

It's not just blokes, either. My wife, who is also my manager, found time during her third caesarean operation to discuss a new contract she'd been sent that morning. I'm not joking. She was lying there, with her stomach open to the elements and needles in her spine, wondering if 15 per cent of the back end was good enough, or if she should push for 20.

That's the sort of attitude that has made the country

strong. We work now, all the time, even during child-
birth. We go out at night with Borg-style mobile phone
headset attachments in case the office wants to get in
touch, and as a result we make more money, which we
spend at a greater rate than at any time in history.

And are we thanked? No. Brown comes back from his
paternity leave, or his six-week summer holiday, and lets
it be known that it's all down to him. Yeah, right, and
victory in the First World War was all down to the
generals.

Sunday 25 April 2004

You're all on probation, this is the British nation

A survey last week revealed that the top 10 things that best define Britain are roast beef (which will give you CJD) fish and chips (which aren't available any more), the Queen, Buckingham Palace, cooked breakfast, the Beatles (half of whom are dead), Constable (who's completely dead), the Houses of Parliament, Marks & Spencer and drinking tea.

Is this why half of eastern Europe is on its way here over this weekend: because they fancy a cup of tea? Because they want a new pair of underpants? Because they like to start the day with a hot meal?

I can only assume that the people who responded to this survey are living in the past or living in Worthing. Anyone who's seen a newspaper recently would come up with some very different ideas about what defines Britain. With apologies to E.J. Thribb, I'm going to have a stab:

The Tipton Three, deep-fried brie
A difficult charter renewal for the BBC
Hospital rashes, endless train crashes
And a spot of closing-time thuggery.
Everyone's at university so you can't get a plumber but
    school leavers are getting dumber and dumber.
Footballers are roasting, cars are coasting and exactly when
    will we get some summer.

Teenage girls with 'juicy' on their arse and let's not forget
the Tony Martin farce.

Provincial chefs cooking, traffic wardens booking, sneak
into the bus lane when no one's looking.

The cameras will catch you if you go too fast, buildings
are never meant to last, here comes a soap star with her
knickers on show, too much sex, Beckham's bloody
texts, and the one-eyed mullah refuses to go.

We suck up to the Yanks, we've closed all the banks, and
everyone talks like an EastEnder.

Our idea of a real night out is a complete and utter
bender.

When the world was in trouble, we were there in a trice,
we've beaten the Germans solidly twice.

But now in battle our guns don't work and the guys on
the subs have started to shirk.

We still like to think we're a major world power, but in a
war today we'd barely last an hour.

Yet again the Social failed to come up with the goods,
government scientists dead in the woods,
cockle-pickers, rate-capping bickers, and the CCTV
defeated because the thieves were in hoods.

Plus we're happy to sit and work at the bureau, but there's
no way we're having that bloody euro.

No one makes things any more, it's all call centres; what a
bore.

By day the streets are full of PC bull, at night they're full
of lads on the pull.

You can't post a letter, it won't get there at all, and bosses
are sued should a worker fall.

Talk proper on telly and Cilla will call you a nob and you
   daren't go out because of the mob.
Dido's warbling on Radio 1, and now what's this?
Oh, Concorde's gone.
I'm a celebrity and I want to get out, have your face
   altered, get a trout pout, be famous for doing nothing at
   all, get called a hero for kicking a ball. While you, dear
   reader, are out chopping logs, the whole damn
   country's going to the dogs.
You like to think in your middle-class home that all is
   well, apart from the dome.
But the whole place is wounded and the wound's starting
   to swell.
The Band-Aid's failing and it's beginning to tell.
I therefore have a message for you, if you're arriving here
   to begin anew:
France is wonderful, France is best, from Alsace in the east
   to Brest in the west.
Their wine and fizz are second to none and remember the
   footie they've recently won.
Their cheese is completely out of sight and St Tropez's a
   lot better than the Isle of Wight.
They've sunshine and châteaux and tits on the beach.
When you're down in Provence, life's really a peach.
Go there instead and leave us alone.
We're rubbish, you know it, we're pared to the bone.
If you don't believe me, consider this tome:
We may have ID cards – but we're fresh out of bards.

Sunday 2 May 2004

Comrade Clipboard won't let me crash the car

Making *Top Gear* used to be easy. I would drive a car round some corners, spin its wheels on the gravel, make a couple of cheap sexual metaphors and then garnish the result with a spot of Bruce Springsteen. Today, though, things are very different.

The new series returns to your screens tonight, but in Tony Blair's weird world the sheer effort of getting it there would have defeated Hercules.

You see, the problem is that, while we weren't looking, an insidious coup has taken over all our main institutions: schools, government, television stations, the police and even the army. Yes, it's not the head teacher or the general who's in charge any more; it's that quiet little man (or woman) in the bad jumper, the one nibbling away at his (or her) one-world, fair-deal polenta crisps.

As a result, the gallery at a modern television studio is like the bridge on an old Soviet submarine. Even the director is now under the direct control of a political commissar whose sole job is to make sure that nobody falls over, trips up or says anything which might possibly cause offence.

So, during the recording on Wednesday, when one of the presenters used the phrase, 'taking the mickey', the lights went up, the shutters came down and the cameras were turned off. With klaxons blaring, we surfaced, special forces took the presenter away and now he, and his family, are living with Ron Atkinson and Robert Kilroy-Silk in a Siberian gulag.

Why? Well, we've known for some time that n★★★★★ is the fourth most offensive word in the English language and, of course, saying all Arabs are terrorists is as silly as stripping in front of a webcam. But now someone has decided that 'taking the mickey' might upset the Irish.

In fact, the Mickey in question has nothing to do with Micks in general. It's an abbreviation in cockney rhyming slang for Mickey Bliss. Taking the mickey is therefore an inoffensive way of saying taking the piss.

But there we have the problem with political commissars. They are not bothered about truth or accuracy: they're there to right the wrongs perpetrated by Oliver Cromwell and General Dyer at Amritsar, and to find all the little problems that Health and Safety have missed.

Ah yes. Health and Safety. For one programme in the new series, each presenter bought a car for less than £100. We filmed a series of tests to prove they were roadworthy and reliable. As a finale, we decided to show their integrity by driving them into a brick wall at 30 mph.

Can you see a problem with that? I couldn't. It's not as if we were asking black or Irish people to have the accident on our behalf. But that didn't concern the political commissar, who called in Health and Safety, who thought we were taking the mickey.

We promised we wouldn't sue if we were injured. Our wives promised they wouldn't sue if we were killed. We produced letters from the head of safety at Volvo, saying there was no danger whatsoever, and we talked to James

Bond stuntmen, who agreed. But Health and Safety were not interested. They knew, because they'd read about it in the *Guardian*, that crashing a car into a wall at 30 mph was dangerous, so they insisted that we spent £8,000 – of your money, I hasten to add – moving fuel tanks, employing paramedics and buying neck braces.

Great. If we abandoned the project, we'd have wasted the money already spent. If we went ahead, we'd be wasting even more on ludicrous safety features that every expert said were simply not necessary.

I offered to stage the crash in my free time and to employ a camera crew myself. I said that I would give the resulting footage to the BBC for nothing. But the political commissar referred to his little red book, smiling that cruel KGB smile, and said, 'No.'

In the end we went ahead, crashed the cars on his terms and, as a result, had no money left to make any more items. Result: a show where nobody was hurt. But a show that nobody wants to watch.

It gets worse. Before anything can be transmitted these days, you have to fill in a compliance form which makes sure that you're complying with every single piece of PC nonsense, no matter how stupid or trivial. The trouble is that, by the time you've done this, and the health and safety form, you have no time left to film the programme.

Actually, you don't even have time to fill in the forms because usually you're away on a course, watching safety films of Anthea Turner catching fire. I thought that it would make the cornerstone of a great show – *When TV Stars Combust* – but apparently it's supposed to demonstrate how things can go wrong.

My latest plan is to take part in some Siamese banger racing. You race in pairs with your car chained to your partner's. I knew Health and Safety would have a fit but, long before they could step in, the plan was quashed by the party commissars. 'We're worried about using the word Siamese,' they said. 'Could you call it "conjoined" banger racing?'

Not really, no.

Sunday 9 May 2004

Noises off can turn a man into a murderer

On Thursday a group of hot-air fanatics floated seven enormous balloons over the centre of Birmingham and, as dawn broke, drenched the city with music that had been specially composed to change the way people sleep.

I should imagine that the change was profound. Instead of waking up dreamily at about seven or eight o'clock, it seems entirely likely that the city's 2 million inhabitants were out of their beds at 6.30 a.m., wondering what harebrained lunatic had sanctioned such a thing.

That these balloonists lived to reach land shows the people of Birmingham to be exceptionally tolerant. If the Sky Orchestra had bombed my house with its 'audio landscape' at dawn, I would have shot its members out of the sky.

I do not mind if something makes a noise while engaged in a pursuit that is practical and useful. People, for instance, who buy houses near Heathrow and then whinge about aeroplane noise need to be larched.

I also despair at those who complain about low-flying RAF jets. One farmer in Wales became so fed up with the sound of the man-made thunder that he wrote 'piss off Biggles' on the roof of his house. Happily, every fly boy went over there for a look-see.

And as for the man who complained last week that Paul McCartney's rehearsals at the Millennium Dome were too loud: come on, mate. Complain about 'Ebony and Ivory' by all means, but don't complain about an event that brings life to Tony Blair's great white elephant.

It's the same story with traffic noise and the din made by farmers when it is time to harvest the crops. These are simply by-products of the modern age. I don't even mind other people's mobile phones, unless they're using the Nokia ring tone.

What I cannot abide, however, are people whose hobbies are solely designed to make a noise. I'm talking about born-again motorbikers who come to the countryside on a sunny Sunday specifically to make as much racket as possible. One day I will silence them by stretching a piece of cheese wire across the road.

I'm also talking about campanologists who wait for the country to have a monumental hangover before polluting the Sunday morning stillness with their infernal bells.

Why? If God thinks getting a bunch of beardies to play 'Home Sweet Home' on six tons of brass at seven in the morning is a sensible way of summoning his flock, he can get lost. It's all very well banging on about peace and love, but what I want on a Sunday is a bit of peace and quiet.

I wouldn't mind, but church congregations are now so small that everyone would fit in the vicar's Ford Fiesta. So why doesn't he pop round to pick up everyone personally? And quietly. No leaning on your horn like an idle minicab driver, thanks very much.

I also think it's about time that something was done about microlights. Sure, an RAF jet is much louder, but by the time you've got back on to your chair, it's already knocking people over in Cornwall. A microlight, on the other hand, struggles to make headway in even the gentlest of breezes so it just sits above your garden all day.

I think it's fine for people to have their own aircraft but I would impose a minimum speed limit up there of, let's say, 600 mph. This minimises the inconvenience for those of us on the ground.

That's a simple solution. What's not simple is what I should do about the blackbird that has nested in the eaves, just six inches from my pillow.

This morning its chicks woke me at 5.20 and I spent the next two hours trying to think of what might be done.

My wife suggests that we get a cat, but this is impossible because I hate the way their bottoms look like dishcloth holders. Mostly, though, I hate them because they give me asthma, which would keep me awake even more than the birds.

It would be much easier to blow the nest, and everything in it, to kingdom come with my 12-bore. Yet I cannot bring myself to do that. I'm not even certain it's legal.

It probably *is* legal to remove the nest gently and put it in the dustbin. But, again, it seems wrong. Weird, isn't it? I would enjoy beheading a biker but I cannot bring myself to kill five baby blackbirds.

I thought about taking a leaf out of the Birmingham Sky Orchestra's book and bombarding them through the night with old prog rock from a Sony Walkman, in the hope that they would sleep during the day.

But I'm told that baby blackbirds aren't like baby people and that this won't work. Nor will milk laced with heroin, apparently.

So what I'm going to do is feed them with lots of grain until they're really fat.

Then I shall drown them in armagnac. And then, after they've been in the Aga for eight minutes, I shall pop them into a baked potato and eat them.

It's called payback and, if it works, I shall try the same thing with the bell-ringers.

Sunday 16 May 2004

The lusty lads have left me feeling exposed

It's easy for women. When they are in the newsagent's at a railway station they can buy pretty much any magazine that takes their fancy, safe in the knowledge that they will be able to read it on the forthcoming train journey.

Woman and Home. Home and Garden. Garden and Hair. Hair and Beauty. Beauty and Slimming. Slimming and Slimmers. Slim Women. Slim Home. Slim Garden. Slim Hair.

They're all fine.

It's not so easy for a man. We know we should pick up *The Spectator* or a book on Victorian poetry because this will make us appear sensitive and clever. And yet, what we really want is to spend the journey looking at naked Australian surfers, especially if they have been the victims of shark attacks.

That means buying a lads' mag, which used to be fine. But now, unfortunately, it's no longer possible to do such a thing, not if you want to read it in public.

The first time I saw a photograph of someone who had been eaten by a shark, I was pretty impressed. The second time was enjoyable too; but now, thanks to the proliferation of the lads' mags, I'm bored witless by South African lifeguards who have lost their torsos.

Shark attack photos have been the staple diet of men's magazines since they arrived on the scene, 10 years ago. But with the launch, and apparent success, of *Zoo* and

Nuts, which are weeklies, the old monthlies have had to up the ante a bit.

With a circulation of 600,000 or so, *FHM*, the biggest seller, has the most to lose, so this month you can feast your eyes on a cow with two extra legs growing out of its neck, and a man who was born with his head on back to front. Also, there is a horse-shaped boy, a bloke with testicles the size of prize-winning pumpkins and a man with what appears to be a sack of red potatoes growing out of his face.

Fine, but this kind of stuff doesn't really work on a train. I mean, it is hard to savour the shots of a man with elephantiasis when you have a stranger who may be a nun sitting next to you.

And it is no good turning the page because whoa, it's a double-page spread of Abi Titmuss wearing nothing but a sheen of baby oil.

This is another problem. In the early days of lads' mags, it wasn't hard to find someone from a soap opera or the pop charts who, for a small fee, would appear in the centre pages, wearing nothing but a swimming costume. But now, with paparazzi on every beach in the world, the tabloid newspapers and celebrity glossies can quench our thirst for shots of G-list celebrities in their G-strings. So the lads' mags have to go further.

That frightens away serious actresses from *Casualty* and *Coronation Farm* and means we are left to gawp at girls who once went out with someone who sold a dog to someone who lives next door to Richard and Judy.

This week, for instance, *Zoo* has printed a picture of Lisa Snowdon's bottom. Who is Lisa Snowdon? I have absolutely no idea. *Nuts*, meanwhile, has pics of Anoushka and Steph who, we are told, are presenters on MTV.

Would you read *Asian Babes* on the train? Would you pull out the *Playboy* centrefold and nod appreciatively? Precisely. And it's no different with Anoushka and Steph, even though, it turns out, they have been to a 40th birthday party, hosted by someone called Shane Richie.

So this brings us back to the newsagent's at the railway station and the quandary of what to buy.

GQ has columns by Boris Johnson and Peter Mandelson, which gives it an upmarket, serious feel, but there are visual landmines in there, too. You turn the page expecting to find a piece on starvation in Africa, but oh no, it's Kate Winslet's thrupennies, and the nun's giving you daggers.

So what about the *New Statesman*? Well, yes, but it pretty much guarantees that you'll wake up in Wakefield, 200 miles from your intended stop, with a bit of dribble hanging down from the side of your mouth.

Specialist publications do have a certain allure. Sit on a train reading *What Computer?* or *Autocar* and you can be pretty much assured that nobody will sit next to you. The downside, of course, is that you will have to read *What Computer?* or *Autocar*.

All specialist publications assume the reader knows as much about the subject as the staff. I recently bought a home cinema magazine and there was not one single word that made any sense at all.

Socially, it is possible to buy a magazine such as *Arena* or *Wallpaper*★ but it's hard to work out what they are about. Mostly, they seem to be full of rather trendy people leaning on bicycles in alleyways, and they are not what you'd call funny – which brings me to the solution.

Being British, and male, we may like reading about gardening or food, and we do have an extraordinary appetite for television listings magazines. But what we like most of all is a damn good laugh.

This means that when I get to a railway station I always buy the two funniest magazines you'll find anywhere in the world: *Viz* and *Private Eye*.

Sunday 23 May 2004

Mobile phones that do everything – except work

After Margaret Thatcher announced she'd be privatising water, she probably thought there was nothing left to sell. But there was – the air.

Tony Blair and Gordon Brown were quick to realise this and so, in 2000, they sold it at auction to a group of multinational companies for a whopping £22 billion.

Now those multinationals are selling it back to us in the shape of third-generation (3G) mobile phones that allow you to check prices on the Italian stock exchange, email naked girls in Vietnam, watch the BBC news, and remind you that next Saturday is your wedding anniversary.

In essence, if you buy one of these phones, you are getting a Filofax, a television, a cinema, a portal to the internet, a computer, a video camera and a photograph album. Great, but is it necessary?

My mobile phone man tells me that, according to his accounts, only 3 per cent of his customers use their current phones for sending photographs. So why should anyone, apart from Rebecca Loos, want a 3G phone that lets you talk, face to face, on a video link?

On *Tomorrow's World* years ago, Raymond Baxter told us that such a thing was possible. So did Judith Haan. And so did Philippa Forrester. But video calls never caught on, because we use the phone primarily for lying and it is much harder to tell porkies when you're being watched.

So why, if we don't want video phones at home, might we want them when we are out and about? And how long do you suppose the battery will last?

What's worse is that you still won't be able to use the phones as phones because, as has always been the way with mobiles – except the Nokia 6310 – people on the other end sound like Daleks and, just before you have a chance to sign off, the call will end. So you have to ring back just to say goodbye.

It is easy to see what is going on here. Having spent a Nasa-sized fortune on the radio waves to handle all this data, the mobile phone industry is attempting space travel before it can walk.

When the motor car was invented, people did not sit around, wondering how a washing machine and a tumble drier could be attached to the back. They honed it and refined it. Only now, 100 years down the line, are we seeing the fitting of extras such as television screens and satellite navigation.

This is plainly not happening with mobiles. Last year, I bought my wife a Sony Ericsson Something Or Other for about £1 million. It turned out to be a fantastic personal organiser and video game console, but for speaking to other people she might as well have used a chair leg.

'Ah, yes,' said the man in the shop, when I complained. 'That particular model isn't very good.'

Not very good! For the past 12 months, she's rung me up, we've said 'What?' at the top of our voices a lot and then, when she's inadvertently moved more than two inches from a base station, the line's gone dead.

I have a Motorola that has several thousand features, all of which are jolly useful, I'm sure. But the speaker is so quiet, I can't even hear the beeps and static coming from my wife's Sony. The damn thing would make Brian Blessed sound like a hamster.

It will have to go, which means the two hours I spent reading the instruction manual will have been a waste of time, and now I'll have to spend another two hours reading a booklet about whatever I buy instead. But I don't have time to do that because I'm in the middle of the book about my wireless internet. Honestly, that's all I read these days – instruction books for gadgets that don't work.

What I want from a cooker is the ability to cook food. What I want from a washing machine is the ability to make clothes clean. And what I want from a phone is the ability to speak with someone else without them thinking I'm the love child of an unusual relationship between Stephen Hawking and Telstar.

I want a telephone that is full of telephone technology, not cameras and internets. I want it to be a Ryanair-no-frills phone. A Ronseal communicator that does only what it says on the tin. In other words, I don't want it to stop working every time I go behind a tree.

I'm not kidding. My phone cuts off – at least I think it does; it's so quiet, I can't be sure – where the M40 meets the M25. This is not the middle of the Gobi Desert. It's not the bottom of the Mariana trench.

Predictably, health and safety is the problem here. The reason why our phones are so useless as communicators is because if they were more powerful they'd fry our heads.

Fair enough, so how's this for a plan? When we go abroad, our phones hook up to whichever service provider has the strongest signal at that time. So why can't they do that when we're at home? When I'm in Devon, where Orange is strong, I want to talk via Orange; and when I'm in London, where Vodafone provides the best coverage, I want to use Vodafone. Is that impossible?

Technically, the answer is no. But financially it's 'difficult', so we're stuck with phones that shtwang lang. krzzzzz. Hello. Hello, hello . . .

Sunday 30 May 2004

We really have to draw a line under tattoos

As the rugby World Cup drew near, Jonny Wilkinson upped his training regime a notch. He was at the ground 12 hours a day for six days a week so that when the big day came he couldn't, and wouldn't, miss.

David Beckham seems to have taken a rather different approach as he prepares for the forthcoming Euro 2004 football tournament. Instead of wasting his time at the training camp, he has got himself another tattoo. His tenth, apparently.

Worryingly, it didn't seem to do him much good last week when England were held to a one-all draw by a Subbuteo team of Japanese little people.

But then it's hard to see how a tattoo might improve anyone's footballing skills.

In fact, it's hard to see the point of a tattoo at all.

I remember, when I was a local newspaper reporter in the late 1970s, writing a piece about unemployment in the wake of some strike or other. One interviewee told me he had all the right qualifications but was always rejected after an interview. He couldn't see why, but I could. It was the enormous spider's web that had been tattooed on his face.

There was a time when a tattoo would demonstrate that you had been in the nick or the navy, but now pretty well everyone I ever see has what looks like a huge Harley-Davidson motif peeping out of their trousers.

Has Camilla Parker Bowles got a giant eagle with a man's skull eating a snake on her backside? I wouldn't be at all surprised.

No, wait. Actually I would be surprised because despite the notable exception of Lord Lichfield, who has a sea-horse on his arm, and Sir Winston Churchill's mother, who had a snake round her wrist, tattooing is still very Club Yob. It's still the preserve of pole dancers and people with England flags fluttering from their car aerials. Abs, formerly from the band Five, has a tattoo on his nipple and I think that says it all.

Of course, when I was 16 I fancied the notion of having a small red Che Guevara-style red star permanently etched into my left buttock.

I didn't, for two reasons. First, the law states that you can't get a tattoo unless you are drunk. That's why 18 is the minimum age.

Second, a tattoo artist once ran his needle over my forearm to show me just what a painless experience it was. He was lying. It felt like I was being stabbed in slow motion.

What would I have ended up with? Aids, probably, and a smudge on my bottom. What's the point of that? Why endure all the pain and expense when you'll have something that you'll never see. That's like manhandling a giant Bukhara rug all the way back from Uzbekistan and then using it to carpet your loft.

You see these people, in *Heat* magazine usually, with half a yard of gothic symbolism plastered all over their back and you think: Do you hang your curtains pattern-side out for the neighbours to admire?

There are other problems, too. Tattooing has been around since the dawn of time, but if we examine the work of all the great artists – Leonardo da Vinci, van Gogh, Monet – we find they would apply their skill and dexterity to just about any surface: walls, ceilings, canvas, paper. But not the human body.

At no point did Constable ever think, 'I know, I'll paint *The Haywain* on Turner's arse.'

Tattoo art is invariably awful. David Beckham today is beginning to look like an Iron Maiden album cover. But then, look at the average tattoo artist.

Maybe, if my children were being held hostage, I would let Tracey Emin loose with the needles, but not a bald, 18-stone Hell's Angel with most of Travis Perkins's stock-room stuck through his nose.

I wouldn't mind, but most proper artists spend weeks thinking about their work and how it should be approached. What you get from the Hell's Angel is a five-minute consultation, and what you end up with is a doodle. Furthermore, most successful artists learnt their craft by wearing berets and walking along river banks. These tattoo guys, you know, learnt their craft by customising vans.

The only good thing is that when the subject dies, the tattoo dies too. Except in Japan, of course, where you can buy dead tattooed people to turn into furniture.

Interesting idea: yakuza scatter cushions.

I doubt if anyone would believe that a friend of mine's love for Ferrari was so intense that she had a prancing horse tattooed just above her G-string. Now, whenever she bends over, people say, 'Er, why has someone drawn a donkey on your back?'

It's rubbish, and she is stuck with it for ever. Oh, I know there are all sorts of procedures these days for having tattoos removed, but they cost – and hurt even more than having the damn thing implanted in the first place.

Do they work? Well, you only have to examine a blotched and botched London Underground train that's had its graffiti washed off to see the answer is no, not really.

Sunday 6 June 2004

Life itself is offensive, so stop complaining

Following two complaints from outraged Muslim leaders, a poster showing four young ladies in nothing but Sloggi G-strings has been removed from sites near mosques.

It's jolly easy to get all frothy about this. There will be those who will say that if Muslims don't want their children to see pictures of girls in their underwear they should have stayed in Uzbekistan. And doubtless those of a *Daily Mail* persuasion will point out that if a British person moves to France and complains about the local café serving horse burgers, he'll be told where to get off.

There are other issues, too. Christians claim that they've been complaining to the Advertising Standards Authority for years about 'lewd posters' to little or no effect. And yet all it takes is a raised eyebrow from a mullah, and Sloggi gets an eviction notice.

Sloggi, of course, maintains that it's difficult to advertise underwear without actually showing it. Although it could take a leaf out of Superman's book and have someone wear their thong on the outside of their trousers.

My problem with this, however, has nothing to do with race or positive discrimination or even the ASA. No. My problem is with the sanctimonious, mealy-mouthed, holier-than-thou, underemployed twerps who do the complaining.

Remember that 'Hello boys' advertisement for Wonderbra? That got 150 complaints.

Then there was the ad for Velvet toilet tissue with the slogan 'Love your bum'; 375 complained about that. Five hundred moaned about FCUK's logo and 275 worked themselves into a dizzy lather about Club 18–30's ad: 'Discover your erogenous zones'.

What you have to remember here is that all these people had to telephone directory enquiries for the number for the ASA, get the address, write a letter, buy a stamp and walk to a postbox.

It wouldn't be so bad if they merely wished to register their disapproval but, having gone to so much effort, they always say they want action and results.

It's not just in the world of advertising, either. Only this week the *Points of View* programme on BBC1 brought a dribble of complaints about excessive speed and what-have-you to the producer of *Top Gear* and asked if, in the light of these letters, he would be effecting changes in how the presenters drive and treat speed in future. Happily, he was bold enough to smile and say, 'No.'

But let's just imagine for a moment that he'd said yes. Let's imagine that we lived in a world where a handful of people could have something altered or banned by saying in a letter: 'I don't like this very much and I want it stopped.'

I could write to the Church Bells Standards Authority and, as a result of my complaint, campanology would be outlawed immediately. And after a second letter, all American tourists arriving at Heathrow would be turned away. How long do you think Bill Oddie would last in a world like this?

And not just Bill, either. I'm sure that the Queen, with her palaces and servants, upsets and annoys someone somewhere so let's ban her, too, and her family. And while we're at it, I know a handful of people who don't like that enormous new gherkin building in London, so let's pull it down, along with the British Library and Preston.

Cats give me asthma and I find their bottoms offensive, so everyone would have to put their beloved moggy in a sack and bash its head in with a croquet mallet.

Providing, of course, croquet hadn't upset someone in the meantime. In which case you'd have to use a frozen leg of lamb. Or, more likely, a nut cutlet.

Oh no, wait. Nuts can make some people swell up. So you see, already we've run into a problem. You've got your cat in a sack but no way of killing it.

I'm struggling to think of anything which would be permitted in a world where nothing was allowed to cause offence to anyone. Cars, condoms, Christianity.

Everything would have to go, except perhaps Michael Palin and maybe David Attenborough.

You probably think this is silly but I'm afraid it's not. When you go to the cinema these days, you're given a synopsis of the movie before the MGM lion has roared.

'This film contains scenes of flashing lights and strong language, and there's a bit of mild violence when the German's goggles fill with ketchup. Oh, and there's some semi-nudity when we see Susannah York in her stockings and I'm afraid there's a dog called Blackie.' This is because the audience may contain nuts.

And let's not forget, shall we, where this whole thing

started. Following just two complaints – that's two, not 2 million – the ASA has asked Sloggi to be more careful in future about where it places posters featuring girls in their underwear.

Happily our great leader, Tony Blair, is still a beacon of hope in this sanitised world. A million people complained, in person, about his plans to bomb Iraq, but he paid not the slightest bit of attention. We should all take a leaf out of his book.

Sunday 13 June 2004

Put the panic button down now and walk away quietly

A friend called last week in some distress to say that his VAT bill was a little larger than expected. Then I had lunch with somebody who spent the entire meal agonising over which school is best for his daughter.

Meanwhile, in Lambeth Palace the Archbishop of Canterbury is to be found, pacing his sitting room, wondering whether or not to make a guest appearance on *The Simpsons*. It's not exactly up there with Thomas à Becket's problems, is it?

The trouble is that, after about four billion years of worrying about sabre-toothed tigers, the plague, having your heart ripped out by religious zealots and being bombed by the Germans, we've been left with an inability to stop worrying when actually everything's fine.

We worry today about the onset of baldness and cellulite with the same intensity as people in 1665 worried about the Great Plague. Today, for instance, the sun is shining, the sky is a cobalt blue, the thermometer is nudging 75°F, I have received an unexpected windfall from a video distribution company, there are three parties lined up for the weekend and the children are well. Yet I'm sitting here worrying about the amount of junk there is in space. Only the other day a French rocket was destroyed when it hurtled into a partially eaten hamburger left in orbit by one of Neil Armstrong's mates. Or it could have been a speck of paint.

There are apparently 100,000 pieces of flotsam and jetsam whizzing round the Earth; and soon, experts say, somebody will be killed when his spacecraft crashes into a spanner dropped by some clumsy Russian, back in 1969.

I'm also worried that my daughter's skirt is too short, that Nigella Lawson may be turning into a man, and that the enormous quantities of Diet Coke that I drink in a day will give me tooth cancer. And I don't even read the *Daily Mail*.

The *Mail* sees terror and pain in just about every aspect of our lives today. Cornflakes will kill you unless an immigrant from Albania gets you first. Farmed salmon will rot your children's eyes, genetically modified wheat will invade your garden and eat your pets, and heaven help those who don't maintain an efficient oral hygiene programme. Because they're going to have killer mushrooms growing out of their gums.

I'd like very much to blame the newspapers for whipping up our worry genes into an undoable knot, but actually, I fear, the real culprit here is everybody aged over 40.

I, for instance, am plodding through middle age, convinced that the perfect world we enjoyed in, oh, about 1976 is being taken away and ruined. I don't see a need for speed humps and navel piercings, and I can't understand why I have to be called Jezza.

Every day I read the newspapers with a growing sense that the lunatics have taken over the asylum and that every single thing, from the Kyoto treaty to the endless bans on garden weedkillers, is designed to put the world into reverse.

It's sad, but older people always believe that life was better when they were younger. Hearing tales of my mother's upbringing is like being immersed in a warm bath with Enid Blyton. It was all one big Noddy story, with ruddy-faced constables chasing ragamuffins for scrumping apples.

The thing is, though, that her mother will have painted an equally fuzzy picture of *her* childhood, and so on. But in every single way, life at this precise second is better and more comfortable than at any time in the whole of human history.

We're told that entertainment is getting worse but even *Big Brother* is better than sitting in the front room watching grandad washing in a tin bath. My granny may have enjoyed her sun-drenched *Cider with Rosie* romps in the haywain, but when she had a toothache she had to go to the local barber, who hit the tooth with a hammer. When her husband lost his job, the family starved. And when her friend had a placenta previa, she died.

Back then you didn't worry about the Sats at your daughter's school or the length of her skirt, because the chances are she would have succumbed to something unspeakable at the age of four. And even if she did make it into double figures, she wouldn't have been allowed into a school or a polling station.

I look today at those people on *Oprah* prattling on about their tormented love lives and I can't help thinking: 'Yes, it can't have been nice to come home and find your son in women's underwear, but not that long ago you might have come home to find him in the sabre-toothed tiger.'

Then we have today's army of stress counsellors, who are on hand to iron out the emotional creases after some minor accident at work. They tell us that life in the twenty-first century is more complicated than ever before, but it just so isn't.

By encouraging us to fret about minor injuries and bits of the international space station dropping on our heads and the threat posed to mankind's very existence by farmed salmon and cornflakes and bloody global warming, we'll all be completely unprepared for the day when Saudi Arabia goes pop and we really do have something to worry about.

Sunday 4 July 2004

Yes, it used to be grim up north – now it's grimmer

It didn't take long. Just a few days after a report said that the north–south divide in Britain was getting wider, all sorts of commentators have leapt into print to say it isn't.

Bill Deedes, grand old man of the *Daily Telegraph*, argued that life up north in the 1930s was far worse than it is now; estate agents pointed to the burgeoning property market; and Ken Morrison, the supermarket chief, said shelf-stackers up north work harder than shelf-stackers down south.

We're told that Corby, in the London 'catchment area', has the highest percentage of unskilled workers, and Peterborough, just 50 minutes from King's Cross, has more business failures than any other town in the country.

So, people of Richmond-upon-Thames, you can relax. The gritty souls of Sheffield are not being forced through hunger to sell their children for medical experiments, so there's no need to drown in guilt. And there's no danger any time soon of being presented with a German-style reunification tax to keep the north afloat.

Actually, I wouldn't be so sure. I think we're heading for a genuinely serious problem. Because I think the north is in real trouble. When I was growing up in Doncaster, trips to London weren't much of a culture shock. Yes, it was big, but the food was just as lousy, the service was just as hopeless and the carpets were just as patterned.

In those days the people of Doncaster dug coal and operated power stations and built trains and tractors. Sure, they didn't earn as much as the people who ran banks in Tunbridge Wells, but the gulf wasn't that wide. It is now. I've spent the past couple of weeks in my home town and nobody over 40 seemed to have teeth, just the occasional lava-black stump. Worse, those under 40 who asked for an autograph hadn't the faintest idea how to spell their names.

It's all very well saying the housing market has boomed just recently, but the houses in question were going for £500 just four years ago. That they're going for £7,500 now in no way implies that the north–south divide is narrowing. Then there are the towns. Deedes may paint a gloomy picture of life up north in the great recession, but I urge him with all my heart to look at somewhere like Conisborough today. There is nowhere – absolutely nowhere – down south which is quite so desperate.

First of all, on a Tuesday morning in term-time the place was full of children, all of whom tried to sell me stuff – wheels, car radios, security, anything. I've seen this kind of thing in Chad and India and Cuba, but I'm talking about a town that's just 150 miles from Marble Arch.

Of course there are poorer places in London – Hackney, for instance, but in Hackney the badly-off are just part of the mix. In Conisborough there's no Hoxton Square to bring a bit of light relief. It's just mile after mile of broken windows and the bloody Earth Centre.

If a child from Doncaster were to visit London today, he'd have palpitations. He'd notice that everybody had teeth and Range Rovers and could write. He'd peer into the low-voltage world of the capital's restaurants and wonder what on earth people were putting in their mouths. And what, pray, would he make of a Lulu Guinness handbag?

I know, of course, that local newspapers up north, supported by people from Harrogate and Altrincham, will dismiss what I'm saying as the rantings of a spoilt southern media poof. But please don't get all cold prickly, because then everybody down here will continue to think you're all right. And you're not.

I know the north is friendly. I know about the community spirit in places like Conisborough. I know about the gritty resolve. I know about the joyous countryside. But what would you rather have: teeth or a nice view?

There have been calls for some of Tony's barmy army of civil servants to be moved up north, and there has been talk of the BBC shifting some of its services away from the capital. But I think they mean Amersham.

This sort of thing isn't enough. For the past century the south-east has had a gentle gravitational pull on the north, but now it has the tug of a black hole.

The latest figures suggest that if current levels of migration continue, nobody will be left in the north within 40 years.

You have only to look at my family tree for confirmation of this. Since 1780, every one of my forefathers was born and lived in Yorkshire. That's five generations on both sides of the family – maybe 2,000 people – all of whom were born, married and buried within 12 miles of one another.

Today I live somewhere else and so do all my cousins.

Even my mother, after 70 years in Doncaster, upped sticks last week and moved down south. There are many things which could be done to reunite the United Kingdom, but rather than preach I've been sitting here thinking about what it would take to entice me back there again.

I'm afraid it's a long list and it starts with '£1 million'. What about you? Are you a lapsed northerner? What would it take for you to go back? Let me know.

Sunday 11 July 2004

Stars staying alive is really killing rock'n'roll

When I heard that Morrissey was to re-form the New York Dolls for a concert in London this summer, I must confess that I raised a bit of an eyebrow.

The Dolls, when they met in the early 1970s, had absolutely no musical ability whatsoever. None of them could sing, none of them could play an instrument and, perhaps as a result, none of the albums they released was what you would call a commercial success.

Today, however, they are seen by many as one of the most important pieces of the rock'n'roll jigsaw.

In essence, they are credited with being the bridge between glam and punk rock, the band that spawned the Sex Pistols and the Clash in England, and the Ramones and Television in America.

They were punks before punk rock had been invented, so it was only right and proper that Morrissey should invite them over for a reunion gig. What puzzled me was how he intended to do it, because, put simply, most of them were dead.

First to go was the drummer Billy Murcia who, while supporting Rod Stewart on a tour of England, decided that it would be a good idea to make a champagne and mandrax cocktail. While unconscious, his friends put him in a cold bath and poured so much coffee down his throat that he drowned.

Undaunted, the Dolls replaced him with a chap called Jerry Nolan who could actually play the drums. This caused so many rows that he left the band and moved to Sweden, where he died from meningitis.

Meanwhile, the guitarist Johnny Thunders had expired in a blizzard of drugs, which brings me back to this reunion gig in London. Who, exactly, was going to be on stage?

Well, Arthur 'Killer' Kane, the original bass player, was there, but only just. He was completely bald and apparently heavily sedated. This was seen as normal. In the early days he was often so drunk that he had to mime not being able to play the bass, while a roadie actually did play it behind a speaker stack.

It wasn't normal, though. Unfortunately, Killer was suffering from leukaemia and last week he went west, too.

Often there are documentaries on ITV called *The Most Dangerous Jobs in the World*, but it's hard to conceive of any that are quite as perilous as being in the New York Dolls. In fact, being in any band in the 1960s or 1970s made nineteenth-century tunnelling look safe. The Who lost their bassist and drummer and the Beatles their guitarist and song writer. Maybe they should team up and form the Hootles. It's an idea.

Then you have Phil Lynott, Janis Joplin, Jimi Hendrix, John Bonham, Jim Morrison, Marc Bolan, Eddie Cochran, Brian Epstein, Duane Allman, most of Lynyrd Skynyrd, Cozy Powell, Alex Harvey, Ricky Nelson, Pete Ham and Tom Evans from Badfinger, Tim Hardin, Steely Dan's drummer, Bon Scott from AC/DC, half of the Grateful Dead, Chas Chandler, Johnny Kidd, Rory Gallagher,

James Honeyman Scott and Pete Farndon from the Pretenders, John Belushi, Elvis, Patsy Cline, Brian Jones, Stevie Ray Vaughan, Terry Kath from Chicago, and Sid Vicious. Even the Carpenters weren't a safe haven.

Of the 321 well-known musicians who died prematurely in the glory days of rock'n'roll, 40 were taken by drugs, 36 by suicide and a whopping 22 by plane or helicopter crashes. Thirty-five died in cars, 18 were murdered, nine drowned in their own vomit and five in their own swimming pools. Picking up a guitar in London in 1972 was more lethal than picking up a rifle in Stalingrad in 1942.

Coming home from school back then and saying you were going to be a Formula One racing driver would have prompted a sigh of relief from your mum: 'Well, thank God you're not going to be in a band.'

Now, though, things are different. With the notable and noble exception of Kurt Cobain, who blew whatever it was he had inside his head all over the wall with a shotgun, and Michael Hutchence, who went to meet his maker with an orange in his mouth, today's rock stars seem to be in rude good health.

So far as I'm aware, nobody in Duran Duran is dead and, the last time I looked, all of Busted weren't. Pink is in it and even Oasis have managed to steer clear of their swimming pools.

Perhaps this is the problem with music today. Perhaps the declining audience for Radio 1 and dwindling album sales have something to do with a lack of danger. Back in 1975 I would rush to see a band, partly because I liked the energy of a live concert and partly, subliminally perhaps, because there was a sense that they would all be dead by the following week. Usually they were.

You certainly don't get any of that from Will Young. I saw him perform at the Cornbury music festival last weekend, and while the tunes were perfectly jolly there was no sense that he might be found the next morning in a hotel room full of hookers and cocaine.

I see him as a perfect role model for my 10-year-old daughter. But I suspect she'd like him more if he filled his head with heroin and flew his private jet into an oil refinery.

Sunday 18 July 2004

Hoon's thinned red line is facing the wrong way

Three hundred years ago Europe was embroiled in a particularly complicated conflict called the Spanish War of Succession. I have no clue what it was all about – God, probably – but I do know that Britain walked away from the peace talks with a shiny new colony: Gibraltar.

Today, the 30,000 residents who cling to this rocky outcrop are still fiercely British, so, to mark the tercentenary of their liberation from Spain, the RAF is sending, er, its brass band. Which, after the defence cuts last week, is pretty much all it has left.

The navy was planning to send a hunter killer submarine, but that has been melted down and turned into Corby trouser presses. And the army? Well, they have sent their excuses, saying that they're a bit busy at the moment.

Geoff Hoon – how did we end up with a defence secretary called Geoff? – says his dramatic cuts will attune our armed forces to the threats of the modern age – and, of course, he has a point. Why spend billions on extravagant homeland security when the countries that are capable of staging an invasion won't and those that aren't can't?

People say we now have a smaller navy than Johnny Frog, but so what? We realised long ago that you don't have to fight the French for control of Gascony. You just have to find a decent estate agent and buy it.

And while the new socialist government in Spain is jolly angry about the Gibraltar issue, the only armada that it could muster these days has fishing nets.

We know the Germans are capable of atrocities but, honestly, can you see them firing up the Panzers any time soon? It's the same story with the Dutch, who are too busy buying Cuba to be a threat, and all is quiet on the Falklands front, too.

So all we have to worry about are a few disaffected Algerian youths and, frankly, using a nuclear submarine to deal with an angry teenager in Sidi Bel Abbes looks like overkill.

But we're looking no further than the end of our noses. Hoon is trimming the armed forces to meet the threats and responsibilities that he can see today, but trouble usually comes from the most unexpected quarters. Who could have guessed in 1918 as we celebrated our victory over the Germans that, just 21 years later, they would be back for more?

Better still, who in 1970 would have bet that the next three countries to face Britain's military might would be Iceland, Argentina and Iraq? And who could have known, as the 1990s wafted by, that Canada and Spain would be up for a spot of mid-Atlantic gunboat diplomacy?

How can Hoon possibly guess who's next: Belgium? Sudan looks likely but it could be Cambodia or, take a big gulp, Russia.

It's all very well saying that the Soviet empire has crumbled but have you not seen *Fatal Attraction*? You thought Glenn Close was dead, you relaxed and then, whoa, she reared up out of the bath with that big spiky knife.

Hoon seems to think that Russia is safe, though, because he has thrown doubt over hundreds of Eurofighters, believing that this extraordinary plane was designed to meet a threat that no longer exists.

We originally wanted 232 of them but have placed firm orders for only 55. What's more, he has asked for the planes to be reconfigured as ground-attack mud-movers rather than dogfighters. His reckoning is simple. Algerian youths do not have MiG-29s, nor do the Sudanese Janjaweed militia and nor does Robert Mugabe in Zimbabwe. What they have are headquarters that need blasting to kingdom come from hundreds of miles away.

Unfortunately, the Eurofighter was not built to do this. It was built for air-to-air action against Ivan. It was designed to win a knife fight in a phone box; and trying to convert it into something else is as silly as buying a washing machine and then using it as a sandwich maker.

I wouldn't mind, but Hoon has also decided to drop the Jaguar from Britain's arsenal even though it has just been through a massively expensive programme to fit better radar, better weapons and better display facilities for the pilots.

It's hard, therefore, to see what the RAF does have left. I read last week that they've found an old Mosquito in the Wash but, while there's some hope that its mighty Merlins can be coaxed back into life, after 60 years in the oggin its balsa wood body has pretty much rotted away.

Of course, these days you could argue that Britain hardly needs any armed forces at all because we're little more than a bird, riding around on the back of the rhinoceros that is America. We get to feast on the fleas that live in its hide and, in exchange, the mighty US military will stick its big horn into anything perceived as a threat.

That's fine, but what if the day comes when the rhino is no longer a responsible democracy? What if it one day elects a president with an IQ of 92 who decides to pick a fight with some large and fairly harmless state in the Middle East?

We'd have to trudge along, and it would be so expensive that the RAF would even have to think seriously about selling its trombones.

Sunday 25 July 2004

Whee, there's a golden apple in my family tree

It was announced last week that the highlight of your viewing pleasure in the autumn will be a series in which 10 people you've never met trace their family trees. You'll learn all about Moira Stuart's great-great-grandmother and discover that Bill Oddie had a sister he never knew about.

Sounds dull, doesn't it? It certainly sounded dull when the producers approached me last year, asking if I'd like to be one of the 10.

Initially I said no. Your own family tree is a sort of personalised version of Simon Schama's *History of Britain*, and that's fine. But someone else's? That would be as meaningless as Simon Schama's *History of Malaysia*. And watching it on television? That would be like watching a stranger's holiday video.

Of course, I can understand why people trace their own ancestors and why the 1901 census website crashed so spectacularly when it went online a couple of years ago.

It's for the same reason that scientists study black holes. Wanting to know where we came from is what differentiates us from the beasts.

Over the years I've occasionally thought about looking into my family's history because, like everyone, I harboured a secret desire to find it was John of Gaunt, then Warwick the Kingmaker, and then me.

But the reality is that we come from a long line of dullards, so I've never bothered. And I really could not see why my family history should form the basis for an hour-long television programme. Unless it was going to be called *Revealed: Britain's Most Boring Man*.

Actually, it could have been called *Revealed: Britain's Biggest Inbred* because preliminary research showed that my ancestors back to 1780 – and there were about 2,000 of them – had all been born within 12 miles of one another. It's a wonder I don't have one eye and a speech defect.

I argued and argued that there was no point going any further with the programme because none of these people had ever done anything remotely interesting; but my mind was changed when the producers revealed that my maternal grandmother was a Kilner. And the Kilners had been nineteenth-century zillionaires. Rich beyond the dreams of avarice. Owners of mills, ships and half of the warehouses that lined the Thames. Wasn't I just a little bit interested, they asked, to discover what had happened to the money?

Damn right I was, so for the past six months, motivated entirely by greed, I have been charging up and down the M1, unravelling a truly epic tale about the meteoric rise, and calamitous fall, of Britain's manufacturing industry.

While Bill Oddie found that he had a sister he never knew about, I found I'm related to the actor Keith Barron. So stick that in your binoculars and smoke it, beardie.

What amazed me, as the months flew by, is just how easy it is to unearth history in this country. I had a team of researchers to point me in the right direction, but even this would have been no use in, say, Scandinavia. There, all the ancient records were stored in wooden churches which over the years have burnt down. This means all the records are gone.

Here, I was able to stroll into Huddersfield public library and help myself to the original court records from an environmental lawsuit that had been brought against my family in 1870. Then I drove to Warwick University and read all about the strikes that plagued their mills in 1880. I even found the record of a fishing trip in 1780 on which the founder of the Kilner dynasty discovered the site for his first factory.

You can send off to the Probate Office for copies of your great-great-great-grandfather's will, and you can find out from the National Archives in Kew where he lived. Go there and, as often as not, the current owners will have photographs of the people you are researching.

I found one of my great-great-grandfather from 1901. He was sitting in a car he had bought, which then would have been like owning a Gulfstream V business jet. So he didn't give a damn about the environment and he was a petrolhead . . .

Of course the science of genealogy is fraught with difficulties, chief among which is the internet. Some say it's an invaluable resource tool, but the only Kilners I could find on Google were members of an American high school baseball team. This didn't seem relevant.

There are many companies in cyberland who promise to prove that you are the rightful Duke of Devonshire, but when you give them your money all you get back is some half-arsed coat of arms which proves only that you've been suckered.

Even in the real world, life for the history sleuth is hard because eighteenth- and nineteenth-century handwriting and spelling were lousy. I spent one afternoon reading what I thought was a history of glassmaking, but it could have been a recipe for baked Alaska.

Also, while record keeping has always been meticulous in Britain, people were not forced to register births until 1875. Worst of all, you can spend thousands of pounds and travel thousands of miles, only to find you are from a long line of farm labourers. Or, horror of horrors, that you are Bill Oddie's lost sister.

Sunday 1 August 2004

Blame your airport wait on dim Darren and Julie

I guess we've all been through an airport at some point in the past few weeks and I guess we all turned up, as requested, two hours before the scheduled departure time. Why? It used to be one hour, so why is it now two?

We're told that airports need the extra time because, in the wake of September 11, stringent security checks have to be made. Ah, yes. September 11. The one-size-fits-all excuse for absolutely everything.

Sure, in America the twin towers thing has slowed down your rate of progress through an airport to the point where technically you are classified as a missing person.

This is because, before the attacks, Americans treated planes like we treat buses. Security was so slack – the airlines didn't even have to match luggage to passengers, for instance – that I'm surprised Bin Laden's suicide jockeys had to resort to Stanley knives. I'd have thought they could have boarded with a brace of AKs and a box of rockets.

Now, though, the pendulum has swung completely the other way. The Americans won't let you on a plane until they've ruined your laptop, and half a dozen spaniels have had a good rummage round your shoes.

In the civilised world, however, where there are Red Brigades and Baader Meinhofs, we have known all about hijackings for 30 years, so airports have always been run like nuclear research facilities. We've always been bar-raged with silly questions while checking in. Bags have always had to be matched to passengers before a plane can take off. And the policemen have always dressed up like Vin Diesel.

In fact the only difference, so far as I can tell, between European air travel pre-September 11 and post-September 11 is that now you have to leave all your cutlery in a big bin before being allowed on board. So why the two-hour check-in rule?

It is a source of massive marital stress in this house. My wife insists on being there when asked, whereas I think 40 minutes is plenty.

I like to check in last, on the basis that the final bags to be loaded into the hold will be the first off at the other end, and I like to be greeted by a stewardess on the plane who tuts a lot and looks at her watch.

And here's the killer. I've never missed a plane.

Deep down, I've always suspected that the two-hour rule is nothing more than airport authorities using the destruction of the World Trade Center as a means of getting us into their giant shopping malls for an extra hour so we can spend more on currency converters, oysters and inflatable pillows.

My wife, who as I write is packing for our Easter break, says I'm a cynic. So, OK then. If security remains the same and it has nothing to do with pre-flight retail therapy, why? Why does anybody think it takes two hours to walk from one side of a building to the other?

Does it perhaps have something to do with obesity? Are we all now so enormous that we move at the pace of an earth mover? But with all the moving walkways at airports, I hardly think this is it. So why? In two hours, they could unpack and rebuild all the electrical appliances in my suitcase, perform keyhole surgery on my abdomen, do deep searches on all my relations and there'd still be enough time left to buy 200 fags and a tin of horrid Harrods shortbread. In two hours, I could park at Gatwick and have time to catch a plane from Manchester.

I suspect the answer may well be found by examining the class system. If you fly first or business, they tell you the check-in takes 60 minutes. It's only people in cattle class who are asked to get there two hours before the plane's due to leave.

On the face of it, this seems silly. Club-class people still have to get a boarding pass. Their bags still have to get to the plane. And don't say the single fast-track lane moves any faster than the 400 channels for ordinary people, because I assure you it doesn't.

So why should a club-class passenger be capable of getting to the plane in an hour when people in the back need two? Are airport authorities suggesting that people at the back can't read direction signs properly and get lost a lot? Are they saying people in thrifty cannot walk past a burger joint without being overwhelmed with a need to stuff their faces with chips? Are we to understand that the less well-off cannot tell the time?

Well, let's think. It's always the Darrens and the Julies who have to be paged over the airport PA. And it's only mouth breathers in football shirts who queue for half an hour for the X-ray machine and then empty their pockets of scissors and daggers. And when was the last time you saw a businessman fumbling around for his passport after he got to the immigration desk?

I may be on to something here. They want you at the airport two hours early because in Brainless Britain everyone else is too thick to get to the plane any faster.

Perhaps a national IQ standard might be the answer. People from Mensa should be allowed to check in two minutes before the flight goes. Those with worryingly long arms must be there somewhat earlier.

Sunday 22 August 2004

Proper writing is like so overr8ed, innit kids

When asked how he felt about the chaos at Heathrow last week, an American student who had been delayed for 12 hours said: 'I am so exhausted now, it's like, "whatever".'

This is interesting because I went on holiday this year with two 13-year-old girls. Actually no. Let's be specific about this. I went on a holiday where two 13-year-old girls were present. And one, who had been bombarded with text messages from a would-be suitor, said to the other: 'It's like, "whatever".'

In my daughter's world almost everything is 'like, whatever'.

The poor weather is like, whatever. The onset of a new school term is like, whatever. Paula Radcliffe's 23-mile marathon is like, whatever. Mysteriously, though, Led Zeppelin are so like, cool.

I'm sure your children speak the same way; I'm equally sure they deliver longer sentences in a flat monotone with a scorpion tail of rising inflection at the end.

This unbelievably irritating syntax, I suspect, has been picked up from too many Australian television programmes.

Couple these speech patterns with the 'like, whatever' that has come from some exclusively blonde and pink valley in Los Angeles, and we're left with an odd conclusion. A girl born in London and raised in Oxfordshire has developed an accent from somewhere in the middle of the Pacific. Yup, thanks to satellite television, my daughter now speaks Polynesian.

This is not the end of the world because eventually she will grow out of it in much the same way that you and I at some point stopped describing Emerson, Lake and Palmer as 'far out' and Goa as 'groovy'.

What she may not grow out of, however, is her insistence that 'today' is spelt with a 2 and that 'great' somehow has an 8 in it. This new language has now spilt from the mobile phone into her thank-you letters and homework.

Those of a *Daily Telegraph* disposition believe that txt spk spells the end for proper English and are furious, but really it's hard to see why.

Think. When pictograms and hieroglyphics were replaced with letters and numbers, did people paint angry drawings in green ink in the caves of Tunbridge Wells, declaring that this new 'writing' was the work of the devil? Imagine having to "write" to a newspaper wn you've hrd a swllw. How much easier it is to simply draw one.

Throughout history, great men have laboured over the written word, endlessly modifying the letters so they could be transcribed more quickly and read more easily. Nobody, for instance, complained when the Carolingian minuscule came along. They simply used it until they decided Gothic angularity was better. And then they used that.

The alphabet, too, has been endlessly altered to contemporary demands. Not until the invention of the settee and the dimmer switch and thus the introduction of

Nancy Mitford's guide to what's in and what's not was the letter U deemed necessary. It was not until the fifteenth century that we were given a J, and although the W came along in the tenth century, modern Germans still seem to manage perfectly well by using a V instead. Except when the German managing director of Aston Martin tries to say 'vanquish'.

Geoffrey Chaucer wrote 'nostrils' as 'nosethirles' and Shakespeare spelt his name differently on each of the five occasions he is known to have written it. Spelling was not an issue until the invention of school and the consequent need to fill the children's day with something other than rotational farming methods.

Now our days are filled with distractions. You've got to locate a signal for your BlackBerry, download some garage on to your iPod and still find time to work, cook, clean the house and kick someone's head in on the PlayStation. Speed writing is therefore a damn good idea.

At journalism college I was taught Teeline shorthand and although I wasn't very good at it – I cheated in my final exam by using a tape recorder, long hair and an earpiece – I did recognise that it made a great deal more sense than the traditional phonetic alphabet.

Some people, even without the benefit of long hair and earpieces, were happily writing at 110 words a minute, more than twice what could be achieved if they were writing 'properly'. So why, I figured, if this works so well, do we still persevere with ABC, the language of the quill?

We changed the way we wrote when steel-nibbed pens replaced feathers, so why not change now that silicon impulses have replaced the Biro? You can't write shorthand on a conventional keyboard but you can write txt spk. And it is perfectly legible. '2day i wnt 2 c the dctr who sd my bld prssur ws gr8'. What part of that can you not understand? A language without vowels: it's never done the Welsh any harm.

Adopting txt spk as the new alphabet would mean that I could say more each week in this tiny creased corner of your newspaper. And because I'm paid by the word it means that I'd be better off too. This would be 'cool'. And the lovely thing is that the newspaper's accountants would have to dismiss the pay rise by saying it's 'like, whatever'.

Sunday 29 August 2004

I have now discovered the highest form of life: wasps

There was much talk in the scientific community last week about the origins and meaning of an interstellar radio message picked up by a telescope in Puerto Rico.

To the untrained ear it sounds like a Clanger talking to the Soup Dragon, but to those who run Seti, the search for extra-terrestrial intelligence, it could well be 'first contact', the first real evidence that we are not alone in the universe.

The temptation is to reply, but how do we know the message was meant for us? What if it were directed at some other species on Earth? And how would the sender respond if he were to discover that his intergalactic email had been intercepted? I have a horrible feeling that the real recipient may be the wasp, which this year seems to be around in greater numbers than ever. Come on, you must have noticed that since the signal was picked up it has been impossible to go outside without being buzzed.

There's plenty of evidence that wasps are not of this earth. Unlike any other animal, with the possible exception of the owl and the Australian, they serve no purpose. They're not in the food chain, they can't make honey and they're not fluffy. Nature has a habit of extinguishing its more useless experiments. The dinosaur went west when it grew too big and the dodo when it mislaid its wings.

But the pointy yet strangely pointless wasp soldiers on. Why?

There's more, too. Wasps can smell a bowl of sugar from five miles away. How? Sugar does not smell. What's more, they can organise flight paths from their nests to known sources of food. Again, how, unless they have been trained in the complexities of air traffic control?

Here's another nugget. Wasps are vindictive. Pretty well every creature will attack when it's hungry or threatened whereas a wasp will attack if you've annoyed it in some way. Local councils, which tend to be staffed by animal-loving eco-mentalists, are forever producing leaflets portraying the wasp as a benign part of the British summer – a sort of airborne nettle – forgetting perhaps that each year wasps kill more people than sharks, alligators, lightning, scorpions, jellyfish and spiders combined.

And try this for size. A wasp can lay its eggs inside a caterpillar, knowing that when they hatch the baby wasps will be able to eat the creature from the inside out. And here's the really clever bit. Normally, the host's immune system would destroy the eggs before they had a chance to hatch; so, to get round this they are coated with a virus that genetically modifies the caterpillar to ignore the invasion. In other words, a wasp can alter the very being of another creature.

Biologists have examined this virus and found that it exists nowhere else on Earth. They've also worked out that it's been around for more than 100 million years . . . which is when that strange radio message from the stars was sent.

You may be interested to learn that wasps eat garden

furniture. They chew the wood, mixing it with saliva to make paper for their nests. And we think dolphins are intelligent. Furthermore, wasps are pretty much indestructible. I now have an electric tennis racket that turns the art of insect control into a sport. Instead of catgut, the strings are made from metal strips connected to a powerful battery. One touch will kill anything up to and including a large dog, but wasps? They sit there, jiggling around, until you take your finger off the power button, whereupon they simply fly away.

Only the other day, after what I have to say was a damn good shot, I cut a German Yellowjacket in half with a carving knife. Such a devastating blow would have killed Flipper instantly, but the wasp? Its head remained alive, its antennae wiggling, perhaps sending messages to outer space, pinpointing my position.

We need at this point to examine the mating characteristics of the wasp, which are, to say the least, odd. As summer draws to an end the males produce a huge semen duvet in which the queen will hibernate. When she wakes for the spring, she uses the sperm to fertilise her eggs and the cycle is repeated.

This process poses a few questions. How, for instance, does a wasp produce semen? This would involve masturbation, and that's a concept which is difficult to visualise: 10,000 wasps in a nest all taking Captain Picard to warp speed. We know they are making paper for their nests, but what else are they using it for? To print some copies of *Asian Babe Wasps*? 'Ooh, Adolf. After you with that picture of the Norwegian queen.'

It sounds unlikely. It sounds even more unlikely when

you discover that having spent the summer collecting proteins for their young, adult male wasps are free, as autumn approaches, to gorge themselves on rotting apples. This renders them fat, lazy and drunk.

Perhaps this is why the radio message has been received. Perhaps the alien beings that put the wasp on Earth are calling to find out why world domination has not yet been achieved. I doubt they'll be pleased when they find that their army has been defeated by Granny Smith.

Sunday 5 September 2004

The doctors are out to get me

Yesterday I spent the afternoon pretty much naked, in a darkened room, while an attractive blonde applied lashings of warm lubricating jelly to most of my soft underbelly. Sounds like fun. But unfortunately this was an ultrasound test, part of my fourth medical so far this year.

I have been sucked dry, pumped up, bent double and asked a range of questions so impertinent that even Paxman would blanch. I've been probed, hit, tickled, smeared and X-rayed, and I've forgotten what it's like to pee in a lavatory. These days, I only ever relieve myself into small plastic vials.

The problem is that insurance companies like to be absolutely sure you're not at death's door before providing cover. Which, surely, is a bit like asking to see the dealer's cards before making a bet.

To make matters worse, insurance is far from the only reason why you need a medical. You need one for an HGV licence, or a mortgage, or a job. And every single organisation insists that you undergo its bespoke check-up.

Things are so stupid that my local practice employs someone who spends half her working week dealing with nothing but people who want to borrow five grand for a kitchen extension. And she can't even do that properly, thanks to me. Because I have so many contracts with so many people, and because I'm forever climbing into jet fighters, I have become The World's Most Checked Man. As such, I am a leading expert on medicals.

When I went away to school, the doctor held my testicles and asked me to cough. He could have established my reflexes were fine by tapping my knees gently with a small rounders bat, but hey, this was a public school, so into the pants he plunged.

Would that it were that simple these days. Today, the first question you're always asked is, 'Have you got Aids?' Well unless you can catch it from slobbing in front of the television, or going to Cotswolds dinner parties, I very much doubt it.

The second question you're asked is whether you're partial to a bit of same-sex heroin. Can we just get one thing clear. I know there are no Conservative voters in the media, but there are several heterosexuals and I'm one of them. And no, I've never slept with an East African prostitute, and the only hypodermic needle I've seen all week is the one you're about to plunge into my arm to check I'm not lying.

The fact that I smoke 60 cigarettes a day and drive like a maniac for a living doesn't seem to bother them. Not until you get to page 442 on the form.

When they're absolutely convinced that you're not a Glaswegian smacked-up rent boy with a girlfriend in Nairobi, they move on to check your blood pressure. Mine is 100/60, same as it was last week, when the Norwich Union asked the same damn thing.

Then you pee in another jar, and then you sit back as

the nurse hunts around for the tiny bit of blood you have left after the Scottish Widows had their fill the previous month. After all the blood tests this year, I couldn't even be a donor for an injured field mouse. Small wonder the pressure's so low: I'm empty.

After my fluids have been checked, the doctor normally sticks his whole head in my bottom. Well, that's what it feels like. 'Aaaaaaaaaaaaaaaargh,' I normally say, until he comes out again to explain that it was only his finger.

Soon, you will be led to the scales which, in doctors' surgeries, are always set to over-read. I am 15 stone, minus a few pounds for all the blood and urine that's been extracted. But in a doctor's surgery, I weigh about the same as the Flying Scotsman. This, to an insurance company, is a good thing. Whoever heard of a fat heroin-user? And what's more, fat people are *ipso facto* unattractive, which means they're less likely to be having much in the way of man-on-man action.

At the end of the session, by which time everyone in the waiting room has died from whatever it was that brought them there in the first place, you will be asked for the medical history of your entire family, back to the middle of the eighteenth century.

Why? Even after the doctor has hit you in the elbow with his hammer and asked you to read his wall, he will still not know if there are tumours the size of conkers dangling from your brain, but the form will be completed anyway.

And you'll be on your way to a new conservatory.

It's all a complete waste of time, and I haven't finished yet because at some point in the procedure, the GP is bound to uncover something that warrants further investigation. This will mean a trip to the hospital where you will get lost.

I did, and that's how I came to be lying in a darkened room, with a pretty blonde smearing me with KY Jelly. She then ran her ultrasound detector all over my belly, before turning on the light and giving me the good news. I'm not pregnant.

Sunday 12 September 2004

Let's brand our man's army

A new type of training shoe was introduced this week. It is grey, made in Vietnam and costs £39.50. Or £79 if you want one for the other foot as well.

In a world of Nike Motion Control Air Sprung Hi-Loaders, you might expect this rather dour and expensive new product to be a commercial flop. But, because the shoe was tested by someone's mate in the forces, it's being sold with an army insignia on the box. That makes it a 'British Army' training shoe, and that gives it an appeal Nike can only dream about.

Branding has now reached the point where the product doesn't matter; only the logo. Already you can avail yourself of a JCB cardigan and pop down to the off-licence for a litre of Kalashnikov vodka – guaranteed to blow your head clean off. And how long will it be before Cadbury gets into romantic fiction, and Louis Vuitton into cars?

Even the dullest and most useless products are enlivened by the right name. A hotel, for instance, can raise its prices if it provides Gilchrist & Soames shampoo in its bathrooms. Who are Gilchrist & Soames? God knows, but the handle has a nanny-knows-best ring to it. There's a sense that it'll bring a well-scrubbed gleam to your secret gentlemen's places.

I have no problem with this. If I'm in a shop, faced

with a choice of two cardigans that seem similar, I'll go for the JCB option because there's a subliminal assumption that Anthony Bamford has personally inspected the sheep from which the wool came and his wife, Carole, has done the knitting. For sure there's a suggestion that the company wouldn't waste 50 years of hard graft by sticking its badge on rubbish.

A prestigious badge gives clueless shoppers a sense of well-being, a sense that their money is not being wasted on tat.

The perfect life, then: suit by Knight, Frank & Rutley, mobile phone by Boeing, car by Bausch & Lomb, furniture by Holland & Holland, kitchen utensils by Mercedes-Benz, children by Uma Thurman, armpit hair by the mysterious Gilchrist & Soames and, best of all, shoes by the British Army.

This is the first time the service has endorsed a commercial product and there's no doubt it's entering a minefield. Colonel Robert Clifford, head of the Queen's Own Light Sponsorship Brigade, said this week: 'We need to be exceptionally careful about what we link ourselves to.' Too right, matey.

You could probably get away with a 'British Army'-branded Land Rover or some green 'British Army' binoculars – the Swiss Army has sponsored penknives for years. I think 'British Army' lager might be worth a go, too.

But I don't think 'army' meat pies or 'army' haircuts would go down well. Also, I probably wouldn't want to spend time on an 'army' holiday. It might have worked 100 years ago when they were in Ceylon and half the

Caribbean, but today they only go to Belfast, Belize or Basra.

This leaves us with a problem.

The small income that could be generated from Land Rovers, binoculars and lager would in no way compensate for the inevitable outcry that such a scheme would provoke.

However, what if the deal were to work the other way around? Instead of the army sponsoring commercial products, why not get the makers of those products to sponsor the army?

Everyone looks up when an Apache gunship heaves into view, so why not sell advertising space along its flanks? Obviously, in times of war you'd have to cover up the Pepsi logos because they're a bit bright, but in peacetime, why not?

All the forces could join in. We could have easy-Destroyers and Lastminute.com transport planes. Marl-boro, I'm sure, would cough up for the already Red Arrows, and local firms could get in on the act, too, sponsoring individual soldiers. Sergeant Brian Griffiths is brought to you by Cartwright & Jones – family butchers since 1897.

It's all very well saying this is a ludicrous plan, but what would you rather have? HMS *Persil* or no warship at all? Because soon that might very well be the choice we face. And let's not trot out the tired old argument that sponsorship would undermine the dignity of the most successful armed forces in the whole of human history.

Where's the dignity in being allowed to fire only 10 live rounds a year? Where's the dignity in not being able to afford to take the ships out to sea? And running them on one engine when they do? Where's the dignity in flying a fighter that has no gun because the MoD can't afford one? We keep being told that soldiers in Iraq use their own mobile phones because the army's radio equipment can't even pick up Terry Wogan, and I'm sorry, but that doesn't sound very dignified either.

I'm not suggesting that a soldier should be made to wade into battle looking like a Formula One racing driver, but there is a happy medium. I'm thinking, as a guide, of the discreet but effective logos allowed at Wimbledon; a little patch on the epaulette that lets the watching TV cameras know that the wearer drives an Audi.

Sunday 19 September 2004

Go to school, see the world

Every morning, it seems, I open the papers to be confronted with a photograph of yet another bronzed gap-
year student 'with the world at her feet' who's been
murdered while trekking through some fleapit on the
wrong side of the equator.

If I were the parent of teenage children today, I'd advise
them to stay home in their year off and experiment with
heroin instead. It's a lot safer.

Happily, my children are far too young to be stabbed
in the Australian outback and, even more happily, by the
time they are old enough they will have been on so
many exotic school trips that the world's wildernesses are
unlikely to hold much appeal. 'Oh, not the Kalahari again.
I did that in Year 2.'

The trips run by my school, back in the 1970s, weren't
remotely exotic. Once we were taken to Matlock Bath
with a Penguin biscuit, but this was an exception.

Mostly, they'd load us on to the school minibus, which
would then be driven by a certifiable lunatic to the Peak
District, where we'd be made to walk five miles through
a peat bog to look at a millstone grit outcrop.

'In geology,' the psychopath would bark, 'this is a series
of sandstones, grits and conglomerates, resting directly on
the carboniferous limestone . . .'

'Hmm,' we'd all think, 'but is it big enough to hide behind while we have a fag?'

Then you had the Combined Cadet Force, which was public school code for genocide.

Large numbers of boys were bussed in eighth-hand army lorries to the Yorkshire Dales, where we were told to leap to our deaths from cliffs, or walk around with millstone grit outcrops on our backs until we collapsed from heat exhaustion.

Anyone who did actually die was given detention.

Today, things seem rather different. My kids are only at prep school, and already they're talking about whether they want to go bear-baiting in Alaska or skiing in the Urals. Or maybe both. 'Oh please, Dad. Aramoctavethia and Phoebocia are going, so why can't I?'

Well, one of the reasons is that parents budget for the school fees without realising that, in fact, we'll need half as much again for Icelandic windcheaters, horse rental in Argentina and a Unimog for the South Pole. Seriously, by the time my eldest leaves for 'big school' she's likely to have more Air Miles than Henry Kissinger.

And big school, of course, is much, much worse. School magazines in the olden days – i.e. the 1980s – used to show photographs of well-scrubbed boys and girls at their desks, learning algebra. Now, school magazines look like brochures for Kuoni.

They're full of boys and girls building box girder bridges in South Africa and sensitive radio telescopes in the jungles of Costa Rica. I'm not sure this is a good idea, because if a child has tackled the Zambezi, rescued

14 Colombian tribes from McDonald's and colonised Mars by the time they're 18, what's left?

Mostly, when I was young, we went on holiday to Cornwall, although, once, I seem to remember spending a fortnight in the shadow of a gasworks just outside Jedburgh.

So when I reached adulthood I went berserk. The stamps in my passport became so prolific that I needed another, and because that was always away having visas stapled in place, I had to get a third. In the space of 10 years, I visited more than 80 countries and spent at least one night in each of the US States. I made Hemingway look like an agoraphobic and Alan Whicker like a slugabed.

As soon as the door to China was just slightly ajar I was bounding through the Forbidden City with my Nikon, and it was the same story in Vietnam, and Cuba. I went to Norway once, simply because it was the only European country I hadn't visited, and I vacuumed up the Mediterranean islands like a dog vacuums up the crumbs from a five-year-old's birthday party.

Eventually, though, the ants in my pants settled down and I realised that, while the world can offer many beautiful and wondrous experiences, home is where your friends are. And no experience is ever quite as rewarding as being in the gooey, firelit bosom of your family.

As a result I now sigh and mooch around with shoulders like a bent coathanger if I even have to go to Oxford; but that's fine. I'm 44 and that's a sensible age to pack away the pith helmet and pick up the secateurs for a spot of light gardening.

But 18?

I have a horrible feeling that my kids are going to leave school not prepared for the world but sick of it.

Obviously they will be far too tired for any further education, which doesn't matter because by then universities will be allowed to take only working-class children. That means there will be no gap year either, and that means they won't be stabbed in Sudan.

Instead, they'll come home from their A-levels having done much too much, much too young. This will mean they'll spend the next 10 years of their lives eating crisps and drinking beer while shooting aliens on the PlayStation.

Sunday 26 September 2004

Space virgins need chutes

If someone were to build a passenger-carrying rocket for joyrides into space, would you go? Of course you would, unless you're a farmyard animal or A. A. Timid Trousers Gill.

So let me put it another way. If Richard Branson were to build a passenger-carrying rocket for joyrides into space, would you go? Hmm.

In the '90s, barely a week went by when we weren't treated to the unedifying spectacle of Branson's rat-like little face being winched, at our expense, from some vast expanse of ocean. His speedboats kept running into lumps of wood, and his balloons were always too heavy for sustained flight. 'Shave off the face fungus, Beardy. That'd lighten things up,' I used to shout as his capsule plummeted into the oggin yet again.

Secretly, though, I've always had a bit of a soft spot for His Richardness.

Despite his Virgin Cola, which is an affront to the sensibilities of any twenty-first-century being, I like the way he's made it in business without a pinstripe suit or an obvious predilection for golf and freemasonry. And despite the often disastrous attempts to go across the Pacific on a small horse, or up Everest in a washing machine, I do like the way he kept on trying.

There are those who say he's a publicity-hungry

monster but, you know, there are easier ways of getting your phizog in the papers than hurtling across the Atlantic at 50 knots. He could have chosen to sit in a jungle while two goblins from up north pour maggots into his ears, for instance. So let's give the poor bloke a break and look more carefully at this space programme of his.

He says that within three years he'll be in a position to offer seats on a spaceship at something like £150,000 a pop. Apparently it'll be no more risky than early commercial jet flight, which, if you remember the Comet, means it'll be extremely dangerous and very many rich people will be killed.

But once we've buried what's left of Elton John and Bill Gates, the economies of scale will kick in, and soon poor people will be able to die in the freezing radioactive wasteland of space, too. The idea of putting ordinary punters into space was kick-started by the $10 million Ansari X prize for the first private venture that could put a passenger-carrying craft 62 miles above the Earth, twice, within two weeks.

Because we've all grown up with Nasa absorbing more money than the Third World, the notion of any individual doing space travel on the cheap seemed as preposterous as DIY brain surgery. But back in June, a machine called SpaceShipOne, funded in part by one of Microsoft's founders, managed to break the 100–kilometre boundary.

It was an elegant solution. A conventional plane took off with the spaceship on its back. And then, at 47,000 feet, where the air is already thin and the fuel-consuming part of a journey is already done, the spaceship lifted off and was blasted by a rocket motor out of the atmosphere. It then glided back to Earth, ready to go up again.

It didn't, because the pilot reported several anomalies, chief among which was a huge bang midway through the flight. Finding out what it was, and fixing it – which they did by painting one of the panels white to reflect heat – meant the second flight was delayed to this week. Early reports suggest that this went flawlessly, apart from the mother ship going into a perilous spin after separation.

So now we have Branson stepping into the breach, saying that by 2007 Virgin Galactic will be using larger versions of SpaceShipOne to transport paying passengers. I do have some concerns about this, none of which has anything to do with perilous spins, loud bangs or Branson's previous failures. No, my main worry is that the passengers will conform to Branson's relaxed style and be allowed to fly in jumpers and corduroys.

If I went, and I would, I'd want the full Michelin Man suit, with an aqualung and a parachute. And I'm not being silly.

Back in August 1960 an American pilot called Joe Kittinger climbed into the open gondola beneath a balloon called Excelsior III and floated up to 102,800 feet. At this point, 20 miles above the Earth in what is technically space, he jumped.

Moments later he became the first man to go through the sound barrier without the benefit of a plane. It was, and still is, the highest parachute jump ever, and it proved you can 'abandon ship' even when you're in space.

I met Kittinger a couple of years ago and he's adamant

that if the crew of the Challenger had been equipped with chutes, some might well be alive today.

Branson ought to bear this in mind. It's all very well promoting a relaxed service; but passengers are going to look pretty silly if they're stuck in space wearing nothing but a nice V-neck and a pair of slacks.

What's more, a 62-mile parachute jump through the furnace of re-entry would certainly add pizzazz to what otherwise might be a once-in-a-lifetime op . . .

Sunday 3 October 2004

Call that a list of best films?

Another day. Another chart listing the best British films ever made.

The last time I looked, the British Film Institute was busy claiming that something called *The Third Man* was at number one, though I couldn't for the life of me work out why, since it was about a man who went to see a friend who was dead.

In second place it was *Brief Encounter* in which a man meets a woman in a railway station, and in third we had David Lean's *Lawrence of Arabia*, which was about a homosexual who rides a camel round the desert. And then crashes his motorbike and dies.

I can't be doing with David Lean. First of all, his ears were far too big, and secondly all his films feature lots of locals in loincloths and too much dust.

And as for *The Bridge on the River Kwai*. God almighty. Jesus took less time to die than Alec Guinness.

Last week, however, *Total Film* magazine said that the best British film ever is *Get Carter*, in which Michael Caine wears a mac and goes up north.

Other notables in the top 20 are *The Wicker Man*, in which we saw someone pretending to be Britt Ekland banging on a wall, *A Clockwork Orange*, which was mad, and *If*, which I always thought was a scientific experiment to see if you can actually die of boredom.

The only Bond film to make the grade was *From Russia With Love*, which came in at number nine. Why? With the possible exception of *Moonraker*, this early Sean Connery flick was one of the worst 007 adventures.

Of course I know these surveys are supposed to prompt debate down at the pub. I know that listing the top 10 coolest windmills and the top 10 zaniest animals are all meant to be the start of an argument, not the end.

But when it comes to British films there is no debate because the best one ever made, without a doubt, is *The Long Good Friday*. A movie that *Total Film* doesn't even put in the top 25.

They credit Michael Caine with genius in *Get Carter*, but for real simmering violence you just can't beat Bob Hoskins and the immortal 'I put money in all your pockets'. As a general rule, I like to watch this film at least once a month.

The second-best British movie was *Local Hero*, starring no one you've ever heard of, apart from Burt Lancaster, who was brilliant, and set right up at the top of Scotland.

There have been (a very few) funnier films, but none has been quite so touching.

When I first saw it I left the cinema, turned round and went straight back inside to watch it again.

In third place it's *The Killing Fields*, which was about . . . well, just about everything actually. Hate, war, friendship, hope, desperation, evil, incompetence, genocide, journalism and platonic man-love, all crammed into 141 spellbinding minutes.

It took David Lean 141 minutes just to get Peter O'Toole's camel from one side of a sand dune to the other. And it took even longer for Alec Guinness to fall on that plunger.

Like many British films, *The Killing Fields* was gently peppered with actors from the small screen. We had Bill Paterson from *Auf Wiedersehen Pet* and Patrick Malahide, who was Detective-Sergeant Chisholm in *Minder*. This would normally be something of a credibility hurdle, but I was so wrapped up in the story I wouldn't have minded if Amos from *Emmerdale Farm* had wandered into shot.

In fact I could make a fairly watertight case that *The Killing Fields*, along with *Local Hero* and *The Long Good Friday*, are not just the best British films of all time but the best from anywhere in the world.

Obviously there have been many wondrous cinematic events from America but, generally speaking, Hollywood movies are designed for 15-year-old youths from North Dakota who, intellectually speaking, are on equal terms with a British zoo animal.

As a result, US films tend to be rather too full of explosions and everyone's teeth are too white.

Then you have French cinema, in which a man meets a woman. They spend about two hours looking at one another, in black and white, over a cup of coffee. And then the man goes off with another man to have some graphic sex.

I would never argue that all British films are better than all foreign films. As often as not, our directors and screenwriters got their funding from FilmFour, handed in their notice at the *Guardian* and went off to make what looked like a social services training video.

Of course it always got rave reviews from the frizzy-haired critics and the compilers of best-film-ever surveys, but in America the audiences were usually not that interested in the fortunes of a Manchester drug addict. They would have preferred it if Manchester had simply exploded, and as a result the film almost always flopped.

Trainspotting was only rescued because the writer remembered to include a plot.

Trainspotting, by the way, was the fourth best British film. And you can work out the rest over a pint at lunchtime.

Sunday 10 October 2004

Two fingers to the pension

Life used to be so easy. At the age of 65 you retired with a nice carriage clock and went home to spend your pension on potting plants and pipe tobacco. Then, 10 years later, you died.

Now things are very different. You retire at 63 and go home to spend your pension on kickboxing classes and cocaine. You have no plans to die at all.

This, as I'm sure you read last week, is having a dramatic effect on pensions. The country can afford to keep its senior citizens in old shag for 10 years but not coke for 30. Not when the number of retired people exceeds the number working.

As a result, the young people of today have been told to expect some harsh changes. They will have to save 30 per cent of what they earn and hand over 70 per cent to the government. They will be expected to work down the mines until the age of 127 and even then they will be expected to die, in poverty, in a puddle of vomit.

Stern-faced men are saying the country must find an extra £57 billion a year for pensions by 2050 if old people are to enjoy the same standard of living that they have today.

It all sounds very gloomy, but £57 billion is nothing. We learnt last week that the government has spent £30 billion on a computer system for the NHS.

In the past few months I've watched Oxford Council spend what must have been £57 billion inserting bollards to make life harder for motorists, then taking them away, then building them again.

Thanks to changes made by Margaret Thatcher in 1979, we're going to fall short of the pensions bill by only 5 per cent. In France they'll miss it by 105 per cent. In Germany it'll be 110 per cent. Then there's the United States.

I read a book by Niall Ferguson while on holiday this year. It's called *Colossus*, it's about the American empire and it argues that already the gap between what America has and what it needs to keep its old people in burgers is $45 trillion.

Now, I don't know what a trillion is, but I do know that $45 trillion is roughly 10 times more than the total combined wealth of Germany, France, Italy and Britain.

It seems there are three ways this vast deficit can be covered: they can either increase taxes, immediately, by 69 per cent or cut medicare benefits by more than a half, or stop all federal purchases for ever.

I haven't seen either John Kerry or George W. Bush suggest they'll be doing any of these things. And that's bad news, because the situation is becoming more critical.

If nothing has happened by 2008, taxes will have to go up by 74 per cent.

No president, of course, will ever impose any such increase, which means that with the certainty of *Titanic*'s fate once it had hit the iceberg, America will go spectacularly bankrupt. It is, according to the author, an inescapable fact.

Long before that happens, however, the US will renege

on all its foreign debt, which will bankrupt the entire world, causing famine and maybe even some kind of holocaust. So you'll look a bit of a Charlie if you've spent the previous 40 years squirrelling away £30 a week for your old age.

This is the fundamental problem with pensions. You are saving for a future you don't yet know. You're taking care of something that might never happen – your old age. You could live a life of thrift and then, the day before your pension matures, you could be trampled to death by a horse. Or win £17 million on the lottery. Or watch America go bust, taking the International Monetary Fund and your pension fund with it.

What's more, how do you know that the people you entrust with your savings will look after them wisely? How do you know they won't raid the fund, spend it on a boat and then jump off?

Every night commercial television is littered with multi-million-pound advertisements for pension companies. That's your money – your nest egg – they are spending, trying to attract more suckers so they can build a taller, shinier office block. From which they can plan more adverts.

The government's no better. If ministers take our money, saying we can have it back when we're old, how do we know they won't give it all to Oxford Council so it can knock over bollards to make way for new ones?

Believing that the chancellor will have a special ring-fenced fund to be spent only on pensions is as silly as thinking your road tax is spent on the roads. It isn't. It's spent on new NHS computers and, of course, on the civil service, which I see now employs more people than live in the city of Sheffield.

Of course they'll be fine. They are on the I'm All Right Jack Civil Service Pension Fund. But what about you? Well, I suggest you buy something stupid like a plasma television and sit in front of it with a big Twix and a packet of killer fags.

Because, do you want to end up poor in a bankrupt world, full of civil servants? Thought not.

Sunday 17 October 2004

This is how the world ends . . .

Crikey. Out of absolutely nowhere the Danes have announced that they own the North Pole, and just in case anyone gets any fancy ideas that they don't, they're embarking on a series of surveys which will prove it.

Over the next few years they will spend £13 million demonstrating that the top of the world is connected by a vast underwater mountain range to Greenland, which is one of Denmark's dependencies along with, er . . . the Faroe Islands and, um . . .

Iceland. Oh no, hang on a minute. They lost that.

So why, you may be wondering, after two centuries of sitting in a sauna have the Danes suddenly decided to get themselves an empire?

Well, they reckon that, thanks to global warming, the ice cap will soon melt, allowing man to access a subterranean lake full of black gold. Brilliant. Denmark becomes Europe's Saudi Arabia and everyone in Copenhagen will have a big Cadillac.

Unless, of course, it turns out that there is no oil up there. And I foresee some other problems, too, chief among which is the notion that states can claim parts of the world just because they're connected by some kind of underwater geology. I mean, on that basis Ireland could claim ownership of Tunisia.

There's another issue, too. According to a new(ish)

book called *Doomsday Just Ahead*, the North Pole has not always been where it is now. And at some point in the next 30 years it'll be on the move again. According to its author Ian Niall Rankin the last Ice Age was caused by what he calls a polar shift, and now apparently another shift is on the way, because the Earth's magnetic field is dying.

Fearing that he may be a loony, I've checked and, sure enough, in the past 35 years the field has lost 235 billion megajoules of energy.

I don't know what a megajoule is, but I bet you could run a kettle on it. And nor do I know how many mega-joules the magnetic field had, to start with. But having spent an hour in the local library I've found that between 1835 and 1965 the magnetic field lost 8 per cent of its strength. So maybe Rankin is right. Maybe we don't have much time left.

Then what? Well, as I understand it, the molten middle bit of the world stops spinning and won't start again until the world quite literally falls over. Somehow – and I really cannot be bothered to find out how – this restores the magnetic field again and all is well . . . except for one tiny detail.

Nobody can predict where the top of the world will be. The new North Pole could be in Cardiff or it could – please God – be in Washington, DC. Scotland could be on the equator, along with Argentina, in which case the South Pole would be about 200 miles west of Hawaii.

Or it could be in the middle of downtown Baghdad. Imagine the joy of that. Bush has his nasty little war to secure all the oil, which is promptly buried under two miles of ice.

It would be prompt, too. There'd be no gradual shift to the new climate. If you woke up tomorrow to find Nuneaton was at the new North Pole you can be assured that your car wouldn't start. It would immediately be 120° below and it would stay that way for the next eight or so thousand years.

If this has happened before – and, according to Rankin, it has – then it would explain what Titchmarsh has been on about these past few weeks. In his series *British Isles* he's been stomping about in the nation's pretty bits, telling us how, before the drizzle came, Britain was jungle-hot and full of hippos, and then freezing cold and full of polar bears.

It didn't make much sense to my children. They learnt, long before they could multiply two by two, that man in general and General Motors in particular have been solely responsible for climate change. And yet here was Northern Alan telling them that the world has been heating up and cooling down for millions of years, all by itself. It was like learning that the answer to two times two is Paris.

I've loved it, because this was Alan Titchmarsh, of all people, doing more damage to Kyoto than a whole herd of coal-fired power stations. In fact I've been watching the show with the engine of my car turned on. Just for fun.

Sadly, he didn't explain why Britain's climate has been so topsy-turvy recently, but I must say Rankin's theory about polar shift does look plausible.

It would be good news for the Danes because if they do prove they own the seabed at what is now the North Pole, they may not have to wait for global warming to melt the ice. When the Earth falls over, they could well end up drilling in the tropics.

The bad news is that when the Earth tilts, the sea, and I mean all of it, will wash over all of the land, killing every single living thing instantly. Unless you're at the top of Everest, or in a mine.

This means that it may take a while for Denmark to recoup its initial investment. More disturbingly, it also means that the world will have to be repopulated by Arthur Scargill and Chris Bonington. This concept is as ugly as it is unlikely.

Sunday 24 October 2004

Fight terror and look good, too

So the Houses of Parliament are to be ringed with steel in an attempt to keep out terrorists – and burglars after those juicy expenses.

All of the proposals seem jolly high-tech, but I assure you they won't work. The boom that's to be anchored in the Thames may well stop baddies from crashing a barge loaded with explosives into the outdoor tea room. But not if it's a particularly large barge. And certainly not if it's a hovercraft, which will simply ride over the obstacle and right up John Prescott's trouser leg before exploding.

Then you have the proposals for CCTV cameras throughout the Palace of Westminster.

Why? So that security experts will be able to work out what the suicide bomber looked like before he became a thin veneer on the walls.

Outside, the entire building will be ringed with an electric fence, but you can bet your children's eyesight that the Health and Safety Executive will ensure it does not carry a death-dealing 4 million volts.

Sure, a lower, less lethal voltage may deter Greenpeace beardies and Otis Ferry from breaking in and making their point, but I doubt a 'slight tingle' would be much of an obstacle for someone who's spent the past three years in a cave dodging daisycutters and A-10 tankbusters.

The intelligence services are said to be worried about

someone driving a car bomb into the clock tower, which could then fall over, landing 13.7 tons of Big Ben on Tony Blair. But then our spies were worried about Iraq having nuclear weapons, so we can take these concerns with a pinch of salt. And anyway, if His Tonyness has to spend the next few years trapped inside a gigantic brass bell, it wouldn't really be the end of the world.

Anyway, I've looked, and if you had it in mind to bring down Big Ben you'd be better off with an aircraft. And this is not the World Trade Center. A Piper Cherokee would do the trick.

The fact is that all the new security arrangements may well stop 100 terrorist attacks. But if they fail to stop the 101st, they will all have been a waste of time and money.

The BBC, for instance, is supremely well guarded. The security personnel are programmed to allow nobody in, at all, ever. And if you do make it to the electric revolving doors, they will respond only if presented with a computerised photo ID.

To get round all this, I simply enter the building every day through the post room.

And I feel certain it's the same story at Heathrow. Yes, it would be very hard to smuggle a pound of Semtex through the terminal, but I bet you could get access to the runways, and therefore the planes, by waiting till nightfall and strolling through the Terminal 5 building site.

They can take as many precautions as they like at Westminster but they won't think of everything, and one day someone out there will. More worrying, however, is what all these security arrangements will look like.

Have you, for instance, seen the American embassy in Grosvenor Square recently? It's been surrounded by hideous crowd-control barriers and by concrete blocks that, I know from personal and painful experience, can be barged out of the way by a small Peugeot so are unlikely to stop a large articulated lorry.

Anyone wishing to gain entry to the building itself has to pass through the sort of prefab hut you might normally expect to find on a Nuneaton building site.

I suppose there's something to be said for making the security measures look temporary, otherwise people could get it into their heads – heaven forbid – that this Middle East business might drag on for years; but does everything have to be so ugly?

The Palace of Westminster is one of the most famous and photographed buildings in the world, a position it may well lose if Britain's notoriously low-rent civil service is allowed to decorate it with anti-aircraft guns, mines and concrete mantraps.

Now I know money is tight. I know that artists are having to give their pictures to the Tate and that the £400,000 an hour being handed over to the Treasury by BP is being spent on MPs' seventh homes; but is this not an occasion when some spare cash could be found?

Could Richard Rogers not be employed to design fencing which blends the traditional lines of Sir Charles Barry's building with the modern world of counter-terrorism? And instead of a boom trailing out into the middle of the Thames, why not build an elaborate sand-bank, such as they've done in the sea off Dubai?

Then there's the question of the serjeant-at-arms's

tights. We're told this is inappropriate combat gear and that they'll have to be replaced with Vin Diesel's body armour. Why? Can Paul Smith not design an eighteenth-century-style frock coat with a built-in machine-pistol holster?

It'd be a worthless gesture, but at least we could lose our battle with the terrorists in style. Not from behind a chunk of nasty pre-stressed concrete.

Sunday 31 October 2004

The Cheshire charity rip-off

Is the money going to charity or to the people who cooked the horrible food?

I read recently that the noble people of Cheshire give more to charity than anyone else in Britain. But knowing Cheshire as I do, I worry a little about what it is they're actually giving.

I suspect that if such a thing as Cheshire Aid were to exist, it would not try to bring grain or farming equipment to the under-privileged of the world. The organisation's lavish video would paint a different picture. 'This small homestead in the Sudan had no water. But after all our hard work, look, we have built them a swimming pool, with a Jacuzzi in the shape of a Cadillac.'

In a recent edition of *Cheshire Life* magazine the publishers ran a competition where readers could win 'another fridge full of champagne', and I fear this kind of thing could have an effect on where those readers might place the poverty line. 'This poor African village had nothing. But thanks to the efforts of our fund-raisers in Wilmslow and Alderley Edge, it now has electric gates. Better still, the people who live there were all brown. Now, as you can see, they're bright orange.'

Still, 400 packs of Dale Winton face cream and half a million gallons of chlorinated swimming-pool water are better than nothing. Which is what I reckon normally gets raised at a charity event.

I guess we've all been to the sort of evening where you're expected to buy raffle tickets at £20 a pop and then, throughout dinner, girls in charity T-shirts arrive just before every one of your punchlines inviting you to place more £20 notes in one of their buckets. And then, with the auction, they start on your credit card.

All these auctions are pretty much the same. Someone makes a heartfelt, tear-jerking appeal on behalf of the charity, and then up pops some sweaty, half-cut, minor-league celebrity who's a mate of someone on the committee. That'd be me, usually.

The first item for sale, which is normally a weekend for two at some godforsaken golfing hotel and country club, goes for £60,000, as someone desperately tries to impress everyone on his table with how much money he's got, and how fervently he wants an MBE for giving it all away.

I once sold a year's use of a Jaguar at one of these do's for more than the car was worth, simply because two blokes in the room were each determined to prove that they were considerably richer than the other.

Better still, I once sold a weekend on a boat in Monte Carlo for £250,000, and the chap was so keen to impress, he handed over the cheque and said he couldn't be bothered to go. I auctioned it again and got another £200,000.

Of course, as you sit there with your slimmed-down wallet, full of spindly canapés, you begin to feel so poor and hungry that you wonder if you shouldn't be on the receiving end of some aid. But you forgive the vulgarity because, of course, the money's going to help some blind teenager in Rwanda whose entire family was butchered by an Aids-ridden terrorist.

Is it, though? Or is the money going to the waiters, and the people who cooked the horrible food, and the people who printed the invitations, and the florist and the band, and the owners of the nasty country house hotel where the event is being staged?

Time and again I've asked the charity representatives at these events how much money they hope to raise and time and again I've been told that they don't expect to get a penny. Just a mention in the local glossy magazine or, if they're really lucky and some people from *Holby City* have turned up, maybe even half a page in *Hello!*

What good's that? How can a small photograph of some P-list celeb like me, with his arm round a bosomy, half-dressed soap actress, be of any possible benefit to the blind and cancerous orphans in Rwanda?

And the problem's getting worse, because there are now so many charity evenings – I have invitations to 23 on my mantelpiece – that the competition among organisers to be more and more lavish is fierce. Some are even employing PR firms, who regularly ring me offering big money – thousands – if I'll turn up for the night and drink their Krug. This means the auction prizes have to be elaborate just to cover the costs.

Soon you will be invited to buy a weekend for two on a nuclear submarine, simply to meet the expenses of the

Brazilian fire-eaters who've just abseiled into the marquee from a helicopter gunship.

I suppose I had better say at this point that some events *do* raise money. My wife, for instance, would certainly like it to be known that the cost of staging her annual do is entirely underwritten by Honda or Ford or Audi, and that every penny raised does go to the local children's hospice.

And this, I think, gives us an inkling of the way forward. When you're faced with the choice of what events to attend, don't ask which footballers are going and what sort of peacock will be used to garnish the roast swan. Ask only how much of the proceeds will actually be going to charity.

And if you're in Cheshire, what those proceeds will buy.

Sunday 7 November 2004

Now I'm an artificial hipster

I know that in recent days we've lost Howard Keel, Yasser Arafat and Emlyn Hughes.

I also know that the Americans are having a hard time in Falluja and that someone from *HolbyEnders* has been caught with her nose in the devil's dandruff. But all of this pales into insignificance alongside the news that I am beginning to disintegrate.

After a lifetime of man-sized hypochondria, where every cold is ebola and every light bruise a shattered limb, I was informed last week that I have finally got a proper, grown-up disease.

About a year ago, my left hip started to ache, so, knowing it was bone cancer, I decided to do nothing. It's better, I figured, to wake up dead one morning than go to a doctor and be told when that morning might be.

Eventually, though, it became difficult to get in and out of my car, which is tricky when you're the host of a television programme that mostly involves getting into and out of cars. So with a heavy heart I went to see the doctor.

'I've caught cancer,' I said Eeyoreishly. But he wasn't convinced and, after a bit of poking around, said he thought it was more likely to be osteoarthritis, arguing that my hip joints may have simply worn out.

This seemed unlikely. My hips have never done anything. I am not a Ceroc dancer or a downhill skier, and the only exercise I ever take is chewing food and typing.

But the X-ray pictures he took are now back from Boots — and blow me down, he was right. I do have osteoarthritis in my hips, and as a result I shall need some plastic replacements.

Apparently this is funny. On learning the news, one friend said I should avoid leaning on any radiators when I have them fitted in case they melt. Another pointed out that they're hollow and could be used as a sort of time capsule. 'You could fill them up with newspaper cuttings and Robbie Williams CDs,' he said, helpfully.

My wife simply phoned our lawyer, saying she really didn't want to be married to a cripple and could he organise a divorce.

More worryingly, I cancelled my health insurance recently because, so far as I can see, they take your money every month and refuse to give it back. So I can either go private, which will cost £25 million, or use the NHS. This would mean waiting until the end of time, and then being given two joints that the 14-year-old doctor, on the advice of his line managers, had bought on the way to work from a plumbers' merchants.

With a view to getting round this, I had a look on eBay and guess what? You can buy second-hand sex toys(!), some naval anaesthetic and even a Vulcan bomber. But nobody is flogging off their dead mum's joints.

That's stupid. Why burn the old dear when you could whip out her hip joints and auction them on the internet? And what's more, with no hips you could bend her legs double and not have to buy such a big coffin. I'd pay up to £30, providing the joints had been washed thoroughly. But there weren't any, so that's that.

The producer of *Top Gear* suggested I contact one of the Formula One teams to see if it could run me up a pair in carbon fibre. Sounds great, but I'm not sure I want to spend the next 40 years hobbling around with a pair of McLaren suspension units in my legs.

And anyway, here's the clincher. Apparently I can't have the operation for another 15 years because plastic wears out even faster than bone, and it's not like changing the battery in a torch. The doctors therefore want to make sure that the replacements I'm given will last until I really do catch ebola.

So that's it. For the next 15 years I have to hobble around with disfigured hips, in huge pain, being laughed at.

This sounds gloomy, but actually, given that all middle-aged people are bound to start going wrong, arthritis really isn't such a bad lucky dip prize. It knocks the socks off cancer, for instance, and it's a damn sight better than the osteoporosis that crippled my dad.

First, it won't kill you or make you run around town in a bee suit blowing raspberries and, better still, it only hurts when you move. Which means you can get a doctor's note saying that you mustn't.

This in turn means you will never again be allowed to bring in coal or carry suitcases. And you will be excused from those stupid bracing walks that your wife is forever suggesting after a hearty Sunday lunch.

I'm not sure, but I'd like to bet that I am now entitled to one of those handy orange stickers that let me treat all pavements as parking spaces.

The only trouble is that to park a car you must first of all get into it, and that really does hurt like hell. I tried to film a road test for *Top Gear* yesterday, and it was like being pulled in half by two tractors. What I'm going to do about that, I really don't know.

Sunday 14 November 2004

Bullies were the making of me

As I understand it, the latest state initiative will force school bullies to wear blue plastic wristbands so the weak and fat can see them coming and have time to take evasive action.

Already I can see some problems with this. For instance, what happens if the cunning and wily school bully decides to get round the problem by simply leaving his wristband at home? Then you wouldn't know he was a bully until you found a large dog egg in your satchel and an unusual stain in your maths exercise book.

Perhaps I've got the wrong end of the stick, though. Perhaps you wear the blue plastic wristband to show you're against bullying, in the same way that people wear little ribbons on their lapel to show they're against Aids or breast cancer or cruelty to moss.

Again, though, I can see some problems. In the same way that a small CND badge would not have protected the wearer from a nuclear fireball, I feel fairly sure that, if you turn up to school with a blue plastic wristband, it's not really going to prevent the bully from pushing your head down the lavatory.

My biggest problem with the scheme, however, is that I have nothing to wear to show that I'm cautiously in favour of bullying. I, for instance, would love to put some sand in Piers Morgan's lunchbox. And nothing would give me more pleasure than spending an hour or so flicking Tony Blair's ears.

Sure, it has its bad sides, of course – nobody likes to think that someone will draw a huge penis on their children's homework – but there are upsides as well. Like if you've spent all day with your head in a lavatory you don't need to wash your hair that night. And you will be a better, sharper, cleverer person.

This, I fear, is what the schools minister Stephen Twigg absolutely will not understand. He'll have listened to a bunch of idealistic town council do-gooders with all sorts of nonsensical degrees in child welfare, and he'll have decided that it was time to break out the blue plastic wristbands. So now all the loony welfare workers will have *carte blanche* to stamp out bullying, in all its forms.

You know where this is going. They started the war on speed by going after lunatics who drove around at 130 mph, and ended up nailing little old ladies for doing 31. They go after people who hunt foxes, and soon your dog will be prosecuted if it kills a mouse. They put health warnings on cigarettes, and now they want to stop you from lighting up in a pub. For the social worker there is no spirit of the law – only the letter.

This means we can wave goodbye to the socially important pursuit of teasing. I tease people for being too short. I tease people for reading the *Guardian*. And in return people tease me for looking like a human toffee apple and liking Supertramp. I'm 44, for heaven's sake, and I still find another man's new haircut funny. So I'll spend the day ribbing him about it.

Teasing is a good thing. It sharpens the mind and

punctures the ego. Teasing, at its best, is faster than Chinese ping-pong and funnier than a really good skiing crash. Teasing is what separates us from the beasts. You never, for instance, see wildebeest laughing their heads off when one of their number falls in the river or gets eaten by a lion.

But of course the stupid do-gooders will see it as a sort of cannabis, a seemingly harmless first rung on the ladder, and try to stamp it out before the teaser takes up some heroin-style bullying.

Well, I was bullied at school, mercilessly and endlessly, for nearly two years. I forgot what it was like to wake up normally rather than as a result of someone letting a fire extinguisher off in my face. And I was thrown on a daily basis into the school's unheated plunge pool.

I remember one night being dragged out of bed at 3 a.m. and told that, because the school would be a better place without me, I would have to be killed.

There was a very good reason for all this. I was a very annoying, very spoilt 13-year-old prig. I had the capacity to irritate before I'd even said anything, and I was the owner of a biblically idiotic haircut.

Eventually the bullying became so awful that I confided in my mother, who said that if everyone was picking on me then I must be doing something wrong. So I grew my hair very long, took up smoking and tried my hardest to make everyone laugh.

It's not easy when you've got a mouth full of dog dirt, but eventually I succeeded, and the bullying stopped.

I really, genuinely believe that were it not for the bullies, I would now be a humourless estate agent in some godforsaken provincial town. Bullying, in other words, saved my life.

And it can work for fat kids, too. You can ban them from watching crisp advertisements on television, and put health warnings on their cheese, but there's nothing more guaranteed to make them lose weight than having their hair set on fire from time to time.

Sunday 28 November 2004

100 things not to do before you die

I've done a power slide in an airboat on the Florida Everglades. I've seen the sun set over the Perfume River in Vietnam. I've flown an F-15E fighter bomber, and I've ingested pretty well everything there is to be ingested. While doing 180 mph. In a Ferrari.

In other words, when I read those silly magazine features listing all the things you're supposed to do before you die, I'm left feeling hollow and empty. I'm only 44 and I've already seen Etna explode. I've swum with the bloody dolphins in Tahiti and I've tried my hand at bobsleighing.

I've even done the odd eightsome reel, which is as close as anyone should get to folk dancing. So now, what are you saying? That I should go off into a corner and commit suicide?

Apparently not. Because last week we were presented with a new list of 100 things to do before we die. Only this time around, the authors are not drunken magazine hacks back from a long lunch; they're all eminent scientists, boffins and inventors.

The idea behind the scheme is simple. James Dyson, who designs purple vacuum cleaners, says he wants to make schoolchildren think of science and engineering – and vacuum cleaners, presumably – as cool. I thoroughly approve of that, but I must say that most of the suggestions he and his colleagues make are either difficult, revolting or impossible.

Let's start with something simple, like extracting our own DNA. All you have to do, apparently, is gargle with salt water and then spit it into a glass of washing-up liquid. You then dribble ice-cold gin down the side of the glass and watch as spindly white clumps form in the mixture. This is the essence of you.

Of course, coughing up phlegm is not quite as glamorous as driving a hovercraft over the glaciers of Tibet, but think what you could do with a thimbleful of your own DNA. You could nurture it, and keep it in a warm place and then, who knows, one day it may grow into a perfect replica of you. Or, if you smoke as much as I do, a perfect replica of a Marlboro Light.

Well, it gets worse, because one of the other things the boffins suggest is that you turn yourself into a priceless jewel. Apparently there's a company in Chicago that exposes cremated human remains to heat and pressure for 18 weeks, after which they have turned into a brilliant one-carat diamond.

Can you see a drawback with this? Yes, that's right. And frankly I'm surprised to find that some of Britain's biggest brains failed to notice that this was supposed to be a list of things to do *before* you die.

Here's a worrying one. You can link your computer to that huge radio telescope in Puerto Rico, then spend your spare time listening for signs of extraterrestrial life. This, I imagine, would require quite a lot of patience. So much, in fact, that on balance I think I'd rather be a diamond.

Certainly I'd much rather go to Tennessee, where the

donated corpses of murder victims are available for would-be forensic scientists. Anyone can have a go, apparently.

You'd have thought, wouldn't you, given the brain-power of the team behind this list that they could have come up with something a bit better than poking around in a dead American's liver to see what killed him. Or slowly turning into a diamond as you while away the hours listening out for something that's too far away to be audible.

Permit me then to suggest something better than they've managed, something more exciting than anything you've ever done. Or even heard about.

Find a group of friends, preferably people you don't like much, and catch the next flight to Los Angeles. Once there, hunt down the company that organises dog fights for paying customers, whether those customers have any flight experience or not.

You will each be strapped into a Marchetti trainer and taken by your co-pilot to 3,000 feet where he will open the throttles as wide as they'll go and ask you to hunt down your friends.

Each plane has a laser on the nose and is coated in the same material you find in those laser-quest games. So, you get another chap in your sights, pull the trigger and, unless he can manoeuvre out of the way, which will involve pulling more Gs than you, he's toast. His co-pilot releases smoke to show he's hit.

And, as a side effect, you'll come back more interested in the science of flight and the theory of aerodynamics than you ever thought possible.

Sunday 5 December 2004

Let's break all Tony's laws

I see that pretty soon parish councillor henchmen will be prowling round our villages at night, handing out £50,000 fixed-penalty notices to those whose lights are keeping people from getting to sleep.

Well, now; I live opposite a football pitch that, each evening, is illuminated by several starburst gigawatt lamps. They're an eyesore, for sure, but since I understand that it's jolly hard to play football in the dark, I have not complained. Instead, I've simply hung two pieces of material in front of the window. I like to call them 'the curtains'.

I have tried, really I've tried, to understand why legislation is needed to prevent people from using lights at night, but then I've tried hard to understand why dogs aren't allowed to kill foxes any more. And I don't get that, either. Or why I can't use my mobile phone when I'm stuck in a traffic jam.

Every single day there is a small piece in the papers that announces the introduction of a law banning something which you thought was harmless. And here's the thing. You raise your eyebrows momentarily, and then you turn the page.

It's only when you add up the number of new laws that have come along since His Tonyness grinned his way into No. 10 that you realise just how much of our freedom he's tried to erode in the past seven years.

Last week Boris Johnson told us that you may not legally fix a broken windowpane in your own home unless you are a qualified broken-window mender, and that when the work is done you must get it inspected by a broken-window inspector from the local council. Furthermore, it is against the law to change or tamper with the electrical sockets in your own kitchen.

There's so much more to come as well. Greyhound tracks will soon need new super-licences, you will not be allowed to tread on a stag beetle, you will not be able to have unprotected sex or a few drinks with your friends after work. Cheese will have to be marked with a government health warning and you will be prevented from telling jokes about homosexual men, lesbians, Muslims, Catholics, the Irish and foxes.

Gary Lineker will be allowed on television only after the watershed, in case children are enticed into his dangerous salt-and-vinegar world; you will not be allowed to get your dog to kill a rat — because it's a wild animal — and you will be banned from giving your mum a headstone when she dies in case it falls over.

Naturally you will also be banned from smoking in public, owning a Bible, sending Christmas cards that feature the nativity, and smacking your children. Happily, you will be allowed to drive a car, but not at more than 20 mph, not if you've had a piece of sherry trifle, and certainly not if it has four-wheel drive.

All of the above will be covered by legislation; but, where this is not possible, Tony uses the Hoxton Thought Police instead. As a result I was told last week that I am now 'not allowed' to talk about Siamese twins and must in future refer to them as 'conjoined'.

Why? Down's babies used to be called mongoloid because it was felt some of their facial characteristics made them look as if they were from Mongolia. And I can see why that might be upsetting. For both Mongolians and those with Down's.

But the expression 'Siamese twins' is used because the first pair ever to reach the world's consciousness – called Chang and Eng – happened to be from Siam. So who's going to be upset? Siam doesn't even exist any more. Are these idiots now saying I can't refer to Dutch courage? And if so, who will stand up for the right of measles if I call them German?

To be honest, however, none of this interference is going to make any difference to my life. That's why I'm not whingeing, because I shall continue to call people while driving, and tell them stories that Cherie Blair would find offensive.

Furthermore, I'll carry on calling two people who share body parts Siamese twins.

I will eat as much cheese as I like and I will still give my dog a whole packet of prawn-cocktail-flavoured crisps whenever she rips a rat to pieces.

This evening I'm thinking of smacking the children. For fun. And then, when I go to bed tonight, after I've altered all the wiring in my kitchen and drunk two bottles of wine, I'll leave the outside lights on. And dream about the glimpse of G-string I saw in the office last week.

In other words, in a single day I will break 14 laws and

seven social taboos that simply didn't exist before Tony came along. And I shall do so with impunity because there's no way in hell he can possibly enforce all his Big Ideas.

Sunday 12 December 2004

Sharks, you're dead meat

Last Thursday an 18-year-old Australian surfer boy was eaten by two great white sharks which, according to onlookers, tore his body in half and then spent a few minutes arguing over who'd get which bit.

As usual, various wildlife experts were interviewed, and they all said the sharks in question should be let off with a caution, partly because they're protected and partly because such attacks are extremely rare.

But they're not. In fact, not even a week had passed since another surfer had been eaten on exactly the same piece of coastline. Meanwhile, in California the surfing community has reported that shark attacks have tripled in recent years and it's a similar story in South Africa.

So what's going on? Well, some say the great white has developed a taste for humans because we've eaten all their usual prey – tuna and so on. Others argue that it's because boards look like seals from underneath. Or it could be these shark attacks are simply God's way of telling surfers to get a job.

But I think I've worked out exactly who's to blame . . . and it's the soppy sentimentality of the National Geographic Channel with its Disney-style ethos of 'no animals were harmed in the making of this programme'.

When David Attenborough does a wildlife show on the television, we see nature in the raw. We see the little thing's big dewy eyes and its wobbly legs when it's born. We see it finding a mate, and relaxing in the sun after a hearty meal. And then we see it being eaten by a lion.

Who can forget the horror of that poor little penguin in *The Blue Planet*? He'd gone off to find food for his wife and been attacked, in gory, close-up detail, by a leopard seal. Terribly wounded, he tried his hardest to make it home, but the journey was too long and the slope too steep. So he died, pitching, beak first, into the ice.

Now, had this been made by the Americans, Mr Penguin would have found lots of food, all of it organic, successfully swum past the waiting leopard seals and made it back to the rookery where he and Mrs Penguin would have opened a fair trade shop and lived happily ever after.

I watched a wildlife show the other night which had been infected completely with the American Way. It was all about the Andes, and guess what? None of the animals had any sex and none of them ever died. Not even the fish. The gannets dived into the water and came out again.

Pumas chased llamas pointlessly. And the foxes just hung around, looking cute.

This is why we now have a hunting ban: because we're living in a world where foxes have vegetarian cubs that frolic around in the woods, playing non-competitive tag.

Certainly, I have never seen any footage, ever, of a fox breaking into a chicken run and killing the lot. And it's why the world is full of surfer boys who scour the planet for decent waves, oblivious to the peril that lurks beneath the surface.

Today, great white sharks are always called 'magnificent', and now we have Peter Benchley, author of *Jaws*, saying he wished he'd never written the book because it gave everyone a sense that the great white was 'a bad guy' when really it was 'fragile'. One can only guess, of course, but I bet the 18-year-old who was pulled in half by sharks this week didn't think, as those teeth sank into his thighs, that the shark was magnificent or fragile.

It's the same story with the mosquito. But because it's never been the subject of a soppy, tree-hugging, natural history show, even the biggest veg-head weird-beard is at liberty to run around his bedroom at night with a rolled-up newspaper and a can of bug zap, shouting: 'I'll get you, you little bastard.'

A great white is no different. It's a dangerous, ugly, killing machine that takes a chunk out of you and lets you bleed to death before coming back and deciding that actually it doesn't like human very much. It's a 23-foot aquatic mozzie, an underwater monster with razor-wire teeth, and it should be treated as such.

We should therefore turn the tables round. Instead of letting the damn things cruise around eating us, we should start eating them. Of course, this would mean hunting them to extinction, which would cause all sorts of loonies to wave their arms around, saying that we were changing the world. To which we could reply: 'Absolutely. We're making it better. And then we shall start on the tigers.'

Sunday 19 December 2004

The ghost of wife's present

Obviously I know you should never buy your wife anything that needs a plug, but this has always presented a
problem. Because I've always had some understanding of
stuff that needed electricity to function, and had no clue
about stuff that didn't.

Scent, for example. Have you actually been into the
perfume department of a shop recently? Not only do you
have the traditional choice of about 10,000 from the
well-known names such as Chanel and er . . . Charlie, all
of which, to a smoker at least, are exactly the same, but
now you have celebrity-endorsed products as well.

Does your wife want to smell like Beyoncé or Celine
Dion?

Or would she like to spend the year strutting around
with a whiff of Cliff Richard behind her ears?

Horrified that you might trip over the great smell of
Kilroy – or Cuprinol, as it's known in hardware stores –
you make a beeline for the clothes department; but this is
an even bigger mistake, because you'll Buy the Wrong
Thing. And, to make matters worse, you will Buy the
Wrong Thing in the Wrong Size.

So, jewellery then. Well, no, because for reasons I've
never fully understood jewellery shops never advertise
their prices. Which means you need a basic grasp of the
Stanislavski technique as you try to pretend the reason

you don't want the necklace is because of the clasp, not because it costs £16,000.

Personalised luggage or stationery is fine, but this needs to be ordered in March.

And it's much the same story with furniture. Plus, it's hard to carry a tallboy home on the train.

Of course, the shop can deliver, but this involves filling out a form, and then another. And then some more. And then the information has to be typed on to a computer, and by the time that's been done the daffodils are out. Why can't they just write your address down on a scrap of paper and give it to the van driver?

At round about this point the modern gentleman will start to think about getting some candles. We all know that girls like to spend hours having baths in the semi-darkness, and we cannot imagine what they might be doing in there. Well, we can, actually, which is why I always say no to candles.

I'm afraid I'm similarly selfish when it comes to music. My wife is forever buying CDs by bands I've never heard of and I know she wants the new Killers album, but if I were to buy it for her, she'd play it, and then I'd have to listen to it as well.

Books? Oh, come on. It seems a bit mean to spend only £7.99, especially as the sort of books my wife likes don't even come with a plot.

This is why I didn't even bother window-shopping for my wife this year. I just headed straight for the electrical department in Selfridges, where I knew I would feel safe and warm and comfortable.

Unfortunately, I must have blinked and missed some

kind of technological burp, because it was full of various brushed aluminium boxes that didn't seem to do anything even remotely worthwhile.

In essence, there are three things you can do with all this modern technology. Listen to music. Take pictures. And communicate with other people while you're out and about. But the combination of these three things has driven the world's techno-nerds into a complete frenzy.

Take the much-talked-about iPod as a prime example. Even if my wife had 5,000 songs in her mysterious CD collection, and even if she had the time to copy them all on to the chip, what would be the point exactly? Why copy something you already have?

So we move on to the new breed of three-chip digital video cameras. Yes, the quality is vastly improved, but answer me a straight question. Have you ever watched anything you've ever shot on your Handycam? Thought not. So who cares if you can now zoom in on your husband's nose hairs from six miles away?

And why would you want a phone that can download clips of movies from the internet? When have you ever been in a position that you're on a moor and suddenly feel the need to watch three seconds of Tom Cruise dangling upside down?

I suppose it might be quite fun to video your genitals and send them to your lover. But if I did that to my wife, she'd think I'd gone mad.

Disappointed, I came out of the electrical department fearing that, while I wasn't looking, the world had moved on. And that it was still moving on, towards Christmas, and that I needed to get something. So I ended up buying my wife a dead rabbit.

Doubtless when the shops open on Wednesday she'll quietly take it back and exchange it for 'Saigon', the great new smell of Henry Kissinger.

Sunday 26 December 2004

Who's afraid of the nice wolf?

With devastating but quiet savagery, the countryside is being destroyed by a million-strong herd of marauding deer. Surveys have shown their numbers are spiralling out of control and that they're now tearing through crops and woodland like a pack of horned locusts.

Worse still, deer were responsible last year for 15,000 road accidents in Scotland alone. Ten people died, pinned to their headrests by those antlers after the animal came through the windscreen. Not a nice way to go.

A similar number were killed in East Anglia, and on one stretch of road through Cannock Chase in Staffordshire a deer is apparently hit once every three days. He must be getting awfully fed up with it by now.

Anyway, the government has decided to act. Amid howls of protest from gamekeepers, ministers have decided that a well-orchestrated nationwide cull is needed. But this being New Labour, they've got themselves into a right old lather about it.

If it were a bacterium, or a Conservative, that was eating all the trees and killing 50 people a year, they'd act instantly to wipe it out. But deer have big, brown, soulful eyes. And that gives the luvvies a problem.

I mean, this is a government that has publicly declared undying love for foxy-woxy, so even though the deer is engaged in wholesale slaughter of mankind, you can't really visualise Tony Blair running around the Highlands in a pair of stout wellies, hosing down Bambi's mum with a hail of machine-gun fire.

As a result, ministers are going to great lengths to point out that the deer is a fine animal and must not be viewed as a pest or a nuisance. But that hundreds of thousands must, nevertheless, be shot in the face.

They're even talking about allowing carefully selected and heavily licensed deer killers to roam the Highlands in the close season, shooting expectant mums. Quite something for a government whose local councils all over the country employ 'deer liaison officers'.

Quite what a deer liaison officer does, I'm not sure. Personally, I'd rather spend his wages helping victims of the Asian earthquake, but there you go.

My favourite part of the government initiative is watching them agonise over what should be done with the mountain of carcasses. Because, of course, they're all vegetablists, and as a result it simply hasn't occurred to them that they could be garnished with onions and eaten.

You can even eat the muntjac, which looks like a big rat and barks like a dog. But, like crocodile and snake, it tastes of chicken.

This would be an ideal solution. Fat, poor people who spend their limited resources on crisps and lard could be encouraged to roam around the woods at night, killing deer. This way they'd get some exercise and a free meal.

But I fear that it won't catch on, so I'm drawn to an idea that was first mooted two years ago by a wealthy Scottish landowner called Paul van Vlissingen. He spent £300,000 of his own money looking into the deer problem, and has decided that the best way of keeping their numbers in check is by reintroducing wolves.

There's no doubt that a pack of wolves gallivanting around the Highlands would keep deer numbers down, and this would save the trees and crops. But I can't help wondering what else Mr Wolf might eat.

Obviously Johnny Fox would be a tasty target, which is fine, now that man isn't allowed to hunt him any more. But what about the sheep? In the Alpine region of France, a pack of just 30 wolves does its level best to keep lamb off the menu in most local restaurants; and we see a similar problem in Sweden, where wolves, tired of eating deer, are helping themselves to pretty well anything that moves.

This brings me neatly to the wolf's favourite *amuse-bouche* – us. Van Vlissingen says humans have nothing to worry about, because in the last hundred years there hasn't been a single recorded case of a person, or even a part of a person, anywhere in Europe, being eaten by a wolf.

He also argues that in Alaska and Canada humans and wolves live happily together.

True, but that's because in Alaska and Canada most people pack some kind of heat in the parka. Here, however, we're not allowed to walk around with a blue-steel .44, so I suspect the reintroduction of wolves would mean the odd rambler would go west.

This means everyone wins. The government keeps deer numbers down without turning its deer liaison officers into murderers. We will be able to drive faster in greater safety on the roads; the countryside gets an interesting new animal; and the rambling queen, Janet Street-Porter, gets eaten.

Sunday 2 January 2005

Bowling for the beautiful people

You'd imagine that the world ladies' bowls championship would be a genteel affair, brought to you by Werther's Originals, Rover, Saga Holidays and Thora Hird's stairlift.

But no. Seven of the eight quarter-finalists chosen to represent Britain are aged between 21 and 37. One, an extremely comely young lady, was pictured in the newspapers last week wearing an unzipped leather biker's jacket and very little else.

This has prompted commentators to come out from behind their tea urns and remark that the team has perhaps been chosen for its televisual appeal rather than its ability. I'm sure they have a point.

You see, in the olden days, when most bowls players were born, there were no photographs in the newspapers, so people were allowed to be fat and ugly. Joseph Whitworth, the great gunsmith, was a national hero because no one knew he had the face of a baboon. Isambard Kingdom Brunel achieved success because the great British public had no clue he was a midget.

Back then, skill and intelligence were what you needed to get on. But now, with the zoom lens and the tabloid newspaper, neither thing matters a jot.

We're entering a whole new world where, to get on, it's not what you know or who you know, or even what you know about who you know. All that matters is what you look like.

David Beckham, I'm told, is far from Britain's best footballer. But he has become a global success because he's a handsome chap. Then you have Tony Blair. He became leader of the Labour Party simply because he is better looking than Robin Cook and John Prescott. What's more, he will win a third term because he has more sex appeal than Michael Howard. And Gordon Brown will never be prime minister because the hinge on his lower jaw appears to be loose.

Then there's Sienna Miller. Who, I hear you ask. Well, she's the bit-part star of two films you haven't seen, but because she's so unbelievably pretty her engagement to another woman called Judy managed last week to knock the Asia catastrophe off the front pages.

I understand all of this. You wouldn't deliberately buy an ugly sofa or an ugly car, so why would you invite an ugly person to peer at you from the other side of the electric fish tank?

By the same token, I'd rather watch my new crush, Fiona Bruce, reading out the Cumbrian lambing reports for 2004 than Reginald Bosanquet, with his florid nose, telling me about the tsunami. I have a friend whose car dealership was staffed entirely by astonishingly good-looking girls. When asked why, he said with a grin that pretty ones cost the same as ugly ones. I understand that, too.

There is, however, an enormous drawback to all of this. You see, Ben Affleck, Brad Pitt, George Clooney and Denzel Washington may look good in leather miniskirts and Roman armour, but where would we have been 30 years ago if the only qualifications needed for Hollywood superstardom were perfectly square, perfectly white teeth and big arms? Without Gene Hackman, that's for sure.

You can be assured, too, that the over-hootered Dustin Hoffman would still be eking out a living in some New York dive, along with Jack Nicholson and Anthony Hopkins.

At the moment the only possible hope for the facially challenged or the stomachularly enormous is comedy. Good-looking people only had to smile to climb into a stranger's pants, whereas the Stephen Frys and Jimmy Carrs of the world needed to tickle the humour bone before they were allowed near another person's pelvis.

I'll give you a challenge at this point. Name me one slim, attractive girl who's famous for being funny. Dawn French? Jo Brand? You get my drift here.

Comedy, however, has only a limited number of openings, which is why, in the not too distant future, I can see a backlash coming. It used to be the case that a person's social standing caused jealousy and bitterness. People would wonder why the idiotic fourth son of the Duke of Nether Wallop could have peach and peacock for supper while his bright manservant had to make do with a cup of mud.

Well, how long will it be before the world's ugly people start to wonder why Kate Moss is a millionaire and why their television screens are full of orange men and pneumatic blonde girls when their own children, who have double firsts in Latin, can't get a job on the bins?

Certainly I hope the backlash comes soon because, unless that bowling bird unzips her jacket and puts the other competitors off, Britain is very likely to get knocked out of the tournament.

Sunday 9 January 2005

Wild weather warnings

Well, as Britain's pop stars predicted, there was no snow in Africa this Christmas, but, strangely, there was quite a lot of it in Texas, and Saudi Arabia.

Last year gave Australia its driest summer since records started in 1859, there were wasps in the Yukon, huge swarms of rain-fed locusts in the Sahara and temperatures in Iceland hit 76.6°F.

Closer to home, big chunks of Cornwall were washed away, Carlisle sank and Scotland was blown clean off the top of Britain. Meanwhile, my cottage in the Isle of Man, which has braved the elements without a scratch for 150 years, was deprived of its roof.

As a result, a great many earnest young men have been cropping up on Channel 4 News, wearing an 'I told you so' expression and explaining that we've got to stop driving cars and eating strawberries out of season. They say that man-made global warming is driving the weather nuts and that if we don't radically change our ways everyone on earth will be boiled.

Well, let's just say we all part-exchange our cars for horses and eat only what happened to have been in the garden that afternoon. And let's imagine the world's governments and multinationals sink billions into finding new ways of propelling aircraft and heating our houses.

Let's imagine we do everything the greens want . . .
and the temperature keeps on rising. Then what?

This is the problem. The earnest-faced young men
want us to have carbon credit cards and nut-fuelled
boilers. They want radical change to combat something
over which we might have no control. You see, none of
the recent weird weather events is weird. There was a
flood in Boscastle 400 years ago. Texas had a white Christmas in 1922. And last year the average global temperatures
were only as high as those in 1649, which was long before
the invention of the Yorkshire Electricity Board, the Airbus A320 and the Ford Fiesta.

Man's total contribution to global carbon dioxide emis-
sions is just 3 per cent, which might be enough to kill the
world. But it might not. Nobody knows. And it seems
rather silly to spend billions developing cauliflower-
powered cars when they might not make any difference,
and half the world is starving.

'I'm sorry, Mr Nboto. We'd love to build a well in
your village, but unfortunately Mr Porritt is spending all
our money on a new type of possibly unnecessary engine
that runs on saliva.'

Of course, there is no doubt that the world is warming
up, but let's just stop and think for a moment what
the consequences might be. Switzerland loses its skiing
resorts? The beach in Miami is washed away? North
Carolina gets knocked over by a hurricane? Anything
bothering you yet?

We keep being told that in just 20 years there will be
no snow in the Atlas Mountains, but honestly: who cares?
And so what if the sea level rises by five inches? I can

appreciate that this would be a nuisance if you were Dutch. But you're not, so relax.

Finding out that global warming will change the landscape in a part of the world where we don't live is as relevant as finding out that the lesser mottled Tasmanian butterfly is on the verge of extinction. It isn't even worthy of a shrug.

In fact, in Britain more ferocious and turbulent weather would be a good thing because it was 57°F and drizzling yesterday, and it'll be 57°F and drizzling tomorrow. And yet, despite the sameness, we are the only people on earth who use prevailing conditions as an ice breaker at parties.

'*Ici qu'il fait frais pendant cette période d'année,*' is not something you will hear at French social events. And nor have I ever heard a German say, '*Es ist ausgefallenes nettes.*'

Last week, every news channel in Britain cut live every 15 minutes to some dizzy bird in wellies, standing in a puddle, saying the wind was very strong and the sea was very rough. No other nation would do that – not just two weeks after the definition of a rough sea had been rewritten by that tsunami.

An Englishman's home is not his castle. An Englishman's home is, as Bill Bryson once pointed out, a large, grey, Tupperware box. A constant, year-round sea of endless misty greyness. So I would therefore welcome some proper storms and heatwaves and swarms of locusts sweeping down from the heavens every afternoon.

Imagine the joy, when conversation begins to flag, of being able to substitute 'it's turned out nice' for 'I was sucked into space by a tornado this morning'.

And imagine being told on the weather forecast that a glacier had buried Birmingham. Big British weather. Bring it on.

Sunday 16 January 2005

Jumbo, a brilliant white elephant

At a lavish, laser-speckled launch party in France last week, Tony Blair said that the new Airbus was 'a symbol of confidence that we can compete and win in the global market'.

Nearly right, you big-eared thicko. Actually, it is a symbol of confidence that we can compete and win in the global market despite the utter stupidity of your government.

The gigantic wings for this plane are built by British Aerospace in north Wales.

But each one is far too large to be taken to Toulouse by road and far too heavy to be taken there by air. So they are loaded on to barges in the port of Mostyn and floated down the Irish Sea, across the Channel and then through France's canal network.

Plainly, this is idiotic. It would be much easier and cheaper to build them in France, but politically this would be no good at all because the Airbus is intended to show how European co-operation can work. We do the wings and the engines, the French put everything together, the Germans finish everything off and the Spanish . . . actually, I don't know what the Spanish do, apart from gate-crash the launch party and lisp.

You would imagine, then, that Tony's government would be doing everything in its power to make sure that

Britain's contribution was smooth and effortless. But no.

Those wings can be loaded on to the barges only at high tide because the monumentally daft Environment Agency won't let anyone dredge the harbour at Mostyn.

Why ever not? Well, there's the European Union Habitats Directive, you see, that was drawn up to protect worms and slugs from the perils of profit. Elsewhere on the Continent they don't apply it to navigational routes, but in Britain we do. So, thanks to the green-eyed madness of our men in parkas, building the most advanced plane in the skies is governed by the needs of an invertebrate and the orbit of the moon.

I have another problem with Tony's launch speech, too, because he described the A380 as 'the most exciting new aircraft in the world'. Even if we ignore the fact that he can't possibly know since it hasn't actually left the ground yet, I am not sure that he's right.

Technically, of course, we must doff our caps to the engineers who have built a cross-Channel ferry that can fly. It is far from the prettiest machine ever made, but we should marvel at the quietness of its engines, its 8,000-mile range, its ability to take off on conventional runways and its parsimonious drinking habits. It uses less fuel per passenger than a Ford Fiesta.

Yes, at the moment, despite much plastic and carbon fibre in its construction, the A380 is four tons overweight, but when the 747 was rolled out in the 1960s, that was 50 tons overweight. So let's not get too worried. They could save four tons by simply removing one American passenger.

Plainly, the weight issue has not worried Virgin,

Emirates and the other carriers that have placed orders. Even British Airways would do the same, except that its long-haul fleet is fairly new and it hasn't got any money.

So the message is clear. For the airlines and their share-holders this enormous plane is marvellous. But I am not sure that it is quite so rosy for you and me.

Certainly life will be worse at airports because, to accommodate these giants, the gates have to be further apart. Walk past four A380s to reach your plane and you will have walked the length of four football pitches.

That is presuming you got past the check-in. I guess you have all experienced the ludicrous queues that build up now. Well, imagine how long they are going to be when there are half a dozen A380s scheduled to depart within 15 minutes of one another. With seating for 550 on each one, that is 3,300 people to be interrogated, 3,300 suitcases to be loaded, 3,300 pieces of hand luggage to be X-rayed, and 3,300 pairs of shoes to be examined.

Do you think that Virgin or Emirates will spend the money that they have saved on fuel by employing more check-in staff? I doubt it. As a result, you will need to arrive at the terminal 3,300 hours before take-off. Then there is the flight itself to worry about.

Airbus made sure that its launch video featured on-board gyms and bars. There were big, squidgy double beds and probably a polo lawn or two. But the reality is that airlines will fill the entire fuselage with seats they've nicked from a primary school to wedge the passengers in like veal.

In other words, being on board the A380 will be exactly the same as being on board any other jetliner. Exciting? I don't think so, Tony.

This brings me to the final point. You see, the cruising speed of the A380 is Mach 0.85 (647 mph), which is pretty good for something with the aerodynamic properties of a wheelie bin and engines that run on mineral water. But the 747 cruises at Mach 0.855 (651 mph). This means that the 747 gets you there faster and you spend less time with your face wedged in an American's armpit.

On that basis, you can marvel at how Airbus has jumped through political hoops and climbed technical mountains to bring the world its shareholder-friendly A380. But you are better off going in a Boeing.

Sunday 23 January 2005

Jackboots rule the countryside

Walking is something that I will gladly do when the car breaks down. In London I have been known to pop out for the papers and not stop until I get to Dartford in Kent. But the notion of treating the exercise as a noun, of going for 'a walk': that has always seemed faintly preposterous.

Still, last weekend the children wanted to play Monopoly, so on the basis that anything is better than that, I went for a proper post-roast Sunday afternoon stride through the rolling vastness of England's achingly beautiful green heart. And, of course, I arrived back where I'd started from with mild exhaustion and a hint of hypothermia.

Each of my wellingtons weighed 200 tons, I had mud in my navel, my lips were royal blue, my face was fuchsia pink and my hair looked as if it had been through a jet engine.

More than that, though, I was angry, riddled with guilt and astonished at what has been done to the countryside while nobody was looking.

You may recall from your childhood those long, lazy summer adventures when you could climb trees, go where you wanted and fall in stuff. It was pretty much a free-for-all, providing you stuck to the 'Country Code'.

Published in 1951, this was a simple set of rules, designed to explain to the working classes what they should do when faced with bits of the world that were not cobbled. In essence, it said that you must not pull faces at the sheep and you must remember to shut all the gates.

Last year, however, the code was rewritten as the 'Countryside Code' by representatives from half a dozen government agencies who, plainly, have never set foot outside Hoxton in east London. It's like the instruction manual for the space shuttle.

Then there's the countryside itself, which now looks like Camp X-Ray. You're marshalled by signposts telling you where the footpath goes and, just to make sure that you stay on it, you're fenced in by miles of electrified razor wire.

Every few hundred yards you are reminded of your responsibilities by slogans that would not look out of place in a Soviet tractor factory. 'Kill nothing. Only time', said one.

There was another which said 'No dogs'. But before I turned to my faithful Labrador and said, 'For you ze valk is over,' I took a moment to reflect and thought, why not? If dogs are such a menace, why are these same government agencies so keen to look after foxy-woxy?

Well, I've had a look at the new code, and it seems that the problem isn't dogs.

It's what comes out of their bottoms. Now, I know that in the parks around Islington, north London, dog dirt is a menace; but the countryside is almost entirely carpeted with excrement. We are ankle-deep in, er, produce from sheep, cows, horses, foxes, chickens, organic llamas and pigs, so why should your household pooch be expected to put a cork in his backside until he gets home?

And why are there so many hills? Why is there a stile every 2½ feet, over which you have to haul your six-year-old, whose hair is standing on end because she keeps bumping into the electric fencing?

I could sue for this, and I would win. I know this because my tree surgeon told me the other day that if some town boys fall off one of the sycamores in my paddock, I can't just hose their broken bodies into the soakaway. I would have to compensate their parents and pay for a proper funeral.

Legal action, however, was the last thing on my mind as I strode onwards and into what was plainly the front garden of someone's very nice private house.

Now, one of the pillars of the new 'Countryside Code' is that we should consider other people: 'Don't openly laugh at the beardy's purple cagoule. Wait until he's passed and then crap yourself.' Fine, so why not move the footpath round the man's garden, rather than through it? It wouldn't be difficult.

But no. The sign steering me right past his sitting-room window had been knocked in with special vigour by someone who, you just knew, had absolutely relished the way that it would direct all his communist mates from the Ramblers' Association straight on to the rich bastard's lawn.

And if the rich bastard complained? Well, he could be told that these footpaths are ancient thoroughfares and cannot be moved just like that. You can't just change the practices of the countryside, you know . . . unless you're waging class war, of course.

Out there, in the quiet of the twenty-first-century

Cotswolds, you're only as free as a bird if the bird you have in mind is a budgerigar. You're as marshalled and governed, and as unable to go your own way, as a piece of Great Western rolling stock.

However, I think I have worked out a solution.

If you must go for a walk, forget the green bits that have been colonised and sanitised by Tony Blair's urban army; do it in the middle of your local city.

There is no mud, there are more visual diversions, you can go where you want without fear of electrocution, your dog is welcome, and you won't come home covered from head to foot in shit.

Sunday 30 January 2005

Found: a cure for binge drinking

On the eve of the 1982 Monaco Grand Prix I was dining with friends at a small restaurant called the Potato of Love in La Napoule when I found a slug crawling through my lettuce. 'Regardez,' I said to the proprietor. 'J'ai trouvez une er . . . um, une escargot sans une maison dans mon salade.'

He was horrified and whisked the plate away, saying that by way of recompense we could drink as much wine as we liked. On the house.

Now, I should explain at this point that I've never been a big drinker. That said, every once in a while I would be happy to indulge in what's now known as a binge-drinking session.

The next thing I knew, I was being dragged from the back of a car by several armed and very angry French policemen, who handcuffed my arms behind my back and then threw me to the ground. 'Aargh,' I exclaimed, as I plunged, nose first, into the road.

It became apparent that, because we'd been in a right-hand-drive car, the policemen couldn't remember who'd been at the wheel. So they decided to punch the information out of us.

Obviously, being completely spineless, I'd have grassed on the offender straight away, but I was also completely drunk and as a result had no clue who it might have been. So I was hit. 'Aargh,' I said again.

In fact, I said 'Aargh' quite a lot in the course of the next few hours – mostly, though, when my escape attempt went all wrong.

For some reason that never did become clear, we were taken to a hospital where the cunning plan was hatched. Having no spoons to hand, I ruled out the tunnelling option and began to wonder if it might be possible to go to the attic and build a glider while no one was looking. And then the idea hit me. I decided that, this being a hospital, the window in the lavatory would not be fitted with bars.

I was right, and so – with the policeman waiting outside the cubicle – I made lots of, I thought, rather convincing being-sick noises and eased it open. It was not a big window but I was almost completely out when I felt the policeman's burly hands on my ankles.

Have you ever been dragged backwards through a small window, while wearing handcuffs? Well, don't try it, because it hurts. It hurts nearly as much as being thrown to the floor again.

Perhaps this is why they'd taken us to the hospital. Because, by the time they'd finished with us, it's almost certainly where we'd end up anyway.

But no. We were bundled back in the van, taken to the police station and ordered to strip. Oh, how they all laughed when they saw my sunburn. '*Le rouge Rosbif*,' said one. At this point, I was thinking about effing Frogs, but I fear I may have said it out loud, which is why they punched me again. And because my trousers were round my ankles, I fell to the floor again. And because I was still wearing handcuffs, I landed on my nose again.

The cells in the Cannes Can are like . . . well, to begin with, it was hard to say what they were like since the only light came through a 1-inch peephole in the door.

For all I knew, there were Laura Ashley curtains in there and an elegant ottoman at the end of the bed.

Sadly, as my eyes became accustomed to the gloom, it became apparent that this wasn't so. In fact, there was nothing but a bed made from stone, a mattress made from wood and a hole in the floor near which several previous occupants had relieved themselves.

Boredom set in within about five minutes. I couldn't even pass the time by trying to hang myself because they'd taken my shoelaces and belt. And cruelly, they'd taken my lighter, too, leaving me only with the cigarettes. The solution was sleep, but this was impossible because if I used my jacket as a pillow it was freezing, and if I kept it on I got a cricked neck.

Sleep was also impossible because one of my friends in the next cell had decided to run, noisily, through a list of battles in which the English had beaten the French. Sadly, we ran out of ideas after Quiberon and Agincourt and, anyway, my enormously swollen nose testified to the fact that in the only battle that mattered that night, we were losing badly.

At around seven in the morning – though because they had taken my watch as well, it might have been four – I decided to order breakfast. So I waded through the effluent and, through the small hole in the door, said I'd like toast, buttered to the edges, poached eggs, some fresh orange juice, a double espresso and my bloody lighter back. What I got instead was a burly French finger in my eye.

Eventually, though, the door was unlocked and, having been made to sign the visitors' book, I scarpered, leaving my hosts to wonder if they really had had Donald Duck in the cells all night.

So did the painful and humiliating experience cure my occasional twentysomething need to binge drink? Well, exactly 12 months later I was in the back of a police car in Greece, planning another escape attempt. So you'd have to say no.

What did cure me is what will cure all the youngsters who binge drink today.

I grew up.

Sunday 6 February 2005

Custard, my wife's worst swearword

Those of us who use the c-word need it to be socially risqué. Or it ceases to have a point.

Today there are bare naked ladies in the newspapers, homosexual men in the woods, homosexual bare naked transsexuals on the internet, and I'd like to bet you have no plans to visit church any time soon. Time moves on, habits change, and as a result what would once have shocked the nation to its core is now considered normal.

And yet, while you're happy to watch a televised autopsy, you would be astonished and amazed if Michael Howard were to make a speech this afternoon in which he described Tony Blair as a 'f★★★wit'.

Why? You use the f-word all the time, and so do your children. Buzz Aldrin used it on the moon, and we know it nestles in the vocabulary of both Prince Philip and Princess Anne. We think Alastair Campbell uses it, too, while addressing the *Newsnight* team, but we can't be sure because journalists can't use it in print.

Don't you think that's weird?

I can say a couple copulated, or that they had sexual intercourse. So obviously it isn't the act itself that causes offence, just the word. And I can't quite work out why.

We're fast approaching the fortieth anniversary of the first time it was ever used on British television – by the critic Kenneth Tynan – and at the time four motions were tabled in the Commons, with one Tory MP suggesting the foul-mouthed perpetrator should be hanged.

Eleven years later Bill Grundy was suspended because some of his guests used it during his show; and Sir Peregrine Worsthorne was denied the editorship of the *Daily Telegraph* because on one of his television appearances he'd used it, too.

And things haven't changed. According to the last set of BBC guidelines I saw, it is still more likely to cause offence than the word 'nigger'.

Nigger is a good case in point. When I was growing up, it was no more shocking than 'cauliflower'. You didn't see Bill Grundy being escorted from the building, because you were watching Alf Garnett on the other side, roaring with laughter as he peppered the screen with his racist abuse.

And yet now, just 30 years later, it's gone. In fact, it is just about the only word I simply would not let my children use. So why, if words move into and out of common parlance so quickly, has the f-word been a taboo since the dark, muddled dawn of the English language?

You may argue that this isn't the case. People with pipes and bifocals will certainly claim that in the not too distant past, words of an anatomical or scatological nature were not frowned upon at all, and that the swearwords of the time were religious: Jesus Christ, goddammit and so on. So they would tell you that there has most definitely been a shift in the nation's choice of profanity.

Really? Well, let's take the worst word in the world as a case study. You know what I'm talking about, and you'll know why I can't even camouflage such a thing behind a mask of asterisks.

We know it was used, in various forms, since before the Norman Conquest, and we know it was in common parlance from the thirteenth century. But if it had been socially acceptable, then why, when Ophelia says Hamlet cannot lie in her lap, does Hamlet reply: 'Do you think I meant country matters?'

By beating about the bush, so to speak, Shakespeare is getting a titter out of the worst word in the world, same as he does in *Twelfth Night*. And he couldn't have done that if it wasn't the worst word in the world back then, too.

Even earlier, Chaucer wouldn't come out and write it, hedging the issue by saying 'Pryvely he caught hir by the queynte'. Mind you, this might have something to do with the fact old Geoff couldn't spell.

In 1961 it finally appeared in a dictionary, but, despite this, it's still a massive no-no. In fact it's probably fair to say that this one word is the most enduring taboo in the English-speaking world. When Johnny Rotten used it on *I'm in the Jungle, Send Me a Big Cheque*, there were 100 complaints – and that, speaking as someone who presents one of the most complained-about shows on television, is a lot. And who can forget the furore when the BBC recently screened *Jerry Springer, the Opera*.

This word, then, is Custer's last stand for the morally upright and the tweedily decent. The Guardianistas and the foul-mouthed have crossed the moat, scaled the walls and traversed the bailey. But so long as the keep is held up by the c-word cornerstone, all is not lost.

Frankly, I'm delighted, because those of us who use it need it to be socially risqué. Or it ceases to have a point.

My wife is especially glad because it's a word she uses all the time. She loves it. Sometimes, when the children are listening, she combines it with 'bastard' to create the word 'custard', but mostly it's the full, uncensored version that's hurled in the direction of anyone she doesn't like. Local radio DJs cop for it a lot.

She's even developed it into a test at parties, using it as soon as practicably possible, whenever she's introduced to someone. Her argument is that those who fall into a dead faint and need to be brought round with smelling salts weren't worth talking to anyway.

I think she has a point, because many years ago my grandfather told me that those who swear are simply demonstrating they have a limited vocabulary. That can't be so because when Tony Blair comes on the news you feel naked and underequipped if you don't have some choice profanities in your quiver. Sometimes only the c-word will do.

Sunday 13 February 2005

Go ahead, lad, be a gay astronaut

So, would you wipe someone's backside for £5 an hour? This was the question posed by an angry woman to Mr Blair last week on a politics show on Five.

The simple answer, of course, is no. Because if the backside is sufficiently dirty to need a whole hour's cleaning, we'd all need a damn sight more than a fiver. But actually there's a much better retort.

Not that long ago, the unskilled school-leaver faced a stark choice. Become a nurse and spend the rest of your life wiping bottoms, or become one of those people who've chosen not to wipe other people's bottoms by going down the mine.

Actually, it wasn't just the unskilled who were given limited options. I've just remembered that the careers form I was given at school asked me to tick one of the following options: solicitor, accountant, estate agent, or 'other'. I ticked 'other' and, when asked to give details, displayed the pre-pubescent wit that has stood me in such good stead over the years by writing: 'I want to be the world's first homosexual astronaut.'

After I came out of detention, I explained to the careers master that I didn't care what I did, just so long as it didn't involve wearing a suit.

He was amazed. 'Look, boy. You either wear a suit and

become an estate agent, or you'd better get practising with the Andrex.' And this was only 1978.

Now let's spool forward to 2005, when it's possible to make a decent living putting pine cones in paper doilies and flogging them to bored blonde stick-insect women as firelighters for £11 a pop.

I'm not joking. Someone has convinced the owners of my local farm shop that what they really need to stock are pine cones in paper bun-holders. Isn't that fantastic?

These days it's even possible to be an author, even if you have no real idea for a book, no literary skills whatsoever, and you are due at a coffee morning in two hours' time.

Right next to the pine cone firelighters, I found a small tome called . . . wait for it . . . *The Incomplete List of Cat Names*.

Now look. You can call a cat anything. Gravel. Honda. Stereo. Wardrobe. Cauliflower. Hitler.

Which means that this book is just a list of some words. So, if you're the woman on Five who doesn't want to wipe other people's bottoms for £5 an hour, why not write *The Incomplete List of Food Names*? Just write 'beans, meat and arugula', and you're the next J. K. Rowling.

If you can't think of an incomplete list that needs writing, or your chosen topic has already been the subject of a Channel 4 list programme, which is likely, don't despair. Simply count the number of broken windows there are in your street and sell the information to one of the government's 529 quangos.

A man called Charles Landry was quoted in the newspapers last week. So what's he done, you may ask: cloned a mosquito, solved climate change? No. He has counted how many times the phrase 'at risk' appeared in the papers in 2003 and compared it with the number of times it appeared in 1994.

I don't know anything about Mr Landry's financial circumstances or how much he's paid to count words in newspapers. But even if it's not much, it is better than wiping miners' backsides. Or inseminating turkeys. Or sliding food and household products over a bar code reader.

And it's certainly better than getting an outreach counselling job through the *Guardian*.

Michael Howard tells us that, for every 1,000 people in this country, two will be doctors, three will be police officers and nine will be civil servants. This is why the civil service now employs more people than the total population of Sheffield. And it's why the Tories want to blow it apart.

Of course, those on the Left wonder what all those people from the British Potato Council and the Wine Standards Board will do when the machine-gun fire starts.

Well, look. If someone is daft enough to think that monitoring British wine is a worthwhile way of passing the time, then anything is possible. I once met a man who sexes the Queen's ducks, for instance.

What is more, we read last week of a man who was paid to run around a shopping centre pretending to be a racing car. If the arts appeal, then why not be a ventriloquist? There are only seven left in the whole of Britain. Or you could eat food, and then get paid for saying whether you like it or not. Or you could stuff a heron. I'd pay £200 for such a thing.

And finally there's this business of being a homosexual astronaut. Just 25 years ago, the mere suggestion that I might like to do this for a living earned me a spell in detention, but now there's a lobby group in America called the Organization of Gay and Self-Loving Men in Orbit.

It reckons that homosexual men have better visual-spatial and dexterity skills than straight chaps and that they display a greater number of hyper-masculine character-istics. Plus. They're unlikely to get women crew members pregnant on long journeys to Mars.

I hope His Tonyness finds this information useful. Because the next time he's asked about the alternatives for Britain's bottom wipers, instead of sitting there, look-ing like a complete custard, he can say: 'Go and be a gay spaceman instead.'

Sunday 20 February 2005

Sticking one on the gum summit

Thanks to the weather and Mrs Queen's problems with Charles and Camilla's wedding plans, you probably didn't notice that last week Britain played host to its first ever 'gum summit'.

Councillors from all over Britain trimmed their beards and dug out their finest jumpers for an all-expenses-paid trip to London, where they sat around, deciding what should be done about people who spit out their chewing gum.

Meanwhile, in the Commons, business was taken up by the Cleaner Neighbourhoods and Environment Bill, which will see £75 on-the-spot fines being handed out to chewing gum offenders. Well, come on. With foxhunting dealt with and all the terrorists under house arrest, what else is there for them to do?

Quite who will issue these fines I don't know. Obviously the police no longer have the time, since they're all running around the countryside, looking for wounded foxes, so it's been suggested that the job is given to council employees like bin men and street sweepers. I'm not sure this is a good idea because, if a fat man in a hi-vis jacket ordered me to cough up £75 for chewing gum, I might just set fire to his ears.

It looks, then, like being yet another law that can't be enforced, so we'll now go back to the council summit and ask ourselves a simple question. If you were asked to list the biggest eyesores in most towns today, I bet it'd be a long time before you got to the small, dark, lichen-like splotches on the paving stones caused by discarded chewing gum.

In most urban landscapes you tend to notice the hideous buildings, the nasty municipal flowerbeds, the ludicrous array of signs, the fatness of the shoppers, their statically charged synthetic clothes, the drizzle, the abundance of estate agents, the polystyrene litter, the pavement pizzas, the graffiti, the lime-green 'Win', 'Free', 'Save' poster adverts in all the shop windows and the diesel smoke from the buses, long before your eye is caught by the mild and patchy discoloration of the chipped, cracked, Third World paving slabs.

Apparently, though, the problem is huge. In the borough of Westminster there are 20 pieces of discarded gum per square metre of paving, and on Oxford Street alone there are 300,000 splotches. Around Sir Alex Ferguson's chair in the Old Trafford dugout the gum mountain is said to be taller than K2.

The cost of cleaning up this mess is £150 million a year, so at the gum summit several ideas were mooted. First of all, one bright spark came up with the idea of biodegradable chewing gum, something that Wrigley has already spent £5 million trying to develop. Why? Even I could have told them that this is an impossible dream, because if gum can withstand two hours in Sir Alex's mouth it seems unlikely it'll simply evaporate when exposed to a light shower. I mean, the human jawbone can exert 7 tons of pressure per square inch.

Sure, we could go back to the days when gum was made from natural products, rather than latex, but since Britain alone consumes 935 million packets a year, this would mean uprooting every tree from Tierra del Fuego to the Rio Grande. And I doubt this would go down well with some of the summit's more communistic representatives who suggested that Wrigley, which has a 90 per cent share of Britain's £300 million gum industry, should be made to share the clean-up costs.

Others reckoned that shops should be made to display notices advising Britain's gum-chewers of their responsibilities. Nice idea, but as a general rule gum tends to be chewed by people who can't read.

And me. I'm ashamed to say that I don't always dispose of it in what you might call a socially responsible fashion. This is disgusting, I know. I've had two pairs of trousers ruined by other people's gum and I realise I should know better, but I'm being realistic. It happens.

I'm therefore in a good position to work out what might be done to mend the error of my ways. Obviously, if a refuse collector sees me jettison some gum from the window of my speeding car, I doubt he'll be able to catch up in his dustbin lorry, so that won't work. And I already know that I shouldn't litter the pavement, so point-of-sale literature will be no good either.

Until last year the Singapore authorities gave people who smuggled gum into the country a year in jail. But this seems harsh. And anyway, the jails will soon be full of people whose dogs were nasty to foxes. So what can be done?

Well, I think I have a solution. And even by my own high standards it's brilliant.

Gum trees.

Councils would erect poles at strategic points along the street on to which Sir Alex Ferguson and I can stick our discarded gum. They could even be sponsored, like ring-road roundabouts. And when the pole is full it could be removed and replaced with a new one.

What's more, these gum trees could be placed on Underground trains and in shopping centres. Enterprising companies could even offer stick-on miniature versions that could be affixed to a car's dashboard.

So there you are. At no cost to the taxpayer I find a solution. Sometimes I wonder what our government is actually for.

Sunday 27 February 2005

It's freezing, so go get your sun cream

Every week, another high street retailer tells us that it's in a perilous financial state. Debenhams. Bhs. Dorothy Perkins. Marks & Spencer. Boots. WHSmith. They're all in trouble, and I know why. They don't sell things that people want to buy.

Last week, for instance, I had a nasty cold, but, of course, being a man, it wasn't a cold at all. It was cancer: well, when I say cancer it was a sort of cancerous leprosy. In fact, what I actually had was bird flu of the cancer of the leprosy, with a light dusting of ebola. Had Norris McWhirter been alive, he would have verified that I was the illest person in the world who wasn't actually dead.

To make matters worse, a cruel Arctic wind was blowing and the police were advising motorists to stay at home unless their journey was absolutely necessary. Well, my journey was very necessary because I needed a coat.

Happily, I was slap bang in the middle of London, which is the world's eighteenth biggest city and the largest shopping centre in Europe.

So you might imagine it would be easy to buy such a thing.

But where? I'm too old for the King's Road, I'm too male for Sloane Street and, so far as I can tell, Marks & Spencer only sells pants to sensible girls who play the violin, and sandwiches. Dorothy Perkins didn't sound too hopeful either and what can you buy in Bhs? Table lamps, I think.

My wife suggested I try Selfridges, and so, with the sleet reminding me that I have a big hole in the back of my hair, I trundled over to Oxford Street with a gold credit card and sticky-out nipples. I was freezing.

Initially, the first floor looked hopeful. It's the size, apparently, of four football pitches, or maybe two double-decker buses. Or Wales. Anyway, it's huge and rammed with every designer label I'd ever heard of, and about a million I hadn't. All of which were selling T-shirts.

I'm not joking. Issey & Gabbana, Alexander Saint Laurent, Tommy Farhi, Ozwald Hackett, Joseph Boateng. One was all green and I couldn't get out of the damn thing. Another was full of string. It was all terribly Tate Modern and jolly pleasing on the eye, but not one of them, on a day that Kent was cut off, could sell me a coat.

'We've got this,' said one cheerful woman, holding up something that travel agents advise you to pack for those chilly evenings you might encounter on a spring break in Rome. But I wasn't going to Rome. The next day, I was going to the iced-up *Top Gear* test track, and I had every disease in the world.

Later, I was to be found on Bond Street, where it was the same story. Lots of shops stuffed full of linen, three-quarter-length trousers and endless poster-sized photographs of people playing with beach balls.

Now look. Those people who have catering concessions in the nation's lay-bys are far from the brightest stars in the firmament. But not one of them would have woken up on that Siberian morning and thought: 'Right.

I'll leave the tea urns at home today and take the Mr Whippy van instead.'

They know that when the thermometer is reading 1, people are disinclined to want a 99. And it was the same story with all the street stalls I passed. They were full of scarves and brollies, not sunglasses and swimming trunks. And these, remember, tend to be run by people who have more Asbos than O-levels.

On Friday morning, I opened my newspapers to be greeted with endless photographs of Stella McCartney's new collection. There were lots of women in shawls and chunky polo neck jumpers, and I thought: 'Aha. Here is someone who recognises that people want to buy clothes to suit whatever weather conditions happen to be prevailing at the time.'

But no. It turns out that these new outfits are for next winter and they'll be in the shops for August.

I'm aware, of course, that women can plan ahead. In a supermarket, my wife will buy oven cleaner and new light bulbs because she's aware we're running low. But men cannot do this. In a supermarket I can buy only what I want at that moment, which is usually a packet of Smarties.

Now, I know that Britain's fashion buyers are mainly women and homosexuals, but surely they recognise this. Surely, they know that half the population buy T-shirts when it's hot and that when it's not they want a coat.

I realise, of course, that each square foot of prime London real estate must be made to pay, and that running summer and winter collections alongside one another is messy, both aesthetically and financially.

But how's this for an idea? Fashion is a global business and therefore the big names must be selling winter clothes in Australia at the moment. So why not simply switch them around? This way, I would not have come home that day having spent no money at all. And I would have had a coat. And that would have prevented the cancerous bird flu leprosy from being complicated still further with a dose of double pneumonia.

Which brings me on to Boots. The company announced last week that sales since January had been disappointing, and that demand for cough and cold remedies had been lower than expected.

Rubbish. I wanted to buy half a ton of Lemsip last week, and 5,000 packets of Solpadeine, but the store was chock-full of hay fever pills and sun cream.

Sunday 6 March 2005

Good riddance to green rubbish

When the humourless and stupid Earth Centre opened six years ago, Tony Blair hailed it as being 'greater' even than the dome. His views were echoed by Michael Meacher, then an environment minister, who went on to say that this lottery-funded eco-theme park would be a 'living and breathing example of sustainability'.

Well, it wasn't. Because last week a last-ditch attempt to save the centre failed. Which means it's gone for good, taking £36 million of our money with it.

The Earth Centre encapsulated everything that is so wrong-headed about this government and its frizzy-haired, baggy-breasted advisers, huddled together, oblivious to the fact that all their eye-swivellingly daft ideas and initiatives are thousands of light years away from what anyone actually wants.

So when one of them mined a hitherto unimagined seam of idiocy and came up with the notion of a green theme park where people could actually watch their own excrement being converted into fertiliser and then sprayed on to the vegetable garden, which would produce food for the centre's café, no one said: 'Hang on a minute. Are you seriously suggesting that people will pay £14 to eat someone else's shit?'

This is because they don't like Alton Towers, which smacks of the Great Satan and commercial greed. They therefore end up believing that we'd much rather spend the afternoon tucking into one another's faeces than have another go on the log flume.

So, in a blizzard of ignorance and naivety, the Earth Centre opened on the 400-acre site of my family's old glassworks outside Doncaster and damn nearly drowned in a sea of effusive newspaper articles by yet more frizzy-haired, baggy-breasted women who'd dragged their utterly miserable children up to Yorkshire.

Unfortunately, hardly anybody else went at all. The idiots had reckoned on half a million turning up every year, but in 2004 only 30,000 went through the turnstiles. On the day I went, the place was deserted. And it wasn't hard to see why.

Because if I want to know what it's like to live in a green world, I don't need to go to Doncaster. I could just strip naked and stand outside all day, gnawing on some bark. They had a yurt, which is a tent, and the guide wondered, out loud, what it would be like to live in such a thing. Not as nice as living in my house, love. They also had a big trumpet that allowed you to hear more clearly the sounds of nature.

But there weren't any because, unfortunately, while they were making the place, they'd built an access road right through one of the most important wildlife reserves in the region. So all you could hear through the eco-trumpet was the sound of various yellow ants, little ringed plovers and marbled white butterflies suffocating to death under a million tons of slurry.

This, however, was only part of the hypocrisy. There was also a feature where visitors were reminded of the region's flirtation with coal, and how much damage this had done to the environment. I bet that went down well with the locals.

And then there was the blurb that said the Earth Centre was bound to succeed because it was within 'a two-hour drive' for 20 million people. Yes, except, if you turned up in a car, you were charged £8.50 to get in, whereas if you turned up on a train or a bicycle it was only £4.50.

When will these buffoons realise that if you open an attraction without sufficient free parking, it is absolutely bound to fail? That's what did for the dome. They deliberately made it inaccessible for motorists, because 'I don't have a car, and neither does anyone else I know.'

Unfortunately, 28 million people in this country do have a car, and I should imagine they didn't take kindly to being herded into the Earth Centre's unheated cinema and reminded that they were a pack of planet-murdering bastards.

It wasn't the hypocrisy, though, that annoyed me most about this terrible place, or the waste of money. It was the dour bossiness, the finger wagging and the concept that all fun in life must be balanced with guilt and rage. Their vision of a perfect world looked to me pretty much like the devil's lecture theatre.

They even said that you could use the same solar-powered system as the Earth Centre at your home for 'the price of a motorboat'.

I see. And how many people do you think would say, 'No, I won't buy a 40-foot Sunseeker. I shall use the money instead to buy some stupid power system that means my kettle won't work whenever it's cloudy.' How many people do you think have the choice in the first place?

I am genuinely delighted that the Earth Centre has joined the dome as a shining example of why green issues, political correctness and multi-faith thinking have no place in a modern, civilised culture. And I hope it shows the dreary harridans that there's another, bigger, more sensible world, away from their earnest and fun-free dinner parties.

What I hope most of all, though, is that the site of their latest failure is turned into a lap-dancing, paintballing racetrack. With discounts for those who turn up in a car. I reckon this could be achieved for half what the Earth Centre cost and that it really would be a shining example of sustainable business.

Because it would be packed.

Sunday 13 March 2005

Bury me with my anecdotes on

A study, reported in this newspaper last week, suggests that there's no such thing as a midlife crisis. And that when people reach the age of 40, they become a symphony in corduroy: happy, contented and more popular than ever.

It all sounds very jolly, but I'm afraid it's balderdash, because when I reached 40 I got the distinct impression that I'd outlived my biological purpose, that I would never again do anything worth doing for the first time and that there was nothing to look forward to, except maybe having my Labrador dognapped.

It may be true to say that middle-aged people stop being competitive and self-centred but that's because, at some point in your forties, you reach the top of the ladder and realise there are no more worlds to conquer. So there's no point stabbing colleagues in the back because it's pointless. You know the only way is down.

The worst thing about becoming 40, though, is that your brain's default setting changes from sex to death. We're told that men in their twenties and thirties think about rumpy-pumpy every six minutes and never consider dying at all. Well, for me, it's the other way round.

At 40, the big picture of Jordan's breasts is erased from your human screensaver and replaced by a shadowy figure with a cloak and a scythe.

The other day, some celebrity was in the newspapers

because she'd forgotten to wear any knickers. But I was more interested in the death of Ross Benson. He was 56, for God's sake. That means I only have 11 years left. And while 11 years to a young person is 11 years, let me assure you that when you're past 40, 11 years is about 15 minutes.

I wonder all the time about how I might die and when it might happen. Every morning when I wake up, I'm surprised. And what's more, I've talked to several of my friends, all of whom admit that when they're not really thinking about anything in particular, they think about death.

That's why you see so many old men playing golf. They're not doing this to stay fit. They're sacrificing their dignity in a desperate bid to make the screensaver go away.

However, since death is preferable to golf, I'm not really bothered by the 'when'.

I'm more concerned with the 'how'. And I've decided I definitely don't want to drown, or be murdered with an axe by someone who wants my watch. Most of all, though, I don't want to meet the Reaper with a tube up my nose. I don't want my last staging post on Earth to be a hospital ward full of old, grey people. Because that would be boring.

And I'm not alone. One chap I spoke to said he didn't care how he died so long as it was in a fireball of some kind. Another said he dreamt of dying while doing some good. Charging a machine-gun nest perhaps, or rescuing a group of schoolchildren from a tiger. Me? Well, I'd like it to be the basis of a damn good anecdote.

Last week, for instance, I crashed a racing hovercraft.

As is the way with these things, it all happened in slow motion. The front end dug into the ground and as I was catapulted from my seat, astride the fuel tank, I actually thought: 'Ooh good. My wife should be able to turn this into a rip-roaring story on *Parkinson*. She'll have them rolling in the aisles.'

I had a similar experience a few years ago while flying into Havana on board a 1950s Russian aeroplane that had seen service with the Angolan air force before being sold to the Cubans. It wasn't in very good nick before the pilot flew right into the middle of a massive thunderstorm.

So anyway, there we were, upside down, with our ears being assaulted by that whining noise you always hear on films when a plane is crashing. And I thought: 'Fantastic! My kids will be able to grow up saying their dad was killed in a Russian plane, in a tropical storm over Cuba. They'll be the most popular kids in the class.'

Perhaps this is why 45-year-old men buy Porsches. It has nothing to do with testosterone's losing battle with an ever-expanding waistline. And everything to do with a need to die while doing 180.

Certainly, I'm staggered that only 21,000 people have applied for a place on Richard Branson's new Virgin Galactic spaceship. Of course, with each ticket costing around £100,000, the price is high. But the vast majority of those who can afford such a sum will be at the height of their powers, facing nothing but a steady spiral into incontinence and phlegm. So why don't they sign up and go for the ultimate thrill: a ride into space.

It can only be a fear of death that's holding them back; but what do you want instead? The carriage clock? The secateurs? The coach tour of north Wales? Or maybe 30 years on a golf course, and your last recollection of life on Earth being the burly paramedic's tongue sliding down your throat.

No thanks. Being blasted to the heavens, quite literally, by a couple of tons of rocket fuel is almost certain to get your demise on the news. You'd bring a little excitement to the lives of millions and that's even more selfless than saving schoolchildren from a tiger. It'd also be quick.

And that really is what I'm after most of all. I want to be drunk, and happy, and then I want to explode.

Sunday 20 March 2005

A screen queen ate my pork pie

I suppose we all dream about the day when George Clooney calls to say he's in the area and would like to drop by for lunch. We fantasise about the Dover sole we'd make for starters, and the sparkling conversation we'd serve up with the coffee and mints. And we know it's never going to happen.

Well, last week it sort of did. I was at a seaside holiday cottage when someone I'd invited for lunch rang to ask if they could bring a friend.

Who turned out to be my favourite actress in the world. I dislike the word 'gobsmacked', but that's what I was. Utterly and absolutely bowled into a stuttering, quivering stupor.

And then the practicalities set in. She would be bringing her three children, which meant there'd be 22 for lunch and the Aga was broken. To make matters worse, it was a Sunday morning, which meant all the supplies would have to be bought at the local ShopRite.

And then there are my culinary skills to consider. Given time, and only three small children to satisfy, I can make a fairly decent fist of a Sunday roast. Providing no one wants gravy.

But we were talking here about catering for 22, including a Hollywood superstar, in a small back-up oven, and the only ingredients I could find initially were six bananas. And some ginger.

Is there anything so depressing as a small village shop on a Sunday morning, after the local dopeheads have been through the place with an attack of the munchies and there's hardly anything left?

Well, yes there is, as it turns out. Being confronted with all those empty shelves when your heroine is due for lunch in two hours. It was a good time to panic.

Happily, I'd been joined by the producer of *Top Gear*, who knows how to reduce a jus. But even he was stumped by what on earth could be achieved with nothing but bananas and ginger.

'What about roast banana with ginger sprinkled on the top?' I suggested imaginatively.

'What about shutting up?' he replied, and set off for the meat counter, where we hoped to find something she'd like: a swan, perhaps, or maybe a bit of peacock.

We were to be disappointed. All they had was a jumbo family pack of steak and kidney pie, and a quiche, which, according to a bright green starburst on the packaging came 'with 26% less fat'.

Neither seemed appropriate. But there was a Pork Farms pork pie, and some sausages.

So, a grated pork pie on a reduction of sausage, garnished with a banana and ginger jus. Mmmm. And we also managed to find a jar of mustard, some Branston pickle, a tub of coleslaw, which was perilously close to its 'best before' date and some limes. We had the bones of a lunch here, we felt. If we had been in a Sudanese refugee camp. Rather than catering for a screen diva, a goddess, a globally recognised, Oscar-nominated, drop-dead gorgeous superstar.

Don't you think this is odd? If it had been you turning up for lunch, I'd have invited you to eat whatever you could prise from the cracks in the kitchen table.

I certainly wouldn't have spent the morning painting a mustard sauce on to the Wall's sausages.

And nor would I have filled the fridge with the staple diet of all actresses: gently carbonated mineral water, into which I'd squeezed a bouquet of my ShopRite limes. You'd have had whatever was in the tap.

Fame sends us all into a complete tizzy. I even broke a golden rule and shaved on a Sunday. I think I may also have slipped out of my jeans, and into a smart pair of slacks.

And then she arrived. You've no doubt seen those television commercials where someone wearing a new kind of antiperspirant runs through the jungle without breaking into a sweat.

Well, I use that brand, and, be assured, it doesn't work when you're trying to offer your heroine a drink, only to find that your tongue, which has worked perfectly well for 44 years, has chosen this moment to become as bent and as twisted as a pig's tail.

What if she wants a glass of Dom Perignon '64 with a dash of yam juice? Because this would be the perfect aperitif for the swan and peacock she'd been expecting.

'On Tuesday,' she said, answering a question my tongue had asked all by itself.

'No. What would you like to drink?'

'Oh, mineral water if you have it.'

Thank God. At this rate, the next thing she'll say is that what she really wants for lunch is a pork pie.

'Ooh, Branston pickle,' she said, having spotted the jar on the table. 'I love that with pork pie.' At this point, my whole heart exploded.

Behind the dazzling eyes, and the porcelain skin, she was normal, as down-to-earth as your mum, or mine.

I was expecting a prima donna because we are forever reading about Wayne Rooney's minders, and that bloke from the Halifax commercial who goes everywhere with an entourage. We have grown to believe that celebrities are too busy quaffing champagne in London's glittering West End to be capable of dealing with a sausage.

So each time I meet a famous person, I'm always staggered that they can cut up their own food. Last Sunday hammered the point home even further, so now I can offer you some valuable advice. If George Clooney does call, open a tube of Pringles and give him a can of beer.

Sunday 27 March 2005

Save me from my mobile phone

My last mobile phone was useless. Oh, it could take pictures and connect itself to the interweb, but its battery went flat every 30 seconds, and when it came to the business of wanting to make a call I had to be actually sitting on a phone mast.

Which has probably given me cancer of the bottom.

And then – and this is the worst part – its speaker was so microscopic it was absolutely impossible to hear what the person on the other end was saying. I wanted a tuba, but I've almost certainly ended up with a tumour.

This drove my wife mad, listening to me shouting 'What?' over and over again, so last week she bought me a replacement.

Now, I could, I know, have inserted the battery and been connected to the outside world immediately. But I didn't. I made a mistake. This being a toy, and me being a man, I thought that it might be a good idea to disable the predictive text facility, which is the single stupidest invention since Sir Clive Sinclair's electrical slipper.

You're no doubt familiar with the way it works. You type in 'to' and it spends the rest of time guessing what the rest of the word might be. Tomorrow? Today? Toyota? Topazolite? Tonsil? It just can't understand that you want to write 'to' – because, of course, in text speak that's spelt 2.

Anyway, to disable the facility meant delving into the handbook, which contains 104 pages. Yes, 104 pages. For a phone. I knew I was in trouble.

And I was, because, while searching for the chapter on text messaging, I happened upon a passage explaining how I could download music from the internet straight into my new phone. This sounded exciting, and I'm not sure why.

You see, I can currently play 'Long Train Runnin'' on my record player, my CD player, my iPod, my Walkman, my computer and while I'm in my car. It is hard to think of any environment, anywhere in the world, where I am more than 4 feet from the Brothers Doobie.

But the notion of being able to harness a series of ones and noughts from the ether and then marshal them into a recognisable tune on a mobile phone – it was just too irresistible for someone who began his journalistic career with a Remington typewriter.

So I inserted the disc that had come with my new phone into my computer and sat back while it whirred and generally went about its business. Then things got tricky, because it wanted to know how it should communicate with the mobile.

This required some input from me, and everything started to go pear-shaped. I was an hour trying to hook up Bluetooth before I realised no such thing exists in my computer's chip. So then I took out one of the wires that came with the phone – there were about four miles of flex from which to choose – hard-linked the two devices and tried to forge a link with the net.

And up came a message saying: 'The PPP link control

protocol was terminated.' Now obviously, I have seen this kind of message before, usually in a film where a nuclear power plant is about to explode. But what does it mean?

I'm not a technophobe. I can work a Sky+ and tune a car radio. But I don't know what a PPP link control protocol is and therefore have no idea how best to un-terminate it.

No matter. I already had 'Long Train Runnin'' stored away in the bowels of my computer's silicon heart, so I attempted to upload this into the phone. No joy. It was, said a message, forbidden. What is this? The music police?

It would accept 'Time' by Pink Floyd and I've now made this the dedicated ring tone for the band's drummer, Nick Mason. How cool is that? Should he ever choose to call, it'll actually play one of his tunes.

It would also accept 'Summer of '69', which I've allo-cated to Bryan Adams. And it happily uploaded 'Behind Blue Eyes', which is now the personalised ring tone for Roger Daltrey. But it refuses the Doobies. Maybe it's because I don't know Jeff 'Skunk' Baxter's number.

While searching for confirmation of this in the hand-book – Concorde's, by the way, was four pages thinner – I found that I could take a picture on the phone, then email it via the laptop to a friend. So obviously I tried to send A. A. Gill (who's been given 'Sing If You're Glad To Be Gay') a shot of my genitals. But this didn't work either. I guess the PPP link control protocol was playing up again.

In fact, I spent – and I'm not joking – a whole day playing with all the new and utterly useless features on my phone, most of which don't work. And all I've learnt is that people who have personalised ring tones have far, far too much time on their hands.

I still have no idea whether the speaker is audible or whether it can receive a signal in, say, Fulham. And I also have no idea how to cancel the predictive texting facility. The handbook devotes 12 pages to this, suggesting it is so monumentally complicated that it'd be easier, and far, far faster, to send the recipient a letter.

The only good news is that the Motorola V3's SAR is well within the 2.0 W/kg limit laid down by Cenelec. I found this nugget in the health and safety chapter, and I think it means I won't catch ear cancer.

Sunday 17 April 2005

Ecologists can kill a landscape

Plans to build a forest of wind turbines on an escarpment in the Lake District ran into problems last week when Lord Melvyn Bragg said they'd mess up his hairstyle.

There's no doubt we need to work on a new type of renewable energy because of one single fact. So far, mankind has extracted 944 billion barrels of oil, and there are only 764 billion barrels left.

But, quite apart from the problems with Bragg's hair, I doubt wind turbines are the answer. They mince ospreys, make a god-awful racket and, worst of all, produce only enough electricity to run half a toaster. You'd need 100,000 to provide Britain with all the power it needs, and can you even begin to imagine the visual impact that would have?

Put simply, to preserve the beauty of our green and pleasant land, we'd have to destroy it.

This is the conundrum faced by all environmental effort. Michael Crichton, in his extraordinary recent book, *State of Fear* – you have just got to read it – highlights the case of the Yellowstone National Park in Wyoming which was ring-fenced as a wilderness in 1872.

Unfortunately, the eco-beards couldn't stop meddling. First, they thought the elk was about to become extinct so they shot all the wolves in the park, and banned Indians from hunting. Soon, there were so many elk, they started to eat the trees that the beavers used to make dams, so the beavers upped sticks and moved somewhere else. And without the beavers' dams, the meadows dried up, the trout and the otter vanished and soil erosion became a serious problem. A problem exacerbated by the huge elk herds that were eating all the grass. So they had to start shooting the elk, by the thousand.

This brings me on to a plot of coastal land I've just bought on the Isle of Man.

It is a spectacular place, as wild and rugged and remote as you can possibly imagine. The air is needle sharp. The sea is ice clear. And then there's the wildlife. There are seals, hen harriers, Manx shearwaters, many peregrine falcons, and some sheep.

There's more, too, because the plot is the only European habitat of something called the lesser mottled grasshopper. Which means I'm now the sole custodian of an entire species. And how cool is that?

'Not very,' you might think, if you are one of the grasshoppers. You can imagine them, all huddled round, craning their little necks, trying to see who had bought their home: 'Is it David Attenborough? Is it Bill Oddie? Or David Bellamy? Oh, bloody hellfire, it's that fat yob off *Top Gear*.'

As a result, they all seem to have scarpered. I've been round the entire site on my hands and knees, looking for the damn things, but I think they may be hiding in one of the caves, fearful that I'm some kind of white hunter whose study walls are groaning under the weight of all the dead heads, and that I'm going to bludgeon them all to death with a baseball bat, for fun. Or spray the site with

Agent Orange from a helicopter gunship. And then open a quad bike racetrack to run over the survivors.

They have me all wrong, though. Which is why I've signed a voluntary deal with the government to make sure all the indigenous wildlife survives my tenure. This sounds simple. But it isn't.

The first objective listed in the agreement says I must 'provide the grass length and warm conditions required by the lesser mottled grasshopper'. Now, I know how to keep the grass short – I shall use the woolly lawnmower known in farming circles as a flock of sheeps – but how in the name of all that's holy do you keep an insect 'warm'?

I must also harvest the crops from the middle of the field outwards, so the corncrakes have a chance to flee, I can't use dynamite to clear the gorse, nor can I clear it in the bird breeding season, I must produce dung for choughs – what, me personally? – I must rebuild the sod hedge, I can't use slurry and I must plant 200 berry-bearing shrubs. Naturally, clubbing the seals is right out.

Of course I get a small grant, but it doesn't get close to covering the cost of the work. Especially as I shall now have to spend the rest of time blow-drying all my sheeps, harvesting the barley with nail scissors and providing the grasshoppers with central heating. But I really don't mind, because hidden in all the rules and regulations is the most delicious irony.

You see, for centuries, this bleak wilderness has been popular with weird-beard types who come out to walk their dogs and peer at the hen harriers. On a pleasant Sunday afternoon, the whole place is a technicolor blizzard of cagoulery and livid walking socks.

And the fact is, these rambling types are frightening the birds. They're also inadvertently treading on all my grasshoppers, which means they're not in touch with the wildlife so much as standing on it.

The government wants them gone and, since the Isle of Man has no right to roam, I'm well within my rights to litter the place with landmines. It's certainly tempting.

Greenpeace and Friends of the Earth are forever trying to ban the car because of the damage it does, and now I have the chance for some payback. To save an endangered species, the petrolhead has to ban the greens.

Isn't that wonderful! To protect the environment, I have to get rid of the environmentalists.

Sunday 24 April 2005

What we need is a parliament of 12

Feeding white noise into a prisoner's cell is classified as torture. The practice is banned by all civilised countries because the human mind cannot cope with endless random sound. It causes insanity, eventually.

But that's what we're getting with this election campaign. An endless white noise of promises that can't be kept, statistics that mean nothing, and a smattering of pantomime personal abuse.

Why? Well, put simply, it is very cheap to cover a general election campaign.

Unlike, say, in a war, newspapers and television stations don't have to buy their reporters airline tickets, flak jackets and satellite phones. For the price of a train ticket to the stump in Peterborough, they can fill hours of airtime and hundreds of pages, and if anyone dares to complain about the bombardment, they're told it's important. Really?

When you push the switch on the wall, light comes into the room. When you are hungry, you go to a shop and buy food. When you are tired, you go to sleep. And when you are bored, you arrange to see friends. None of this has anything to do with whatever government happens to be prevailing at the time.

I'm willing to bet that none of the problems you have in life at the moment has anything at all to do with the decision-makers in Westminster. Is your daughter having a rough time at school? Is your wife having an affair? Neither of these things will be solved by the outcome of a general election.

Boris Johnson once claimed that a vote for the Tories would cause your wife to have bigger breasts and increase your chances of owning a BMW M3. He even had some science to back these claims, but it's nonsense really.

The Conservative Party likes to say Tony Blair is responsible for the emergence of MRSA, but this is political arrogance. MRSA is caused by nurses and doctors not washing their hands properly, and personal hygiene is not a political issue. Nor should it be.

On the flip side, I'm also pretty sure that none of the joy in your life has been created by politicians, either. Did they write the book you're enjoying at the moment, or make the film you watched last night? Do they make your children giggle, or your dog wag its tail?

Whatever it is that turns you on — watching a soufflé rise, making an Airfix model of a Mosquito bomber, riding your motorcycle — all will be unaffected by the general election.

What's more, whichever way the vote goes, the sewage network will continue to function and so will the company for which you work. Roads will continue to be fixed, doctors will continue to mend the sick, the police will continue to maintain law and order (except in Nottingham, obviously). We now have a system in this country, an infrastructure, and for the most part it would continue to run even if all the 650 Members of Parliament decided to spend the rest of time dressed as Hiawatha on a remote Scottish island.

Each one of us is now governed by a parish council, a district council, a county council and the European Union.

Unless we live in Scotland or Wales, in which case there's Holyrood or the assembly as well.

So, what is it, exactly, that the House of Commons does? I've thought hard about this, and the only thing that's truly changed in my life since Mr Blair came to power is the M4 bus lane.

Other than that, he's blundered about, making a lot of speeches, but unless you're a Polish plumber, or you're in the army, or you hunt foxes, he and his kind have made no difference at all. We all still get up, go to work, pay our bills and go to bed. New Labour has been, for the vast majority, utterly irrelevant.

And I'm not being party political here. All the main parties are making all sorts of promises about what they'll do if they win the election: 600 border guards, the abolition of top-up fees, a base rate for stamp duty, local income tax. But it's all just fiddling with a finite pot of money. None of it will make any difference.

Unless it's the Lib Dems, who want us all to have wire-wool hair and go everywhere on an ox.

I'm not suggesting we don't need leaders. We shall always need someone to react to American requests for soldiers, or an African need for food. But I do think the finite pot of tax money might be stretched a little further if there weren't 650 leaders, all on expenses.

Could it not be run, perhaps, like a cross between a parish council – which, now we're in the EU, is exactly what it is – and jury service? Can we not just have a dozen people, picked at random from the current electoral register, who sit in a village hall somewhere, making decisions only when they're necessary?

If Ruth Kelly and John Prescott can do it, then anyone can. And in case the random selection procedure does cough up the odd loony who wants to invade France, majority decisions will be taken.

What I'm talking about is benign, reactive government rather than cancerous, proactive government whose endless schemes dominate our viewing and reading pleasure and, with the exception of the M4 bus lane, achieve nothing of significance.

A poet once wrote, 'Meet the new boss. Same as the old boss.' It has become the mantra of the terminally disillusioned. But this morning I offer a solution. What if there were no boss at all?

Sunday 1 May 2005

Why won't shops sell me anything?

Not long ago, I wrote a column saying that high street stores have got completely out of sync and only sell clothing that is in no way relevant to the prevailing weather conditions. So on a cold day in March you cannot buy a coat. And on a hot day in August you cannot buy a pair of swimming trunks.

What I did not realise at the time is that these days, unless you have a spare fortnight or so, you cannot buy anything at all.

Last week, for instance, I was strolling home from my first ever breakfast meeting – it made me feel very important – when I saw a plasma television set in the window of a shop. 'Ooh,' I thought, 'because I'm now the sort of person who gets invited to breakfast meetings, I should have one of those.' And since I had five minutes to kill, I went inside with my credit card greased and ready for a battering.

The salesman opened proceedings with a lot of technical gobbledegook I didn't care about or understand, but I was expecting that. What I was not expecting was the sheer complication of giving him my money.

As a general rule, the only thing I ever buy is petrol. So I'm aware of how credit cards function. You dash into the shop, the Indian man pushes it through a swipy thing, you sign your name and dash back out to the car again. The job's done in seconds.

I've heard that it's the same story in supermarkets. A woman who breathes through her mouth drives your Loyd Grossman tomato sauce through a beam of light several times and then summons a colleague called Janet who goes to the back of the store to see how much it costs. It all sounds very efficient.

But apart from petrol stations and supermarkets, the whole buying process is now littered with an immense amount of needless baggage. I mean, have you ever tried to get something from the internet?

I watched my wife downloading songs from iTunes on to her iPod the other iDay and I reckoned it looked simple. And it is. But only after you've told Mr Apple who you are, where you live, what password you would like, whether you want some Viagra, how much you earn and all sorts of other stuff that is in no way relevant to the fact that I wanted to buy *Radar Love* by Golden Earring.

Back in the real world, things are just as bad. And the worst offenders, so far as I can tell, are those that sell stuff with plugs, the shops that show *Richard and Judy* in a hundred different ways: electrical retailers. What happens here is that the spotty man with enough product in his hair to fry a fish takes your credit card, goes to his computer terminal, logs on and begins to write *War and Peace*.

After a while − it was a week or so − I became so exasperated that I moved along the counter to see if he'd at least got to the bit where Marya chucks Anatole, but guess what? He wasn't writing *War and Peace* at all. What he was doing was all the company's internal accounting and stock control, informing some mainframe in Ipswich that he was in the process of selling a television.

This, I'm sure, is better than having a man in a brown store coat out the back, noticing when the pile of 42-inchers is getting a bit low. A big flashy computer program is something you can talk about with the suppliers at breakfast meetings.

It looks good.

Anyway, when the man with the solid hair had finished updating the company's database, he started to ask me a series of impertinent questions. Like where I lived, my home phone number and my email address, presumably so that his bosses could sell my details to a spammer who, knowing I'd just bought a plasma television, would clock me immediately as someone who has breakfast meetings and therefore is someone in need of a larger penis.

By this stage, he had already taken up the time I usually set aside in a whole year for shopping. And he hadn't even started on the credit card transaction, or the delivery address. Which was different from my home address. Which meant he had to re-program the company's entire software package.

I began to be overwhelmed with a sense of helplessness, a sense that I might be in the shop for ever. So I started giving serious consideration to the idea of popping next door and buying a knife. I'm not by nature a murderer, but I began to visualise the blade in question and how it might look sticking out of the salesman's head.

All that saved him was the sure-fire knowledge that I'd get the same treatment in the knife shop, the same endless pitter-patter of a computer keyboard and the same requests for personal information; the only difference being that, if you buy a knife, you end up with an inbox full of messages from people in America wondering if you'd like to buy some camouflage trousers and maybe shoot a black man.

So listen up, shopkeepers. I am a busy man. I am dipping soldiers with businessmen long before you've got your shutters up and I do not have the time to stand around while your staff do all their in-store financial housekeeping. If you must update your records, then would you mind awfully waiting until I've gone away.

Shopping can never be a pleasant or worthwhile activity. The notion of exchanging money, which is useful, for goods, which by and large are not, is fairly pointless. So please, can you do your best to make it quick.

Sunday 8 May 2005

Fun: the true sign of a good school

It seems like a good week to speculate on whether private education works, or whether it's a complete waste of time and money.

On the one hand, we heard recently about some poor girl who achieved about a million A-levels, all with an A grade, but couldn't find a place at university because, she claimed, they were biased against her paid-for schooling.

Then, conversely, we heard last week that only public school children were getting on to engineering and science-based courses at university because today's state school pupils only learn about hairdressing and how to win a knife fight.

So it's all very confusing. Does private education give children a much-needed leg-up, or do the sneering bitterness and hatred of New Labour's foot soldiers mean your expensively schooled child is taken straight from the examination room to a dacha in the woods and shot?

In other words, do £150,000, plus extras, guarantee a future lined with gold and myrrh? Do the money and the Latin iron out those annoying little creases in life and assure the child of a silky future? Or do you just end up with a floppy-haired twerp who can't even get a job as a pox doctor's clerk?

To find out, I decided to check on the progress of my contemporaries at the large public school I attended

27 years ago. Obviously, the easiest way of doing this is by grazing the Friends Reunited website, but I'm afraid this gives a jaundiced view, since anyone who bothers to keep former friends updated with career and marital progress is either a girl or a social retard.

Instead, then, I turned to the school magazine which, through its old boys' news section, seemed like a good indicator of whether or not a private education has worked.

It hasn't. Which, on a personal note, is wonderful news because, of course, it's only fun to succeed if you can watch your contemporaries fail. Which most of them have done, in spades.

One is working on a special disinfectant to kill mouth bacteria, for instance, while another has written a book called *Guidelines for the Use of Personal Data in System Training*. Then there's a chap who's actually written to his old school magazine, at the age of 39, to say he's been made the East Midlands regional director for a building company no one's ever heard of.

The only fly in the ointment, so far as I'm concerned, is a direct contemporary of mine who's now the director of international security at the Foreign Office. That sounds pretty cool. The bastard.

What I'm trying to say here is that, every year, this school pumps a hundred people into the system and in the past 30 years or so not one of them has ended up being Queen, or in space, or on the silver screen. Whereas the state system has given us Catherine Zeta-Jones, John Prescott, Ant and Lard, and countless others who now live a glossy, chauffeured life of Riley.

Public school used to guarantee you a place under the punkah wallah on an agreeable veranda in Calcutta; but today, for every Hugh Grant, there are a million Denise Van Outens. As the screw is tightened on university selection procedures, the pendulum shows no sign of swinging back. On that basis, then, there is absolutely no point sending your children to an expensive school. They will be denied a place at university, become regional managers for stationery companies and will write to their old school magazine after 20 years to say they have just bought some new decking for the patio. If they go to a state school, at least they stand a chance of becoming a minister, or an actor, or Alan Sugar.

However, the simple fact of the matter is this. School is irrelevant. University is irrelevant. And qualifications are irrelevant, too, because you can put anything you like on a CV and I absolutely guarantee an employer won't check. And let's be honest here: saying you have 12 A-levels is a damn sight easier than actually getting them.

What's more, if I were an employer, I'd far rather take on someone who lied about his academic achievements than someone who wasted his precious childhood by reading John Donne poems and doing algebra. Lying shows you have a bit of nous.

And this brings me on to the whole point of public school. It's not designed to make you cleverer or more likely to succeed. It's all about ensuring your children have the happiest possible childhood.

Mine was. Conjugating verbs, the periodic table, cricket. Yeah, we did all that, but when the lessons were over I didn't slope home to spend an evening with my parents, or in the bus shelter; it was night after night of full-on, Harry Potter-style japes and pranks. With only a light sprinkling of buggery.

This is what we seem to be forgetting with our league tables and our university selection complaints. That when you pay for a child's education, you're not buying jam for tomorrow. You're buying it for today. Success in life is down to what sort of person you are, and not how many chemical symbols you can remember or how casually you can toss a V-neck over your shoulders. Put a dunderhead into the system and it doesn't matter what sort of education they get, you'll get a regional manager out the other end.

Sunday 15 May 2005

Nuts and dolts of an eco-boycott

When someone from Oxford Brookes University called recently to say its School of Technology wanted to give me an honorary degree – for championing the cause of engineering – I was thrilled. It had been only a couple of years since a similar honour was bestowed by Brunel University.

So I would be Jeremy 'two doctors' Clarkson, which isn't bad for someone who barely managed O-levels.

However, much to the delight of the BBC's fanatically pro-fox, anti-car internet news service, my nomination is being boycotted. Because, in this day and age, it's preposterous to honour someone who has a four-wheel-drive Volvo and a ride-on lawnmower.

This means I'm in the same boat as Margaret Thatcher, who was snubbed by Oxford University for stealing milk or something, and Tony Blair, who wasn't even nominated because he accused the dons of being élitist.

Honorary degrees were first introduced about 600 years ago and are still the highest honour that a university can bestow. They are designed for the great and the good, thinkers, men of vision, women of principle. And Alan Titchmarsh.

Noddy Holder from Slade has one, as does Robson Green from everything on ITV.

David Attenborough is reputed to have 19. It's easy to

see why. A celebrity in a floppy hat and a huge red cape does bring a touch of glamour to what might otherwise be a rather dull day.

You may think this devalues the concept of honorary degrees, and I would have to agree. But my nomination is not being boycotted because I'm a two-bit television presenter from some poky motoring programme. Crikey no. I'm being boycotted because I'm seen as anti-environmental.

Craig Simmons, leader of the Green group on Oxford City Council, said: 'Awarding Clarkson an honorary degree devalues Brookes, Oxford and the planet.' Others have been less polite, calling me a 'git' and an 'idiot'.

For a full rundown of my crimes, you need to consult the BBC's internet news service, which, pretty much every week, runs a story charting my sins against left-thinking, *Guardian*-reading, fox-loving people.

It seems I once crashed a car into a tree, damaging the bark. Also, I drove up a mountain, hurting the heather. If that wasn't bad enough, I had the temerity to tear up literature from the pressure group Transport 2000 on television. And do you know what I did last week? To protest about enormous gas-guzzling vehicles clogging up city centres, I chained myself to a bus.

Well, now I'm going to give them something else to write about, because I'm going to explain why I think engineering is more important than environmentalism.

God made the world in seven days, but it was a fairly bleak and hopeless place, full of volcanoes and sharks. On the eighth day, however, man got cracking and, as home improvements go, did a monumentally good job. He created light, warmth, the potato crisp and the dishwasher. And every single one of these things – everything that makes your life pleasant, comfortable, safe and exciting – is down to engineering.

Environmentalists make out that the planet is some kind of wondrous, self-sustaining entity, and engineering has ruined it. They look at the gun, the car and the jet engine as instruments of Satan, but the mosquito has killed more than all three put together. And don't forget that the Boxing Day tsunami killed more than the atomic bomb dropped on Hiroshima.

What's more, it'll be engineering that creates the satellites to make sure that no tsunami ever has such dire consequences again.

There's more. Thanks to the last Ice Age, which was not man's fault, anyone wishing to travel between Denmark and Sweden had, until recently, to drive round the Baltic or use a plane. Neither of which would go down well with the environmentalists. Now, though, God's oversight has been corrected by engineers who have built a massive and staggeringly beautiful 10-mile double-decker bridge for trains and cars.

The thing is, they couldn't just go ahead and build it. They had to make sure the construction project in no way affected the local avocet population. How mad is that? How far do you think Brunel, Stephenson and Watt would have got if they'd had Greenpeace sticking its nose into every single thing they did?

And what about the future? It will be engineers who bring an air-powered jet to fruition, not Stephen Joseph from Transport 2000. And it will be engineers who predict the next volcanic eruption, not Simmons from Oxford Council.

I feel for engineering students these days. When they get a job the pay is derisory. There's no respect. They have to operate with the anvil of environmentalism permanently attached to their left leg. And when they nominate someone other than Bill Oddie for an honorary degree, they're made to look like murderers.

If I'm turned down for the award, it won't make any material difference to my life. But I refuse to remove my name because that would be yet another victory for environmentalism, which has given the world nothing, over engineering, which has given us everything.

Sunday 22 May 2005

Small BBC strike, not many stirred

For most of the people who walked out of the BBC last week, striking was a new and exciting experience. A chance to be part of the 'us' in the never-ending class war with 'them'. A moment when they could be a righteous blend of Che Guevara and William Wallace. For me, however, it was just a wearisome trudge down memory lane.

In my youth, everyone was on strike. Car workers. Tanker drivers. Dustbinmen. Even the sound recordists charged with the not too onerous job of putting microphones in the bras and knickers of the 1979 Miss World contestants decided they'd rather stand outside round a brazier and promptly walked out, forcing the show to be cancelled halfway through.

It was a hopeless time. I'd just started work on the *Rotherham Advertiser*, with high hopes of exposing corruption in the council and industrial nepotism in the steelworks. I was going to be Clark Kent, William Boot and Bob Woodward all rolled into one, fighting injustice and standing up for what was right.

But even before I'd found the space bar on my Remington, I was back on the street, caught up in the seven-week local newspaper dispute over . . . well, it had something to do with Nottingham. But I was never very sure what.

The reasons for last week's BBC walkout were similarly

unclear. Apparently, the unions want the latest round of redundancies to be voluntary rather than compulsory, but that just means the best people leave and those who couldn't even get a job selling televisions in Dixons hang on. The unions, I should explain to younger readers, are a bit like Britain. They still strut about, thinking everyone's listening and that they're a big player. But if push came to shove, they'd barely have enough muscle to overthrow Marks & Spencer.

Anyway, back to the story. So far as I can tell, most of the proposed BBC cuts will be in the health and safety department – whoopee – and in human resources, which should make the redundancy notices interesting. 'Dear Me. I know I have three kids to feed but I'm afraid I'm letting me go . . .'

I might have got this all wrong, of course; but, whatever the reasons, BBC premises up and down the land were immediately ringed with people who really hadn't got the hang of picketing at all. Instead of throwing concrete slabs at the scabs and threatening to eat their children, they sipped a lot of skinny lattes and made their feelings known by tutting. Jeremy Vine was sufficiently frightened by this to stay at home.

There didn't seem to be much public sympathy, either. But then, if you work on a turkey farm, spending five days a week up to your knees in guano and up to your elbow in a bald bird's backside, you aren't going to be all that impressed by a bunch of Prada people who are facing a new life working for a lively independent production company in Soho where the coffee's great and the receptionist is drop-dead gorgeous.

Certainly, none of the passing motorists honked to show support, probably because they were all so wrapped up in the rather good music show that had been cobbled together to replace Jeremy Vine.

Meanwhile, staff in the *Top Gear* office all turned up for work as normal, partly because they didn't know what the strike was about and partly because the net result of staying away would have been a) the loss of a day's pay and b) twice as much work to do the next day.

Of course, all of us feel very sorry for those faced with the sack but this is not 1979. The *Guardian* is chock-full of job adverts, so all of those affected could be highly paid human safety outreach co-ordinators by this time next week.

And therein lies the problem of striking today. It's an axe in a digital world, a completely outdated weapon that doesn't even have an army to wield it any more.

For a walkout to be properly effective, the strikers need to be salt-of-the-earth, horny-handed sons of toil with a simple-to-understand and genuine grievance. But the miners have gone. British Leyland is gone. The steelworkers have gone. And the last time anyone built a ship in Britain, it was called the *Mary Rose*.

Billy Elliot would never have worked if it had been set against the backdrop of the Great BBC Walkout of 2005. And *Brassed Off* would have been far less successful if it had been set among the drinking fountains of a soon-to-be-closed call centre in Brentford. It simply doesn't work when everyone on the picket line is standing under a personalised patio heater from Conran, with a cup of Costa coffee and a Dolce & Gabbana donkey jacket.

I could always support someone if they didn't have an indoor lavatory, and their left lung had been turned into a diseased walnut while digging coal to power my Aga. But Alan Yentob? I don't think so.

Yes, the BBC still commands respect among right-thinking people everywhere, and if there really were plans to introduce advertisements for panty-liners in the middle of *Newsnight*, and farm all programme-making out to independent production companies, I'd have been on the picket line like a Scargill, bashing policemen over the head with my placard and dropping effigies of Tony Blair into my brazier.

But there aren't. So I wasn't.

Sunday 29 May 2005

Twin your town to save Africa

Isn't it marvellous to have wizened old Bobby Geldof back on the scene, poking politicians in the eye and peppering the airwaves with his peculiar mix of profanity and passion?

What he's got planned is huge: the biggest musical event the world has ever seen.

In one day, just four weeks from now, there will be five concerts in five cities on two continents, featuring 100 acts who will play to a million spectators and more than a billion television viewers.

As an added complication, up to 24 bands are being squeezed into 18 slots at the London gig, and all of them have to be finished by 8 p.m., when the ever helpful health and safety mob move in with their noise-measuring equipment.

Choosing who can play has been a nightmare because back in the days of Live Aid, rock'n'roll was a single generational affair, whereas now Geldof has to keep the kids watching while Elton John is wheeled on to the stage, and the parents amused when Baldy is replaced by, oh, I don't know, that bloke with the nose piercings who ran himself over last week.

Then there's the bothersome business of political correctness. Already the organisers have been told that the line-up is far too white and that only one African singer is featured, way down the line-up in Paris.

Of course, sorting all this out would be worthwhile if it raises lots of money.

But this time around that's not the goal.

Twenty years ago, Geldof raised £79,426,252, which was more than enough to buy the poor of Ethiopia lunch. Now, though, he wants to completely refurbish the whole of Africa and he knows the bill for this cannot be met by the Spice Women and A-ha.

So, the plan with the concerts is to focus the world's attention on the forthcoming G8 conference at Gleneagles. In other words, Geldof knows he can't make a difference, but he can bring pressure to bear on those who can.

It's a brilliant wheeze, but I can't help feeling sorry for the G8 delegates, because with Bob on the rampage they'll have to act, and that's not easy when George Bush, the richest man at the table, almost certainly has no idea what Africa is.

The big problem is, what do they do? If you pour money into a dictatorship, the dictator ends up with some gold bathroom fittings and the kids still have flies in their eyes. A year after Live Aid, I was in Mali and asked some villagers if they'd seen any of the money. 'No,' said one, taking me outside and pointing at the soldiers. 'But they all have new guns.'

Then there's the business of Third World debt, which the protesters want cancelled. Fine, but who will lend the poorer countries money if there's no chance of getting that money back? And how does a drug company stay in business if it has to give its medicines away?

It's all very well saying that Britain could easily afford

to help because it's the fourth richest country in the world. But how can a government convince a single mum living in a filthy high-rise on the outskirts of Birmingham that she's well off?

And how do you get the money out there? A recent report suggested that £6 in every £10 of aid is spent on consultants who work out how the money can be spent and on reports, presumably, into how much those consultants cost.

The G8 delegates could try to explain some of these difficulties, but there's little point because, in a battle for the people's minds, a man in a suit making a reasoned point is never going to beat Brad Pitt clicking his fingers every three seconds to remind us all how often a child dies in Africa.

Don't get me wrong. I want Brad Pitt clicking his fingers. I want the concerts. I want a million to march on Scotland. I want those delegates to feel like they're in a pressure cooker and that, to turn down the heat, they have to stop making empty promises and actually do something. I even have a plan for what that 'something' might be.

It's based on those 'Adopt an Otter' schemes you see at zoos. The idea is that you pay £2 a week, and a specific otter, called Fluffy usually, is actually yours.

I'm not suggesting that every single African should be adopted by every single westerner – there aren't enough to go round, for a kick-off – but it certainly could be done on a town-by-town basis.

At the moment, councillors spend an inordinate amount of time twinning themselves with some agreeable little hamlet in France or Germany. Why? So they can go on exchange visits? It is hard to conceive of a more useless way of spending public money.

But what if your local council twinned itself with a town in Africa? I had a similar idea after the tsunami, and I really think it would work.

At the moment, we all just think that there are nearly a billion people in the G8 countries and that if we don't cough up, someone else will. But when your village has been given the responsibility for a specific village in Africa, abdicating your responsibility to keep the people in that village healthy is not an option.

You would make cakes for the bring-and-buy stall.

Without wishing to sound like I'm writing the copy for a banking commercial, poverty is a global problem. But the solution, I suspect, is local.

Sunday 5 June 2005

Rock is dead, long live rock'n'roll

Every Sunday evening 56 million people in Britain find something better to do than watch *Top Gear*. So, statistically speaking, you almost certainly don't know we're currently staging a vote to find the country's best driving song.

I assumed, because I know that the programme is watched by many children, that the list of nominations would be full of bands I'd never heard of and music that, if it came on my radio, would make me want to get out of the car.

But no. The top 10, as it stands at the moment, features AC/DC, Motorhead, Steppenwolf, Queen, Kenny Loggins, Golden Earring and, rather disturbingly, at number one Meat Loaf's appallingly pretentious *Bat Out of Hell*. In the whole of the top 20, there are only three acts from the twenty-first century.

This brings me on to Radio 2. We're told the new-found popularity of Auntie's Light Programme is because all the presenters are different, but that's not it at all. It's because the new music being played on Radio 1 is always irritating and can sometimes be harmful to your well-being. If the nanny puts Radio 1 on in the kitchen when I'm trying to write, I am often overwhelmed with a sudden and sometimes uncontrollable need to hit her over the head with a bag full of snooker balls.

Do you see where I'm going here? There's much talk, especially as the festival season begins in earnest, about which of the new bands are any good. Even the *Daily Telegraph* devotes half a page to the relative merits of Coldplay. But the fact of the matter is that the pearls, and they are few, are drowned in an ocean of absolute rubbish.

I know I have something of a reputation for being a rock dinosaur but you should see my daughter's record collection. Of course, it isn't a record collection as such; it's an assembly of ones and noughts on her computer; but anyway, being 10, she likes Maroon Five and Avril Somethingorother, but mostly her binary ballads are from Led Zep, which she thinks are so cool, and Bad Company.

This means, of course, she doesn't mind at all when Mummy and Daddy go out at night to see artists you thought had gone west in a puddle of vomit and chemicals some time in 1976. In the past couple of years we've seen Roger Waters, Blondie, Yes, the Who (half of whom have actually gone west in a puddle of vomit and chemicals) and then, last week, Roxy Music.

Bryan Ferry is a remarkable human specimen. He is a man for whom the ageing process has had no meaning. He may now be a hundred and twenty-twelve, but there are no man breasts, no spread and no sign of a hair hole. And you should see him move. Be assured, his rebellious pro-hunting son Otis can never say to a mate: 'Hey, you dance like my dad.' Because no one, no matter how athletic they be, is that good.

The man redefines anyone's concept of cool. He even makes whistling cool, which is technically impossible. And what's more, it's rumoured he once ticked off a younger son for swearing while their hijacked jet was in the process of nose-diving. And this iciness comes through on stage as his band of real, proper, clever and talented musicians run through a set of songs that would leave any modern band open-mouthed in astonishment.

The best thing, though, is that the audience was also far cooler than anything you'll find at a teenage rave. There were no football shirts, no spots, and none of that awful greased-down hair that is so popular with tyre fitters. There were one or two rather strange-looking creatures whose barnet had been styled in 1974 and then left to thin out all by itself. I may have also seen some black T-shirts tucked into jeans, which also dated from the early '70s. But for the most part it was bright-eyed, middle-aged people for whom time has been kind.

There was no unduly long queue for the lavatory cubicles, nobody was flogging bags of expensive aspirins, and in the ballads, instead of waving cigarette lighters around, everyone held up their mobile phones so their kids could hear the tunes too. Best of all, nobody was beaten up and murdered on the way out. Everyone just piled into their Range Rovers and went for something to eat.

Now, compare this with sharing a tent, in a field, having spent the day listening to a bunch of teenagers in spectacularly baggy trousers banging bits of garden furniture together. It doesn't even get close.

Rock'n'roll, I'm beginning to suspect, is not a going concern. It's not, as we have always thought, simply a means by which teenagers can annoy their parents but, rather, a one-off, 30-year moment in the development of music. Like baroque and skiffle and oratorio.

Every attempt to change the original formula, be it hip-hop, garage, techno or rap, certainly grates with those older than 12, but that's its only purpose. It's not music to annoy the old. It's just a noise to annoy the old. Which means that when its fans become old it will not survive.

I can absolutely guarantee that, 30 years from now, nobody will be going all the way to London to see P. Diddly, or whatever he's called this week. Whereas my wife and I will be availing ourselves of cheap-rate rail fares and heading to Camden, again, to see Bryan Ferry, again. And you know what: he still won't have any man breasts and he'll still be dancing like a hard-bodied ballerina.

Sunday 12 June 2005

You are about to be devoured

According to the *Daily Mail* you're going to die, and because your husband eats red meat he's going to die as well. This means your orphaned children will be left to die, alone, unless they have already been killed by illegal immigrants, or cornflakes. Or drugs such as cannabis and Ecstasy. Or they may have been boiled alive by global warming.

In our sheltered, cosy, centrally heated lives, we love all this, which is why last week the *Mail* brought us news of a new menace waiting at the French entrance to the Channel tunnel.

This dwarfs all that has gone before. So you'd better sit down because soon, apparently, you will be going to the shops when all of a sudden you will be eaten by a tiger.

This is even better than the swarms of killer bees that were on their way from Mexico a few years ago, or the deadly algae that were on the verge of swamping Venice. But then didn't. That's because there's nothing that scares us more than the concept of being eaten.

Bill Oddie might like to think that nature is a fluffy place, full of doe-eyed badgers and baby birds, and that nothing nasty ever happens there. But it does: 90 per cent of living creatures go to meet their maker via the intestines and stomach of another creature.

This means the fear is in us. Underneath the iPod, and

behind the suit of civilisation, we can think of nothing more painful – or humiliating, frankly – than being devoured by something that has no remorse, no pity and no opposable thumbs.

We can watch a million people being shot, stabbed and quartered, and we won't turn a hair. But we all remember how Robert Shaw went west in *Jaws*.

This isn't something that only happens in Hollywood and South Africa, either. The Mediterranean is full of great whites which often eat humans, despite the risk to their health from digesting uncooked red meat. And now, according to the *Daily Mail*, the peril is on our doorsteps. Except for one small thing. The tiger they're talking about goes 'nnnnnnnn' instead of 'grrrrrrrrr', because it's a mosquito.

Don't be disappointed. Over time, mosquitoes have killed more people than all wars and all car accidents put together. They are the deadliest creature known to man, and the species lining up to invade Britain carries enough disease and pestilence in its tiny proboscis to lay waste to vast swathes of the population. Hospitals won't be able to cope. Corpses will be piled high in the streets. And your house could fall in value by as much as 30 per cent.

Apparently, the mosquito has arrived in Europe in old tyres that have been sent from Asia for recycling, and it is able to survive because of the mild weather. That's a great double whammy for the mongers of doom, because they've managed to blame cars, multinationalism and global warming in one go.

And it gets better because, among the smorgasbord of terror carried in the mozzie's bomb bay, is dengue fever, which killed the man who used to rent me jet skis in Barbados, and the West Nile virus, which causes vomiting, headaches, fever, neck stiffness, a rash, stupor, coma, paralysis, disorientation and blindness. If you feel unwell in any way at all, you've had it.

Anyone who's bitten by a mosquito this summer is urged to catch the insect and send it directly to the Chartered Institute of Environmental Health, unless of course your fingers are too swollen and you think you're Ena Sharples. In which case your family are urged to paint a white cross on your front door and sing 'Ring-a-ring o' roses' until the plague cart arrives.

So why, you may be wondering, are we not being buzzed by crop-dusting helicopters spraying the nation with insecticide? Why isn't Patrick Allen on the radio, advising us all to stay inside when the air-raid warning sounds? Why are people not panic-buying Buzz Off and bottled water?

Well it might have something to do with the fact that the Asian tiger mosquito is a lousy flyer whose habitat never extends more than a few feet from its home base.

So, while it may be in Calais, it would struggle to reach the White Cliffs.

Let's, for the sake of argument, however, say that it did. Well then, it would have to find a creature over here that had been infected with the West Nile virus. And the creatures most likely to carry it are chipmunks, skunks and birds that live on swamps.

Since there are no swamps or chipmunks or skunks in Britain, it is extremely unlikely that the mozzie could pick up the disease. But again, let's say that it did. Then what?

Well, according to the Centers for Disease Control and Prevention in America, the insect would have to bite you within a day or so, and, even then, only 1 per cent of humans who get infected become seriously ill. Mostly, this will be people with HIV.

In other words, you stand a 99 per cent chance of not becoming ill from a mosquito that can't pick up infection in Britain, even if it could get here, which it can't.

That's the truth of the matter. So the Asian mosquito must line up with cornflakes and red meat as something that poses no threat at all to our health.

If this has ruined your day, don't worry, because I have a tip. Try being happy and contented instead.

Sunday 19 June 2005

Death by 1,000 autographs

Like most people, you probably remember Johnny Morris, the talking television zoo keeper, as a genial old soul, with his llama noises and his jaunty cap. So you may be surprised to learn that when news of his death was announced on the radio, I whooped with delight, punched the air and shouted, 'Good.'

This is because when I was four years old I asked him for an autograph and he told me to 'bugger off'.

The indignity of it. I had made him a celebrity by watching his programmes, so therefore it was his duty to drop everything, including the small orang-utan that he was holding at the time, and do as he was told. And if I had pretended to be part of a television news crew and squirted him in the face with water, that would have been fine, too.

Did you see Tom Cruise last week, hopping up and down on his stumpy little legs, just because some Channel 4 pranksters had emptied a bucket of acid into his eyes?

Doesn't he realise that it's the God-given right of 'ordinary' members of the public to say, do and squirt whatever takes their fancy into the faces of those on television? I always used to think that. Right up to the moment I appeared on television myself.

I still remember the first time I was asked for an autograph. It was a middle-aged woman, and I sank to my knees in a mixture of shock, deep pleasure and eternal gratitude. I wanted to bask for ever in the turbulence of her magnificence. 'Thank you. Thank you. Thank you,' I said, clinging on to her ankles with one hand and writing a veritable essay with the other.

As Angela Rippon once said, 'I love it when people ask for my autograph. It's when they stop you have to worry.'

Except today I'm not so sure, because every time I turn round, there's some snotty-nosed kid with a felt pen, half a chewed napkin and an expectant look on his face.

And it's always his mum who does the talking: 'He's ever such a fan of *Newsnight.*'

Even the lavatory fails to provide a safe haven. Only last week I emerged from a stall in the gents at Birmingham airport, to find a couple of kids waiting outside with their dad: 'They love your lunchtime show on Radio 2.'

On an average day I'm asked for an autograph maybe 20 times, usually when I get to the punchline of a story, or when it's raining, or when I'm carrying something heavy.

Of course, I understand the autograph culture. At a charity auction last week, I sat next to a woman who paid £55,000 for a guitar that had been signed by Bono and Sir Cliff. And that made sense, because I have a guitar signed by Jan Akkerman from the Dutch group Focus.

I also have a 100-yen note signed by Bob Seger, and my most prized possession is Monty Python's Big Red Book, signed by everyone on the whole team, right down to Carole Cleveland. In fact, come to think of it, the only autograph I don't have is Johnny Morris's. The bastard.

Signatures bring us closer to fame, and that's great; but can I say, from the other side of the fence, that there are rules.

John Cleese said on the radio recently that he was asked for his autograph at his father's funeral.

And when he said 'No', he was subjected to a torrent of abuse.

I know how he feels. I was given both barrels last week by a woman who said my signature was too much of a squiggle. And when I argued, she stomped off, saying, 'It doesn't look much like "Beadle" to me.'

Then you get the people, usually those with tyre-fitter haircuts and gormless faces, who just stand there, and when you say, 'What's the magic word?' they have absolutely no idea what you are on about.

One man recently sauntered over and said he really didn't like me on television, that I'd never made a good programme, that his wife wouldn't have me on in the house, that he'd cancelled the *Sunday Times* because of me and that I should grow up. 'Still,' he concluded, 'I'd better have your autograph, I suppose.'

And you know what? I'm so fearful of Johnny Morris syndrome that I agreed, knowing full well that the stupid man would sell it for 99p on eBay that very night.

Mind you, even this is better than the request for a quick picture, because the camera that's produced is invariably a phone.

So you wait while a mate tries to turn it on.

Then you wait while it hooks up to the nearest satellite.

Then you wait a bit more while the mate fumbles around in the menu trying to find a camera setting.

Then you wait while he finds the zoom and the brightness setting, and you think, 'Honestly, it would have been quicker to set up an easel and break out the oils.'

Soon, of course, thanks to *Big Brother* and other programmes of that ilk, everyone will be famous. And then you might imagine there will be no need for me to stand around in shopping centres gurning into people's telephones or trying to write my name with one hand while having a pee with the other. This happens a lot.

Strangely, however, even when everyone is famous, I don't think that much will change.

I was at a do the other day when I bumped into the boy band McFly. 'Ooh,' I said. 'I hope you won't mind but please can I have your autographs for my son?'

'Yeah, sure,' said one. 'Providing I can have yours for my dad.'

Sunday 26 June 2005

Oops, £25,000 went overboard

We all know the form at charity auctions. You have a few glasses of wine and then you spend an hour or so trying desperately to not buy trips in hot-air balloons and books that have been signed by TV's David Dickinson.

I especially know the form, because recently I was the auctioneer at a charity event to raise funds for Chipping Norton's swimming pool. The evening went brilliantly, mainly because two hands kept shooting out of the crowd, buying just about everything, no matter how high the price.

Annoyingly, the hands turned out to belong to my children, who had got bored and decided to join in. So we went home with, among other things, two bags of dung, a nylon T-shirt and several signed copies of my own book.

With that experience so fresh in my mind, I should have known better than to stick my hand up at a children with cancer do last week. The lot was a week on a 140-foot superyacht in the south of France. It has two speedboats slung over the back, many windsurfers, two jet skis, 12 cabins, a crew of eight (including a bosun) and the usual range of bar stools coated in whale foreskin. Ordinarily, seven days on this ocean-going gin palace would cost £75,000. Bidding started at £25,000. Or, rather, it didn't. Nobody put their hand up, so, since

I knew the auctioneer, I thought I'd help him out by getting the ball rolling. 'At last,' he exclaimed, in an excitable, auctioneery way, 'a bid of £25,000 from Mr Clarkson. Now. Who'll give me £26,000?'

The marquee, I noted with quiet satisfaction, was stuffed with several hundred extremely blonde women and an equal number of bronzed men who, I figured, would want to show their friends just how rich they'd become in recent years.

This always happens. Only a week earlier, at yet another charity auction, I had gleefully stuck my hand up to buy two weeks' use of the huge, 96-sheet advertising hoarding that dominates Cromwell Road coming into west London.

I wanted it so I could write something rude about a colleague who commutes down that road every day, but I knew in my heart of hearts it would go to someone much, much richer. And it did. And so would the boat . . .

A minute passed and still no hands had gone up. The auctioneer was giving it his all, gyrating and twitching as though he'd become attached to the mains, but nothing.

Then the awful truth began to dawn. The women were blonde because they were hairdressers, not jet-set jetsam. And the men were brown because they work all day in the open air, with scaffolding. Nobody was going to top my bid. And they didn't.

Outwardly I was calm. I'd just given £25,000 to a very worthy charity that seeks to provide a home away from home for the families of children with cancer.

So I acknowledged the applause from the hairdressers and waved cheerily at the auctioneer whose bacon I had so nobly saved.

But inwardly I was in a flat spin. I mean, shit, £25,000 is a colossal amount of money. And I'd just spent it by accident.

Someone next to me tried to argue that £25,000 was cheap. But that rather depends how you look at it. Twenty-five thousand pounds for something that would normally cost £75,000 is indeed a bargain. But, in the same way that I was once offered a fully functional jet fighter for £4.5 million, it's also completely irrelevant.

I just don't have this kind of money to hurl around like confetti. Maybe I'd spend £25,000 on a car. But on a whim? Jesus. I felt sick.

Then it got worse, because my wife, whose face had turned the colour of tracing paper, was busy reading some small print in the catalogue about what the price didn't include.

Fuel, for instance. And on a boat of this type you don't measure consumption in terms of miles per gallon or even gallons per mile. Oh no. When you are topping up a vessel like this, you have to think of the diesel fuel in terms of tons. And then there are the mooring fees which, in a port like Monte Carlo, will be hundreds and hundreds of pounds a night.

'So,' I said to my wife quietly, 'even if we could afford to get the boat to Monaco, and we can't, we wouldn't be able to afford to park it there.'

Yes, and that's just the start of it, because other things that weren't included were drinks, food and, crucially, a tip for the crew, which is normally 10 per cent of the charter fee. Great. I was facing a week on a boat, not eating, not drinking and not moving. Just recovering from the fact that I'd had to walk to the south of France because I couldn't afford the easyJet bill.

You haven't heard the really funny part yet. You see, contrary to what the auctioneer said in his warm-up spiel, it turns out the vessel is only available in the week commencing 17 September.

And guess what? Slap bang in the middle of the week commencing 17 September it's the *Top Gear* charity karting evening. Where I shall be hosting a charity auction to raise money for the parents of children with cancer.

I've examined all the options, and I'm afraid the only solution is for me to commit suicide. Still, at least I'll be going to heaven.

Sunday 3 July 2005

Annoying: I like David Beckham

Every week the glossy supermarket magazines bring news of yet another celebrity who's married a horse, drunk their own urine or thrown a telephone at some hapless hotel receptionist. The message is crystal clear: all famous people are mentalists.

Really? Well, I must say that Steve Coogan has never asked me to share any of his pee, Neil Morrissey has never thrown anything at my wife, and Jonathan Ross is not married to his hair. Quite the reverse in fact.

All the famous people I've met are just like everyone else. David Frost has bad breath. After a night out with Johnny Vegas, he was sick in a teapot. And Anne Robinson lets my children play tag in her bedroom.

Yes, Dale Winton is bright orange, but what's unusual about that? If you were to tour the salons of Alderley Edge, you'd find they were stuffed to overflowing with people who are similarly autumnal.

The people I've met, however, are the angel fish, the small, home-grown stars whose fame is limited to Britain. But what about the whale sharks and the tuna? What about those whose names are etched on the consciousness of every living being on the planet? This is where we find the real eccentricity.

Take Elton John as an example. If he'd become a plumber, would he go around kissing other men on the lips? I suspect the answer's probably no. And Angelina Jolie? Would she have painted her husband's name across her wedding dress in her own blood if her dad had been Reg Arkwright rather than Jon Voight? I doubt it.

So what went wrong? It's easy to blame money, but do Bill Gates and Richard Branson get together once a week to sacrifice a goat? Can you visualise the Duke of Westminster hurling a potted plant at a waiter because his soup's not brown enough?

Maybe it's a combination of fame and money. Maybe that's what makes a normal person turn into an oddball, insisting that all the blue M&Ms are removed and that everyone on your table at dinner should eat with their feet. Maybe money buys the ability to dislocate yourself from reality; maybe it filters out the criticisms and allows only the warming, gentle rays of adulation to shine on the turbulence of your magnificence.

Maybe that's Michael Jackson's problem. He hears only the good things. 'No, no, Michael. By all means dangle your child out of the fifth-floor window . . .'

Last weekend, I was backstage at the Live8 event and discovered the answer. The really famous, really global stars walked around like comets, trailing a tail of 'people' who had been employed to make sure nothing even remotely real got in their employer's way.

These 'people' were like pilot fish, employed to remove the creases from life and scratch the itches you can never reach yourself.

Snoop Doggy Dog, or whatever he's called, had an armada of bodyguards, each of whom was the size of a beach hut. I couldn't work out what they were protecting him from exactly. Peaches Geldof? Nasa?

Then there was Madonna, who had a hundred bossy women with clipboards whose job, so far as I could see, was to yell a lot and make sure nobody got in Madge's way. Which was a problem when they encountered Paul McCartney's entourage coming in the opposite direction.

I tried to take a photograph of the ensuing chaos and was astonished when one of Madge's secretary birds stuck her hand in front of my camera and shouted, 'No pictures.' Apparently one of the public relations pilot fish had decided that Mrs Ritchie could only be photographed with Mr Geldof. So obviously, to enforce this rule, a whole team had had to be employed.

Against this backdrop, even A. A. Gill looked normal, so we went in the beer tent for a drink. And it was here that I encountered David Beckham. Over the years I've made fun of his silly wife, his stupid tattoos and argued, forcefully, that if he spent less time at the hairdresser's and more time at the training ground, he might have been an excellent footballer instead of a one-trick pony. I think that, after he was sent off in a World Cup match, I'd also said I'd like to beat him around the head and neck with a baseball bat.

'Why are you always so nasty about me?' he squeaked.

'Gosh,' I stuttered. 'Well, the thing is that, um, sometimes when you're looking for a metaphor, and er . . . you've got a deadline, you say stuff you don't really mean.

'Sometimes I wake up in the morning and think, "What have I done?"'

'This is pathetic,' tutted Gill, and walked off to find someone with a spine.

'But you were really horrid about me on *Parkinson*,' countered Beckham.

And I had to agree. I had used the poor chap as a metaphor for all that's wrong with the world, on about a thousand different occasions, in newspapers, on the radio and regularly on television.

This is because we are forever hearing about David Beckham rather than from David Beckham. He employs people to speak on his behalf and, when he does talk on his own, it's all been carefully choreographed by other people.

The thing is, though, that when you take the people away, you find a very nice chap: friendly, normal, and not as thick as you might have been led to believe (by me).

So now I have a serious problem. Who to hate? I can feel Jade Goody coming into the cross hairs. What do you think?

Sunday 10 July 2005

My burning hate for patio heaters

What with all the bombs and so on, you might imagine that Britain's environmentalists and health and safety Nazis would give it a rest and stop bossing us all around. But no. While the nation's normal people observed a two-minute silence last week, the busybodies were working out how much damage is done to the planet by tomatoes.

Yes, you thought *Attack of the Killer Tomatoes* was a joke B-movie, but it seems not. Honestly, someone has worked out that less environmental damage is done by eating tomatoes that were grown in Spain and then brought here on a ship than eating tomatoes that were grown in heated British greenhouses.

And while they were doing that, binmen in Fife were told not to turn up for work in shorts, despite the heat-wave, in case – and I'm not making this up – they scratched their knees or were bitten by an insect. It seems health and safety guidelines are clear on the subject.

Meanwhile, Greenpeace has taken a long, hard look at the world. It has noted the alarming emergence of Islamic extremism and the corruption in Africa. It's logged the oppression in Burma and the slaughter in the Middle East. And it has decided that something must be done . . . about your patio heater.

Mark Strutt, a climate campaigner, claims they're a 'frivolous waste of energy', while Norman Baker, the

Liberal Democrat environment spokesman, said the first thing that came into his head. 'Blah blah blah, carbon dioxide blah blah, heating the earth for years.'

Apparently, there are now 750,000 patio heaters in Britain, and together they produce 380,000 tons of greenhouse gases every year. That's nearly as much, in case you're interested, as is generated by the nation's joggers.

Now, I should explain at this point that my wife bought me a patio heater for our tin wedding anniversary, whenever that was, and I've always been slightly nervous about it. Of course, now I know such things annoy Greenpeace, I shall keep it lit 24 hours a day, but still the doubts won't go away.

First of all, there's the word 'patio', which I dislike. And I especially dislike it because, unlike toilet or settee or lounge, I can't think of an alternative. I suppose you could call it a terrace heater but a terrace, as I understand it, must be raised. There's no such thing as a sunken terrace. That's a patio, whether you like it or not.

The main reason, though, why I dislike patio heaters is that they're trying to make Britain something it's not. In Australia you can eat and party outside because the climate is kind and the evenings are balmy. Whereas here the climate is miserable and the evenings are freezing. This is great. In fact, it's precisely because we were brought up on a diet of drizzle and fish fingers that we had the biggest empire the world has ever seen.

And it's still going on today. Because there's almost certainly no such thing as global warming, we still have completely unreliable weather and that's why we have such a powerful economy. While the French and the

Italians and the Australians are at the beach, we are all sheltering from the rain and the cold, at work. The patio heater undermines all that. It brings the possibility of alfresco dining to our restaurants and ends the caveat at the end of all garden party invitations: if wet, in the village hall.

What's more, it encourages families to eat outside. And this, in Britain, never works because it's almost always too cold, and, when it isn't, it's far too hot.

And when it's far too hot, you can't sit out because you're English and you'll burn. Not smoothly either. You'll end up with strap marks, sleeve marks, a 'V' around your neck and a nose like Rudolf's. At work the next day, you'll look like a raspberry ripple. You'll look ridiculous.

Oh, and unless you're very careful, every single mouthful of food eaten outdoors in Britain will contain a wasp, and every slurp of drink a fly the size of Jeff Goldblum.

I should also explain to those who have no allergies that the four most terrifying words in the English language, if you suffer from hay fever, are 'shall', 'we', 'eat' and 'outside'.

Then there's the food itself, which, if you're outdoors, will have come from a barbecue. So, it will be nuked on one side and wriggling with salmonella on the other. And covered all over in a thin film of ash because, at some point in the cooking process, it will have fallen through the bars and into the charcoal.

Being invited to someone's house for a barbecue fills me with the same sort of horror and dread as being invited to someone's house for a fancy dress party.

Especially if they have a patio heater, because then the

guests end up like the food. Heated up on one side to the point where their flesh is starting to melt, and frozen solid on the other.

Greenpeace tells us that it's ridiculous to try to heat the outdoors and that if we're a bit nippy we should wear a jumper. But, as usual, I have a much better idea. Go inside and eat food that has been cooked in an oven. It'll taste better, you won't be eaten by a mosquito, you won't die of food poisoning, it's good for the economy and, if you turn the central heating up a notch or two and eat British tomatoes, you'll annoy Greenpeace even more than sheltering under a hot tin umbrella.

Sunday 17 July 2005

Multicultural? I just don't see it

Over the past couple of weeks Ken Livingstone has explained over and over again that Britain is now a multi-cultural, multi-ethnic society. He paints a picture of Polish plumbers helping Nigerian witches to learn the art of welding, and Greek lady-men teaching disabled Iranian dentists how to play the bouzouki.

Of course I'm sure that Ken's mayoral headquarters in London are a veritable pick'n'mix of ethnical diversity, a rainbow of skin tones and religion. I bet there are a hundred different cultures in there, all working together in right-on perfect harmony.

And naturally, when you work in an environment like this, it's easy to convince yourself that school playgrounds up and down the land are full of little Jewish boys playing football with little Muslim girls. And that every social gathering looks like the crowd scene from a British Airways commercial.

But in my world things are rather different. Because, with the exception of A. A. Gill, who claims to be Indian, pretty well all my friends are white and well off.

They live either in agreeable Georgian piles or in big, Victorian town houses, and most have two or more blond-haired children at private schools.

Only last week I was at my children's sports day and, as I lay in the long grass by the river drinking pink champagne and chatting with other media parents, I remember thinking: 'God, I love being middle class.'

You may call this sort of existence boring and you may have a point. But what am I supposed to do about it? I live in a town which, according to the most recent census, is 98.6 per cent white. Some 75 per cent of the population is Christian, with the remainder made up of those who say they have no religion at all, or they don't know, and one Jedi knight. That'd be me.

So when I go to a dinner party, the guests are always white. All my friends have white spouses. And the only diversity in the office where I work is that three of the staff are left-handed. As a result I never meet any black or Asian people. So, in this country at least, I have no black or Asian friends. Not one.

Ken would be amazed by this, I'm sure. I was slightly amazed, too, the other day, when a Jewish friend asked how many other Jews I could count as mates. 'Oh, loads,' I said without thinking. But then, when I actually looked in my address book, the correct answer was in fact 'two'.

Last week in this newspaper Michael Portillo said: 'Our signature national quality of tolerance has been strengthened, not diminished, by successive rounds of immigration.' This sounds very noble and very wise. But it's simply not true. In my case, and I suspect I'm far from unusual, my quality of tolerance has been completely unaffected by immigration, because it has made not the slightest bit of difference.

What I think of Albanians now is exactly the same as what I thought of Albanians when they lived in Albania. Nothing, because I don't know any.

I'm told things are different in London, and certainly when you look at the photographs of those killed in the bombings two weeks ago it's an absolute smorgasbord of colour and creed. But, away from the public transport system most ethnic groups tend to stick together just as firmly as we do out here in the sticks. Southall High Street, for instance, is almost exclusively Indian. Brixton is predominantly black. Golders Green is Jewish. And so on.

Only the other day I was looking round a large and well-known public school, and I couldn't help noticing that the black kids all sat next to one another in chapel.

And, what's more, we never get mixed ethnic groups in the *Top Gear* studio. Asians come with other Asians. Black kids come with other black kids. Golfers come with other golfers.

In Harrow there's to be a school for Hindus in the same way that in Yorkshire there's one for Catholics. And it's the same story on the internet. There are chat rooms for Muslims, chat rooms for Hindus, chat rooms for Poles. The whole country is full of people carving out a little enclave for themselves. In much the same way that British people living in France tend to eat and socialise with other British people.

Ken Livingstone may have engineered a multicultural environment, but I suspect that Britain isn't multicultural at all. It's simply a land mass on which an unknown number of immigrants and indigenous people happen to live.

We co-exist like birds. You don't find sparrows joining in with a flock of starlings. You don't see yellowhammers swooping down on a cherry tree with a pack of fieldfares. But, crucially, you don't see them fighting either.

This, I think, is the lesson we should learn in these difficult times. Instead of forcing a Pakistani teenager to swear allegiance to the flag and learn English and get some crummy certificate of Britishness from the local mayor, why not let him be a Pakistani who happens to live in Bradford?

Let him go to a Muslim school. Let him support Pakistan when they play England at cricket. Let him be what he wants to be.

If you say that this is Britain and we've all got to be British, that's going to annoy those whose roots lie elsewhere. But it's worse if you tell us that we've got to be multicultural. Because that's going to annoy everyone.

Sunday 24 July 2005

Children really don't want toys

Worrying news from Hamleys. According to the world's largest toyshop, parents had better start saving because the must-have children's presents this Christmas are going to cost three hundred and eleventy million pounds.

Boys are going to want a 2-foot Robosapien V2 that can bark orders, lie down and chase a beam of laser light. This will sell for about £200 and be broken before the turkey's ready.

Girls, apparently, are going to lie on the floor and thrash their legs around unless they are given a pink doll that looks a bit like Jade Goody and has a hissy fit unless you brush its hair. It's called Amazing Amanda and it will cost about the same as a new kitchen.

It all sounds very frightening, but I'd like to bet that in real terms these toys are no more expensive than the stuff my dad was given as a boy. And that, as he liked to remind me, was always an orange and a piece of string. What's more, I bet they are no more pricey than the toys that filled my sack as a boy.

I mean Spirograph. A big box set used to be phenomenally expensive, and could it respond to orders? Did it like having its hair brushed? No; and it was always just as broken just as quickly as the interactive computer toys we're told our kids want today.

In 1965 a small Corgi toy was six shillings, which in

today's money is about what the space shuttle costs. And what did it do? Well, it sat in a sandpit for a few years and then it oxidised. And then there's Paddington Bear. In 1978 you would have paid £25 for one of these, which in real terms is about the same as a Robosapien. Toys are more expensive? I don't think so.

What's changed dramatically, however, is the frequency with which children receive them. As a boy, and my upbringing was far from deprived, I was given presents on my birthday and at Christmas. Today, my children get a present from someone or other once every 24 seconds.

I still own and cherish the first wristwatch I was given, whereas parents nowadays give watches away as throwaway, 'going home' presents. My kids have lost more fountain pens in three years than I've owned in 45.

They're not unusual, either. I watch kids at their birthday parties gleefully ripping the paper off a gift and then completely ignoring it. As a result, every child's bedroom is now stuffed with board games that are still in their cellophane, car parks that are still in their boxes, and a million unopened farmyard animals.

Lego, however, is always opened and then left lying around so adults have something to tread on when they are prowling around the house at two in the morning, in bare feet, looking for the source of a noise.

We actually have enough primary-coloured bricks in our playroom to build a whole new house. And enough dolls, bears and action figures to repopulate the whole of East Germany. My youngest gets through Barbies faster than I get through cigarettes.

Once, my son expressed a vague interest in building a

small Airfix aeroplane. What he meant, of course, was that he'd like to spend a few moments watching me trying to build such a thing before returning to the PlayStation; but that was enough.

Now, all his relations, friends and godparents have taken to buying him model planes. The result: he has more aeronautical components than British Aerospace.

The problem is simple. We talk all the time about how kids are growing up so fast these days. At five they are using the f-word. At 10 they are putting it into practice. Do you know what your 12-year-old is doing on the MSN network at night? Well, for crying out loud, don't go and look because you'd die of fright. And she wouldn't even notice, because chances are she will be off her face on speedballs.

And yet, on Christmas morning, you are going to give her an Amazing Amanda. That'd be like buying Pete Doherty a train set.

Just because you wanted a model Spitfire at the age of nine doesn't mean your nine-year-old will be similarly inclined. It's more likely, in fact, he'll want a digital camera, or an iPod or a gram of cocaine. Or a webcam so he can watch his fiancée getting ready for bed at night.

Today's children have outgrown what you and I would classify as a toy by the time they are five. And before that, as you know, they'd be quite happy to receive an empty cardboard box just so long as it was covered in pretty paper.

It's not worrying news *from* Hamleys, then. It's worrying news *for* Hamleys.

Because it is only nostalgic parents who are keeping

the toy market alive, endlessly buying their kids stuff they don't want.

My eldest breezed into the kitchen the other day and momentarily removed her iPod from her ears to announce that she'd saved up £15. 'Is that enough to buy a car?' she asked.

'Of course not,' I replied scornfully.

But you know what? If all she wants is an old banger, it is.

So there we are. We bought a house with a paddock so our children could have a pony. Instead of which, they are going to tear round it in an old Mini. We wanted Jenny Agutter from *The Railway Children* and we've ended up with the Lotto Lout.

So here's my tip for bringing up children. Stop buying them toys they don't want every five minutes. And buy them stuff they do want very occasionally. On that basis, this Christmas, forget Hamleys. Think more in terms of Bang & Olufsen.

Sunday 31 July 2005

The Catch 22 of taking exercise

I was slightly alarmed last week when an appointment card from my osteopath arrived, suggesting it might be a good idea to turn up with a T-shirt, training shoes and some tracksuit bottoms.

Frankly, in any chart of 'things you don't want to hear', being told to turn up to a doctor's surgery with sports kit ranks alongside your girlfriend peering at a swab and saying, 'Ooh, it's gone all blue.'

Of course, not being a Mancunian drug dealer, I don't actually own any tracksuit bottoms, so I went to Selfridges, which, this being the height of summer, was rammed full of big, thick coats. Happily, these gave me something to hide behind as I approached the sports department.

I grabbed the first tracksuit I saw and was asked by a salesman what sort of sport I'd be doing. 'I won't,' I said loudly. 'I shall be selling cocaine to schoolchildren in it.' This seemed better, somehow. And no, I didn't want to try it on because I would never wear such a thing in a public place, so it didn't matter if it was the wrong size.

Later, the osteopath showed me down several flights of stairs into a basement where there were many implements of torture on the walls and a chap called Mr Wong in the middle of it all. Mr Wong, it turned out, was a 'corrective exercise' specialist. And he had some bad news.

To make my slipped discs better I must wear tracksuit

bottoms every day and move about even if I didn't want to go anywhere.

And so we began. He made me lie on the floor with a pressure pad under my back and told me to raise my legs while keeping the pressure in the pad level and even. It was impossible. Each time I began to raise even one leg, the dial dropped immediately to nought. Mr Wong said my stomach was 'unbelievably weak'.

This, of course, is rubbish. I fill it each day with a great deal of food and wine, and it has never split once. But before I had a chance to tell him all this, I was on all fours. Except I wasn't.

My left arm was not capable of supporting the weight of my unbelievably weak stomach, so the front left quarter of my body was being supported by my face.

Even I was surprised by this.

But having made the discovery, it softened the disappointment of not being able to do a single press-up.

Then I was standing in front of a mirror looking at my tracksuit bottoms, while Mr Wong asked me to gyrate my hips. Now I've seen elderly people in Florida doing this, so I know it's humanly possible. But I couldn't do it at all.

This gave Mr Wong all the information he needed to prepare an exercise programme, which I must follow rigidly twice a day for the rest of my life. And then he began to assault my posture.

Apparently, I must learn to stand like a Coldstream guardsman. Chest out, stomach in, head back. And I've got to stop locking my knees. I must bend them slightly, like you do when you're skiing. I tried this for five seconds and my thighs felt like they'd caught fire. Mr Wong made another note.

It turns out that there's not even to be any respite when sitting down. I must make sure my ears, shoulders and hips are all in a straight line, something that's not physically possible because I have too many chins. Also, I must ensure that the screen on my computer is level with my eyes so I don't have to look down while typing.

Fine, but I use a laptop, and if I get the screen high enough I can't see any of the keys. There are two possible solutions to this. Either I get my co-presenter Richard Hammond to write *Top Gear* from now on or I buy a new computer.

But how can I make enough money to do that if I'm having to spend half the day lying on my back with my legs in the air?

Actually, the main problem with my new exercise regime is the sheer complicatedness of it all. In one routine I must stand in front of a mirror and, while not laughing at my trousers, breathe in while holding my shoulders back. Then I hold my breath while pulling my tummy towards my spine, and then I must bend my knees until my thighs are parallel with the floor. And then I breathe out while standing up straight again.

It is in no way physically taxing, not even for someone whose muscle structure is made up of pure fat.

But the brain power required to remember what comes next is huge. I've flown an F-15 fighter jet, and that, believe me, is easier.

What staggered me about the process most of all, though, is the mind-numbing boredom and the slow rate of improvement brought about by each held breath and stretched limb. So, as you lie there in your silly trousers, stultified by the tedium of it all, you start to intellectualise the process.

And I've arrived at an alarming conclusion. If I fail to spend 27 hours a day lifting things up and putting them down again, I'll be back in a world of pain and misery. And if I do spend 27 hours a day lifting things up and putting them down again, nothing will happen.

In other words, I must spend the rest of time making a massive amount of effort for no reward at all.

Sunday 7 August 2005

A shady person's holiday guide

When I tell people I went to Iceland for my summer holidays this year, everyone says the same thing: 'Ooh. I've always wanted to go there.'

Well, it's not difficult. If you want to spend a week basking in sulphur and riding around on horses with hair like Toyah Willcox, and you've always wanted to know what guillemot tastes like, you just go to an airport and get on an aeroplane.

The fact is, however, that actually you don't want to go to Iceland at all because you've guessed that you'll come home without a suntan. And then your friends and neighbours will think you haven't been away at all. This might lead them to suspect you're poor, which, if you've bought some wine in Reykjavik, you will be.

So instead, you went to Stansted at four in the morning, where you were herded on to some godforsaken charter jet that whisked you to the Med, where you spent a couple of weeks bathing in turds, drinking wine made from old shoes and dining in restaurants that have plastic chairs.

But it didn't matter because you came home with what you think was a tan but actually was a series of pink and red stripes.

Deep down, you know you looked like a raspberry ripple. And now, two weeks down the line, it's all gone.

You have therefore spent what? A thousand pounds? On something that didn't look very nice and lasted about as long as a beach hut in New Orleans.

The history of the suntan is an interesting one. In the olden days, anyone with a brown back worked in the fields, which meant those who lived in big houses spent most of their lives under a parasol or bathing in buttermilk, to ensure their skin remained Daz white.

Even when the seaside holiday was invented (in Biarritz, incidentally), the upper classes would appear on the sands wearing what now would pass for a pretty decent ball gown.

Then, one day in 1923, Coco Chanel stepped off the Duke of Wellington's yacht in Cannes, sporting the full David Dickinson leatherman look, and suddenly everything turned around.

The Americans took note and began to appear on the world stage, having spent a whole summer with their heads in big tinfoil satellite dishes and, because the Americans had tights and cars with fins, we thought they were cool. So when the package holiday came along, it gave every office worker in Britain a chance to look like the amazing love child of George Hamilton and Michael Winner.

Not me, though. I accept that I am the colour of forced rhubarb and I spend my time on hot holidays scuttling from tree to tree. This is because, more than anything else, I loathe the way suncream costs more than a bottle of plonk in Iceland and is so damn complicated.

You need wallpaper paste on your first day and you gradually come down to Castrol GTX. Which must be topped up with a fifty-quid tub of greasy Bovril called tan deepener. I don't have time for any of this, and anyway, is there really a difference between factor 8 and factor 6? Only in the same way that there's a difference between semi-skimmed and skimmed milk, I reckon.

Then, if I do find myself in the sun, I remain convinced that a UV-ray that has travelled 93 million miles through space and survived the blitzkrieg of Earth's upper atmosphere is not going to be defeated by an invisible sheen of coconut oil.

As a result, I panic that I'm burning, which is the fourth worst thing that can happen to a man.

After seasickness, catching ebola and going on a bus.

And of course I usually am burning, because chances are I'll have forgotten to cream some exposed part, like the tops of my feet. So then I have to spend the rest of my holiday wearing socks. I learnt 10 years ago that it's cheaper, less risky and much less complicated to read your book in the shade.

Mind you, you still have to apply suncream to your children who, by 8 a.m., are already covered in sand and won't sit still. And why does children's sun protection have to have the texture and spreadability of Evo-Stik? I make mine play on the beach in frogman suits.

My wife disagrees with this. She will happily spend an hour smearing buttery sand into a child and then another hour rubbing herself down with what, so far as I can tell, is cooking fat. And no, I won't rub it on your back.

Afterwards, she goes to the beach and, using celestial alignment, organises a sun lounger so that she need not move all day. And she doesn't. She just lies there, like a roast potato, basting. The effect, though, I must say, is stunning. In just two weeks she changes from a dark-haired beauty into a leatherback turtle.

And then, of course, two weeks after we come back to England, she changes back again. Which means she may as well have spent two weeks in the Aga.

My message then is simple. If you want a tan, get a job mending the roads. Then you can go on holiday to Iceland. It is a fabulous place; but one word of warning. On one day the sun did come out, and because I was standing within the Arctic Circle, I didn't bother with protection. I still have a slab of heat rash on my neck today.

Sunday 4 September 2005

It's a very fishy world, angling

I've taken up knitting, or 'fishing' as you may know it.
This is not because I don't like my wife any more and
would rather spend six hours playing with maggots on
the side of a canal. And nor is it because I want to eat the
catch. It's much easier, and tastier, and less bony, to buy
fish from a shop, as a finger.

No. I've taken up knitting because I am now a lobster
fisherman. I have five pots, which is the legal maximum,
and each morning they need rebaiting with something
that gives off the oily aroma of a fish in distress.

So, rather than get in the Volvo to buy more mackerel
from the fishmonger, I thought it might be nice in a
natural-food-chain sort of way to buy a rod and catch my
own.

The man in the shop said that the best way to catch
mackerel where I live is to use feathers. Righty-ho. So I
shoot a seagull and use its plumage to catch the fish to
attract the lobsters. Great. And wrong. Feathers, actually,
are little strips of tinfoil, each of which hides a hook.

So I bought a packet, tied them to the line and flicked
them into the sea. Where they became attached with
ferocious limpet tenacity to a piece of seaweed. I pulled
and tugged and yanked until the line broke, so then
I went back to the shop and bought some more.

Soon this became a routine. Get up. Go to bait shop.

Buy feathers. Throw them into the sea. Lose them. Go back to bait shop. Eventually, however, I met a man who said I'd be better off with live bait and a float.

This involves a lot of tying things to other things; but soon, with a lot of making everyone stand back, I made my cast and watched as all the knots I'd tied came undone and the whole shooting match sank. Then I went back to the bait shop again.

Honestly, it would have been easier and cheaper to have thrown my wallet into the sea every morning. The shopkeeper said that in 30 years he'd never known anyone lose so much equipment. And that was before the whole reel came off on one vigorous cast and was lost as well.

Even the short walk to the sea was fraught with complications, because usually the hook would somehow attach itself to some crucial component and all the line would fall off the bobbin and become tangled. This, then, was a typical day. Get up. Walk to sea. Undo knots. Come home.

Luckily, there were many locals on hand to explain what I was doing wrong.

Everything, it seems. Standing in the wrong place. Wearing the wrong-coloured T-shirt, casting in the wrong way.

'You don't want to use sand eels,' said one gnarled and salty sea dog. 'You want mackerel.'

'Pah,' said another. 'What you use isn't as important as when you use it. Slack water's best.'

'No it isn't,' argued his mate.

This was astonishing. Man has been fishing since the beginning of time and yet still there is no definitive list of do's and don'ts. It's been 20 million years of solid arguing.

Eventually, one bloke told me to try spinners, which are shiny pieces of metal with hooks on the end. You toss them into the sea, reel them back, toss them into the sea, undo some knots, reel them back. And so on. Until you die.

It worked. Sort of. Time and time again the rod would shudder as a fish took a snap at the spinner, but since the Spanish have helped themselves to everything larger than a stickleback, all that's left in our waters is a selection of aquatic insects. And plainly my 3-inch spinner was too big to fit in their micro-mouths.

So I tried a smaller one, which flew off because I hadn't done a good knot. But then, guess what, I caught a fish.

All the evidence in my book of fishes suggested it was a firemouth cichlid, except that firemouth cichlids are usually found off Guatemala, not in the Irish Sea.

The mystery was cleared up by yet another salty sea dog, who said it was a wrasse. And then by another, who said it was a pollock. Whatever, the lobsters loved it and that night I had a sizzling thermidor.

The next day I caught more than enough to bait all my lobster pots. And then I kept right on going. Pinching the crumbs from underneath Manuel's big blue table.

I'm aware, of course, that most anglers free whatever they catch, but this isn't as easy as it may sound, technically or morally. Especially when the hook has gone right through the fish's left eye.

It seemed wrong somehow to pull it out of the sea, blind it and then throw it back again. Life for a blind fish can't be that easy.

So I hit it over the head and put it in the kitchen sink. Where it stayed until it had made the kitchen smell very bad. And then I threw it back.

I would like to conclude at this point by saying fishing is a cruel and stupid waste of time. But each cast has the heart-pulsing tension of a blackjack hand. And there's always time for just one more, because that could be the big winner. I loved it.

It's good for you, too, because fishing with spinners means you have to stand up, in the fresh air, and you need two hands. Which means you can't smoke.

Sunday 11 September 2005

The message in a litter lout's bottle

This week, after getting a custard pie in the face, I thought it might be a good idea to write about the environment, so let's kick off with the composition of sea water. There's water, obviously, and then there's some salt, a splash of chlorine, a hint of sulphur and a sprig of magnesium.

As a modern-day garnish, there are also some shoes, a couple of million plastic bottles, several hundred thousand disposable lighters, some Volvos and five and a half trillion miles of nylon rope.

I know this, because I recently bought a cottage at the seaside. It's a wild and rugged place, full of seals and ospreys.

But you tend not to notice the wildlife because after every high tide the whole place is coated with a thick veneer of rubbish.

Don't worry. The phantom flan-flinger has not turned me into a raving eco-nut. I have always had a passionate loathing for people who drop litter. Once, at a level crossing, the driver of the car in front emptied his ashtray out of the window and I became consumed with a sudden need to shave his face off with some kind of linoleum knife.

Sadly, I didn't have one to hand, so instead I scooped up all his fag ends and sweet papers and at the next set of red lights lobbed it all through his open window, saying: 'I think you dropped something.'

Unfortunately, it is not possible to find the people whose rubbish smothers my bit of coastline, which is a pity, because I have some questions. Like, for instance, how in the name of all that's holy do you cretinous imbeciles manage to lose your effing shoes when you're out for a walk?

Then there's all the discarded wiring; miles of it. This really is weird, because if you've got to do some electrical work on a broken toaster, what kind of knuckle-dragger thinks 'I know, I'll stand in the sea to do that'?

In the absence of culprits to question and then kill, I did a survey of which products are most favoured by the littering riff-raff.

In first place it's full-fat Coca-Cola. And then we have BIC lighters and Flora margarine, which begs another question. I can understand that you might take a refreshing beverage and a lighter with you on a seaside walk, but what's with the marge?

'Right, kids. Have we got everything we need for our trip to the beach? Some shoes to lose. Dad's fags. Drinks. Something electrical to mend. And oops, nearly forgot, a tub of margarine in case we get hungry.'

I can also reveal that the litterer has a fondness for salt-and-vinegar Walkers crisps; and so a picture is emerging here: margarine, crisps, full-fat Coke, smoking . . . all the modern-day thicko needs to survive. And you can't train a thicko to put his rubbish in a bin without using a cattle prod as a punishment and some dog biscuits as a reward.

So what's to be done? Well, you can forget the notion of asking a council to clear up because it would just wrap everything in red tape and make it worse, and you can't rely on environmentalists because they're too busy shoving pies into my face.

I try to do my bit, but even on my tiny piece of coastline the volume is overwhelming. And if you try scooping it up and setting it alight, you end up with a field full of eco-mentalists complaining about the smoke and a sticky, glutinous stain. That's the problem with plastic. It never goes away.

So how's this for an idea? Car makers were told recently that when one of their products reaches the end of its life, they are responsible for disposing of it properly. So why can't that idea be widened? If you find a discarded margarine tub, you take it back to Flora, which is then forced to pay you, I'd like to say £500, but 50p would probably do the trick.

This would have a twofold effect. It would make me staggeringly rich and it would force Flora and Walkers to think very carefully about the advantages of paper and cardboard.

And Coca-Cola? Well, what's wrong with glass? It's made from sand, soda ash and limestone, which means it's all completely natural. This means there's no taste transition from the packaging to the product, and that's why Coke tastes better from a glass bottle than it does from a plastic one.

What's more, when a glass bottle is dropped into the sea, it breaks into tiny pieces, which are then worn smooth by the waves until eventually they wind up in a pretty bowl from Conran on your dining-room window-sill.

You probably think the cost would be prohibitive but,

in fact, glass soft-drink bottles cost about 5.5p, while those made from plastic are around half a penny more. Of course, this saving is offset by the problems of transportation: glass breaks. But that's where my money-back scheme comes in. It would price plastic out of the market.

It turns out, however, the biggest problem with glass is that it can be used as a weapon when the pubs shut. Already, Glasgow Council has banned all glass bottles from the city centre, and now the government is thinking of making it law.

This is idiotic, because those who go around at night glassing one another are the sort of fat oafs who are doing the littering. If therefore we switch to glass, they end up dead, and there is less litter on the beach. Everyone wins.

Sunday 18 September 2005

Great no-shows of our time

In these hectic times of long hours and bad traffic I do understand that it's not always possible to be bang on time for an appointment. This is why, if I've arranged to meet someone in a restaurant, I always give them 60 seconds' grace before getting up from the table and going home.

There are many ways of insulting a man. You could snort with derision at pictures of his children or you could chop him in half with a chainsaw. But I've always argued that the biggest insult of them all is to turn up late for a meeting.

It's the stiletto subtlety of the message that hurts most of all, the quiet implication that your time is worth more than the other guy's. That it'll be OK to leave him hanging around because, hey, what else is there for him to do?

Airlines do this, insisting you turn up nine hours before the flight because that makes their life easier. Utility companies do it as well, telling you to stay at home between the hours of nine and February so that their chap can call round when he's good and ready. It's just rudeness. There's no other word.

Recently, however, my eyes have been opened to something that's even worse than turning up late: not turning up at all. It's a disease that seems primarily to affect people in the public eye, people who are probably invited to so many red-carpet do's that the easiest thing for them is to say yes to everything and then make a decision on the night.

When we record *Top Gear*, I live in constant fear that the Star in a Reasonably Priced Car will simply stay at home and I'll be forced to interview the chair.

Doesn't happen? Oh yes it does, and from the most unlikely people. Davina McCall for instance. And, amazingly, David Dimbleby.

Of course, both had entirely proper excuses but even though it was no longer possible for them to turn up we had to find a replacement at very short notice. That's very hard work and usually results in us featuring someone you've never heard of.

And, like turning up late, for me the no-show message is simple. My life is more important than yours.

For the past few weeks I've been helping to organise a charity go-karting event.

Companies pay to bring guests along and are given a celebrity team captain. Then afterwards there is dinner, and the edifying spectacle of watching Johnny Vegas vomiting into a teapot. Well, that's what happened last year, anyway.

I know this is a bore for people on television. I know the last thing anyone wants to do on a Friday night is drive to Milton Keynes to be stared at by a hundred photocopier salesmen.

And so I have no problem when 99 per cent say, 'No thanks, I'd rather spend the evening sitting in a bath full of cold vegetable soup.'

What I do have a problem with are those who say, 'Mmmm, yes, count me in,' and then count themselves out with two days to go.

First to cry off this year was Richard Hammond, the shortish chap I work with, who said he had a corporate gig that night. But when I suggested he gave his fee to the charity, he quickly realised that he could get a helicopter and go to both.

Then James May, the quiet, sensitive one, called to say he suddenly had to go to Scotland. Rubbish. Fighter pilots may find they are suddenly needed somewhere else. And lifeboatmen. But not motoring journalists. And anyway, no one suddenly has to go to Scotland.

No, I'm afraid James now has Jade Goody Syndrome; I worry that he thinks he doesn't need friends because he's got fans instead. And if he loses some of those, there are always half a million more queuing up for a slot, in his address book.

I nearly wrote a strong letter of complaint to his website because his refusal meant I had to spend two whole days trying to find a replacement, someone who I knew would say 'Yes' and then not show up on the day. If Dimbleby can do this, anyone can.

In fact, the only man in show business who is 100 per cent reliable is Michael Winner. He makes the speaking clock look sloppy.

But I can't see him in a go-kart somehow. And that left me with Ronnie Winner, who's also reliable but who is a greengrocer and is therefore not what the paying guests would consider to be a celebrity. As we speak, I'm waiting for Steve Coogan's brother to call back.

Meanwhile, the caterers keep ringing and asking how many will be there for dinner.

I suggested they got Jesus into the kitchen because it

could be five or it could be 5,000. And it was the same deal with the people supplying tables and chairs, and the taxi service.

Organising a party when you have absolutely no idea how many people will be there, or when they'll come, or when they'll go, is like making a salad blindfolded. You don't know whether you'll end up with a Niçoise or a caesar, or even if the mystery ingredients have missed the bowl altogether.

But I know exactly what I'm going to do to James May. I'm going to wait until he has a party and then, with 24 hours to go, show him what real rudeness is by taking his entire guest list on a free holiday to Barbados. But only if they all pee through his letter box first.

Sunday 25 September 2005

I've been seduced by Beardy Airways

The job of a newspaper columnist is to find something wrong with everything. To find discord where there is harmony. To sprinkle a little bit of hay fever dust all over the perfect summer's day.

Unfortunately, it's hard to find fault with something you love. And, strangely, one of the things I've loved most of all over the years is Club Class on British Airways. I love the way that, when you've finished working in some godforsaken Third World fleapit, you're welcomed on board by a homosexual in grey flannel trousers, and you think: 'Aaaah. We haven't even taken off but I'm home already.'

I love their scones and clotted cream. I love the way they have back-up planes for when yours goes wrong. And I love the calmness of their pilots, all of whom have abbreviated Christian names and reassuring three-syllable surnames. 'Welcome on board, ladies and gentlemen. Mike Richardson here on the flight deck . . .'

Oh, they've done their best over the years to shoo me away, ditching the elegant grey-and-blue livery in favour of that terrible pre-Tony multiworld design on the tailfins, and then by buying the tedious and slothful 777 to replace the brilliant jumbos.

Even when I stopped flying quite so much and they demoted me from a card that entitled me to sit on the captain's lap to a card that didn't even get me into the economy class bogs, I still stayed loyal. And what happened when they ditched Concorde? Did I work myself into a frenzy of righteous indignation. Did I rant and rave? No.

I blamed the French.

I chose to fly BA the other day even though I knew the catering staff were on a roundabout in Slough and there'd be no scones. To give you an idea of how devoted I am, the only request I made when negotiating my BBC contract was that I should fly BA whenever possible.

Last week, however, it wasn't possible, and I was sent upper-class tickets for a flight to San Francisco with the enemy. Virgin.

I'd flown once before with Beardy Airways and, having been told to put on the 'funky phones' so I could hear the safety demonstration, I seriously considered opening the door and jumping out. It's an airline, for crying out loud, not a playgroup.

Still, this time they offered to send a car to pick me up, which is something BA has never done. Of course it wasn't the limo in which Helen Mirren luxuriates in the television commercials; it was more a sort of Volvo, in fact.

But, even so, it took me to a check-in zone at Heathrow where, without even getting out of the car, my bag was checked in and my boarding card issued. That was impressive. And then I was escorted by a pretty, slim girl, which is what airline employees should be like, to the Virgin lounge.

My God. It was like walking into the Design Museum.

The whole place was dripping with the sort of style that means you can neither open nor close the lavatory doors, and the wine's Norwegian. It was fabulous.

In the BA lounge you get a cup of coffee and a biscuit, and you help yourself.

Here, there was a restaurant, bar staff, a smoking area that wasn't just a glass box like you get at a zoo, a hairdresser's, several massage parlours, some steam rooms, and a businessman on a mobile phone in a jacuzzi.

He was unusual. When you fly with BA, everyone has a laptop and they model themselves on those idiots you see in airport poster advertisements for American banks. But with Virgin, most of the passengers looked like the sort of people you might have round for dinner. One was the lighting director for the Eagles. Several were women.

I had a massage, which the girl said was like trying to ease the tension in a fridge door – this is because I'd been unable to get into the lavatory and was in agony – and then I rang the office to find out how much it was all costing. 'Oh,' said the girl, 'it's about the same as BA business.'

That's weird. Normally, two similarly priced products designed to do the same sort of thing are roughly the same. A Ford is much the same as a Vauxhall. Evian is pretty much the same as what comes out of your tap. But the gap between Virgin and BA is planetary. And we hadn't even got on the plane yet.

Superficially, it *was* the same as BA. They even had a homosexual man to welcome us on board, and scones, and seats that move around electrically. But on Virgin you have a girl in stockings and a suspender belt to give you another massage, and there's a bar. And I mean a proper bar, on which you can loll.

What's more, on BA you watch the films when they come on. On Virgin you are the master of your own destiny, thanks to technology that's bound to break all the time. It certainly did on the way home but, because we were on a 747, the flight took less than nine hours. I therefore didn't really mind.

So there we are. Finally I've found something wrong with British Airways. They're not good enough. And now it's time to put a superbug in Beardy's omelette with a question. If you can make your airline even better than the best airline in the world, how come your trains are such rubbish?

Sunday 2 October 2005

We are a nation in rude health

Soon it will be illegal to make derogatory remarks about people from other countries. But it isn't now. So we begin this morning with an observation. It's possible, I think, to sum up the people of every nation on Earth with a single word. The Americans are fat, the Spanish are lazy, Germans are humourless, Russians are drunk, Australians are chippy and the Greeks are homosexual.

Fine, but what word, do you suppose, would people from around the world use to sum up the British? I guess, if they've been exposed to our football team or some of our holidaymakers, that word might well be 'hooligans', but I really do think the vast majority would describe us as 'polite'.

There's a sense that we spend all of our time in bowler hats, standing up for ladies and offering our seats to elderly and disabled people on trains. But the perception is far removed from reality because actually, when it comes to politeness, I think the British slot neatly between the Israelis and the leopard seal, a blubbery and vicious bastard that kills penguins for fun.

Last week, *Reader's Digest* provided some evidence to back this up. Its researchers toured the nation's biggest cities, allowing drivers out of side turnings to see if they were thanked and deliberately dropping bags of shopping to see if anyone would help pick it all up again.

Each city was then awarded a courtesy rating and, with the exception of Newcastle and Liverpool, pretty well everywhere did very badly. Birmingham was branded the rudest city of them all; drop your shopping in the Bullring and chances are you will be killed and eaten.

Good. Birmingham is what Mr Blair would call a multi-cultural city and the research shows that the recent arrivals are getting the hang of what it means to be British.

First and foremost it is critical that you do not know the name of your next-door neighbour. Why should you? Living on the same street as someone is no basis for a friendship. In fact, the only time you should be noticed by your neighbours is when you've lain dead in your kitchen for nine months.

That is a uniquely British tradition: the ability to rot in peace. In Italy, you wouldn't even be cold before half the town was beating down your door to see what was wrong.

And I'm not just talking about cities. From my office window I can see half a dozen houses dotted around in the countryside, and I'm proud to say I don't know who lives in any of them. And according to Bill Bryson, things are no different in Yorkshire, which is always billed as a friendly place. He'd lived in the Dales for years before someone from the village wearily waved a hand to acknowledge his presence.

Disagree? Well, just try walking your dog through a field full of sheep and see if you like the rural welcome – which will come steaming towards your pooch from the barrel of a 12-bore shotgun.

If any tourist wanted to experience, first hand, a typically British exchange, they should head for the Grab'n'Go shop at the BBC. Here I am able to buy a bottle of Diet Coke, some cheesy Quavers and a Picnic chocolate bar without exchanging a single word with the cashier. She takes the products, scans them into her machine, points lazily at the amount on the till, takes my money, and I go away.

Think how much time this saves.

It could be argued, in fact, that Britain conquered a quarter of the world simply because no one was wasting their lives telling everyone they met to 'have a nice day'.

This brings me neatly on to my postman. I see him every morning, come rain or global warming, and the only thing I've ever heard him say is, 'Can you sign here?' Actually, nowadays we've moved on from that. Now he just points at his form, I write my name on it, and he gets back into his van. Brilliant.

It's said that true silence can only be found these days in a desert, but that is simply not true. If you want to experience absolute peace and quiet, just step into a crowded British lift. I did just that, yesterday, in Birmingham in fact, and not a single sound was made, even when the doors closed and the damn thing failed to move.

And where else in the world do you read in the newspapers about neighbours going to war over a hedge, or a borrowed hosepipe that was not returned? Can you imagine anyone in Switzerland getting road rage?

They say New York is a rude place but compared with Britain it's just a very tall, noisy version of Lucie Clayton's.

Is there any city outside Britain where young men, and quite a few young women, go out at night specifically to have a fight?

Where else can you have your head stove in for looking at someone, or have a pint glass rammed into your neck for spilling someone's drink? Nowhere I've ever been, that's for sure.

What's more, this is almost certainly the only country in the world where a major newspaper would carry a piece that began by calling the Americans fat, the Spanish lazy and the Greeks homosexual. So, on that basis, Birmingham should be proud to be voted the rudest city in Britain. Because that makes it the most British city of them all.

Sunday 23 October 2005

Four eyes aren't better than two

My eye was caught recently by a photograph in a magazine called *The Spectator*. It showed an old man in a nineteenth-century setting, and underneath it read 'Samuel Hahnemann, the founder of homosexuality'.

This seemed odd, partly because the old man in the photograph, with his mutton chops and his frock coat, looked about as gay as Sean Connery, and partly because I thought homosexuality had been invented long before the 1800s.

I therefore plunged into the lengthy story that accompanied the photograph and pretty soon my curiosity turned to bewilderment. Because it just went on and on about alternative medicine.

Only when I reached the end and turned back for a better look at the old man did I realise my mistake. Samuel Hahnemann was not the founder of homosexuality. He was the founder of homoeopathy.

For some time now I've suspected that my eyes are beginning to fail and that some spectacles might be a good idea. But I've always been nervous about coming out because of a simple truism. Not all people who wear glasses need a poke in the eye. But all people who need a poke in the eye do wear glasses.

Sadly, contact lenses are not an option, because if your eyesight is broken how are you supposed to find them when you drop them on a brightly coloured hotel carpet? Or at a football match? I've seen too many people on their hands and knees, shouting, 'Nobody move.'

There's something else, too. Regularly I appear on television with bloodshot eyes because I can't use eye drops, and I feel physically sick at the thought of having a retinal scan. I can't even watch a close-up of someone's eyes on *Casualty*. So, given the choice of putting in a pair of contact lenses or having my scrotum eaten by a pack of wild dogs, I'd have my trousers off in a jiffy.

And therefore, with an hour to kill at London City airport last week, I sauntered into the shop and decided to buy some spectacles.

It wasn't easy. A notice alongside the display asked me to stand 14 inches away and read various lines of print, each of which was in a different size. Right. So how do you know what 14 inches is in an airport shop? Eventually I figured a Berliner newspaper might be about right, so finally I had a very good reason for buying the *Guardian*.

Having used it to position my nose in the right place, I found I could read the entire eye chart, and who made it, and their address, with no difficulty at all.

So on that basis my eyes are fine.

But they're not. I cannot read *The Spectator* by the 40-watt glow of my bedside lamp. And nor can I read menus in candlelit restaurants. And so, because I didn't want to go through the rest of my life eating the wrong food and muddling homoeopaths up with homosexuals, I selected the weakest lenses and set about choosing some frames.

Now look. It's a fair bet that most people who need

spectacles are no longer in the first flush of youth, so could someone please explain why the choice was so universally cool and anti-fit hip. I wanted something from the '70s, an Aviator perhaps, or maybe a Lennon, but all I was offered was the sort of stuff worn by fierce-looking television executives and Bonio.

None of them, I felt sure, would suit me at all, but for confirmation of this I put a pair on my face and stood in front of the mirror to see what they looked like.

It was hard to say for sure, because all the advertising paraphernalia and health and safety nonsense was hanging like bunting in front of the lenses which, to make things even worse, were covered in stickers. How stupid is that?

After I'd peeled and ripped it all off, I went back to the mirror to find that I was completely out of focus. For all I knew I wasn't standing in front of a mirror at all. It could have been a huge poster of a space alien. Certainly the creature staring back at me had a face that was about three miles wide.

And it was covered in huge, pustulating spots. Jesus Christ. They hadn't been there when I'd shaved that morning, and yet now I looked like I'd been attacked with half a pint of VX nerve gas. And there was what looked like a whole tree growing out of my nose.

How come the girl at the check-in desk hadn't thought to mention this? I always make a point of telling people when they have loo roll sticking out of their trousers, or their skirt tucked into their knickers, so why had no one taken me on one side and explained that there was a giant redwood growing from a moon-sized, pus-filled crater on my nose? Bastards.

Hurriedly I removed the spectacles and felt a wave of relief as everything returned to normal. The spots went away and the tree turned back into a small hair.

Small wonder people with glasses are so irritating. Like vampires they live in a permanent state of fear that they may accidentally catch sight of themselves in a mirror.

They also know that the disintegration has begun. Today it's the eyes, but soon the ageing process will start to scythe its way through something more important.

Spectacles, then, make *The Spectator* and menus easier to read, but in the process they also bring into pin-sharp focus your own mortality.

Sunday 6 November 2005

Naughty nights in heartbreak hotel

Each week on *Have I Got News for You*, a guest publication is used for the missing words round. It could be *Successful Potato Magazine* or, when I hosted the show recently, *Fuel Oil and Tanker Driver News*.

Ho ho ho, we like to think. How amusing that someone should produce a magazine for tanker drivers and those in the fuel oil business. But you know what? Each of these comedic little bi-quarterlies represents the visible tip of a vast iceberg, evidence that below the waterline there is an army of people who want to know about all the latest breakthroughs and management appointments. People for whom fuel oil, and its transportation, pays the mortgage and feeds the kids.

And, like every other industry, there will be an annual exhibition where new stuff can be showcased. This, invariably, will be held at the National Exhibition Centre in Birmingham, which means that once a year those who replenish the nation's boilers will find themselves holed up for the night at the nearby Metropole.

When I checked in there last week, it appeared to be a normal international hotel.

There were revolving doors, lots of plants and plenty of TV pornography in the room. But in fact it wasn't normal at all. The first clue that I had entered what is surely the weirdest place in the world came as I headed for my room and passed a middle-aged woman working on her laptop in the lobby while dressed as an elf.

It turned out that a chocolate company had taken over one of the 'function suites' for its annual knees-up and, to break the ice, had insisted that the entire staff doll themselves up in hilarious fancy dress.

At eleven o'clock or so, they hit the bar and were joined by 60 public relations girls from an agency up north who'd come in little black cocktail dresses and seemed pretty keen to go all the way with Hiawatha, an enormous fork-lift-truck driver.

The elf, meanwhile, had got off with Tonto.

Those who'd failed to pull decided that the best and most amusing thing they could do was set off the fire alarm. And so there we were at 2 a.m., standing in the hotel lobby in our dressing gowns and our under-pants, watching firemen doing their best despite a gang of vomiting Smurfs. It was an eventful and reasonably sleepless night, but no matter, at least tomorrow would be quieter.

It wasn't. Tomorrow brought some girls from an endowment policy complaints call centre in Scotland and a huge number of men who may, or may not, have been involved in some way with fuel oil and tankers.

The courting ritual began again, but this time there was some celebrity spice. Yes indeed. Bill Bailey, the bedraggled comedian, had appeared at the NEC that night with Jasper Carrot and was to be found at the bar, fighting off tanker drivers with a hard stare.

The call centre girls had zeroed in on my doe-eyed *Top Gear* colleague, Richard Hammond. At one point he was wearing about six of them, and two simply wouldn't let go at all. At 2.30 a.m. I received a call from the distraught midget, saying they were following him up and down the corridor and he daren't go to his room.

It didn't matter, though, because at 2.35 a.m. some of the lads beaten off by Bill Bailey decided that the best and most amusing thing they could do was to set off the fire alarm. And so there we all were again, in our underpants, watching the firemen step over the vomit.

Then everyone sloped back to their rooms to finish cleaning the epiglottis of some accounts girl from Rhyl.

Of course, all hotels are an aphrodisiac and all business trips are similarly laced with possibility. So bring the two together, and it's an inhibition-free zone. You check in to the Metropole as a perfectly decent, perfectly normal human being, but you'll leave with an itch. God knows why televisual sex is provided in the rooms, because the real thing seems to be freely available at the bar.

Unlike a drink. At most hotels you simply tell the barman your room number and that's that. But at the Metropole you must provide documents as well, and since my wife had changed my check-in name to try to get me some peace and privacy, and I had no idea what it might be, I couldn't buy a beer.

I sympathise with the management here, because most of the guests are too drunk to know their name and certainly way too sozzled to remember that, while the bed and breakfast account is taken care of, they're picking up the extras.

On the third night I couldn't take any more, so our party went into Birmingham for a curry. We got back at midnight to find ourselves in the midst of what appeared to be every Christmas party ever held.

You can forget Ibiza or the streets of a provincial town on a Saturday night. For round-the-clock, seven-day-a-week drinking and debauchery, it's hard to top the Metropole. If you're young, free, married, old, pretty or blessed with the face of a bull elephant, you can have the time of your life. I mean, it was at the Metropole a few years ago that I saw a girl cartwheeling past the picture windows wearing nothing but a G-string. You don't even get that sort of view at the Carlton in Cannes.

Sadly, though, I'm too old for it now, so on the fourth night I went back to the hotel to pick up my bags and go home. It took a while, because someone had set off the fire alarm.

Sunday 27 November 2005

When the fame game goes funny

Sadly, because of a few lunatics at the top end of the show business ladder – the ones who adopt dolphins and drink their own urine and have tantric sex with bits of furniture – we seem to have got it into our heads that all celebrities are completely bonkers.

Well, sorry, but they're not. You may see Ricky Gervais strolling through London and you may imagine he's off for lunch with Clint Eastwood, but actually he's probably trying to find some filing cabinets.

You may see Steve Coogan driving down the M6, and you may wonder how many lap dancers he has in the footwell of his car, but in all probability he's just spent the weekend at his mum's house, talking about Mabel at No. 23.

People assume that, because I go on television and shout while driving round corners too quickly, I live in a leopard-skin house, being fed cocaine and peacock by girls in PVC. Whereas, in fact, I spend most of my time picking children up from parties. Just like you.

Normally, of course, the misconception is no big deal, but once a year I'm dragged round the nation's radio and television stations to promote my Christmas DVD.

Called *Full Throttle Power Hell Megablast*, or something.

Most of the big-name stars know the game and it's all very jolly. You rock up, tell a short, amusing anecdote, they mention your new DVD/book/play, you talk about it without trying to sound like you're plugging, then you get in the car and head off for your next appointment.

On Thursday last week I began at LBC, then moved to *This Morning* with Fern and Phillip, which is like spending 10 minutes in a warm, pink bubble bath, and then it was off to Simon Mayo on Radio Football.

Unlike anyone else in the business, Simon, who is normal and drives a Volvo, has actually read your book/watched your DVD/seen your play, so the chat is quite intelligent and pertinent, and then on the way out you bump into Ellen MacArthur, who's dropped by to talk about her latest boat.

At Radio 2 you pass Gordon Ramsay, who's doing the rounds plugging his hundred great football cock-ups video. Interestingly, he's not hurling four-letter insults at the coffee machine. And then you're on to Steve Wright, who's genial and cheeky.

And you try to be genial and cheeky too, but it's difficult because you have to remember it's next Wednesday.

It really is next Wednesday in the mind of Danny Baker. Being interviewed by The Man is like having four million volts fed through your hair. Halfway through 'Highway Star' he winds down the volume, announces to his listening public that Franz Ferdinand are not fit to grease the tank treads of Deep Purple, and then explains why he hasn't got a mobile phone and why pilchards have monocles and then, whoosh, you're back on the street, back in the car and on your way to meet someone called Colin and someone called Edith who appear on something called Radio 1.

So, what's the problem? Well, I'll tell you what the problem is. Simon and Edith and Danny and Steve know you're normal and that you're just doing a job. But, at some point in the day, you have to be interviewed by provincial radio station disc jockeys and junior reporters on lads' mags, and they think you live in a big house with Angelina Jolie and Harrison Ford and Kofi Annan, and you while away the hours shooting tigers and taking heroin.

So they try to humiliate you with idiotic competitions and stupid questions. I was interviewed over the phone by a boy from . . . Mars, I think . . . who wanted to know how homosexual I am. This involved answering some phenomenally personal questions about my sex life and, I'm sorry, but I ran away.

And straight into the clutches of some girl fresh from a *Guardian*-sponsored media studies course who didn't want to interview me so much as lecture me on the evils of being male, having a car and wearing shoes. It was all she could do to stop herself actually calling me a bastard man-pig live on air.

One breathy chap from some godforsaken station in the north announced with the tape machines rolling that he was going to ring a local business at random and I'd have to use 'my fame and celebrity' to blag something from them.

Imagine that. Imagine the hilarity of getting Jeremy Clarkson to name-drop his way into getting four yards of plumbing or a photocopier for nothing.

I calmly explained that I don't do blagging. The DJ would have none of it, though. Because he has a Rover

200 with his name, and the name of the dealer that gave it to him, emblazoned in foot-high letters down the side, he was adamant that I wouldn't even buy my own milk. No, really, I explained . . .

But it was no good, I heard the phone ringing and knew that pretty soon I was going to be speaking with some hapless shop assistant who, in all probability, would have no clue who I was and no intention of giving me a rotary washing line for nothing.

I could see nothing but embarrassment for her and nothing but humiliation for me.

So I'm afraid I removed my headphones and ran from that, too. And now the radio station has flogged the story to the local paper. Which will doubtless say I stormed out and ran back to my moated castle, where I keep bears and have a hallway full of stuffed German soldiers. If only they knew.

Sunday 4 December 2005

Cornered by the green lynch mob

Environmentalists, it seems, can't argue like normal people. You may remember, for instance, back in the summer, that a vegetarian girl, whom I'd never met before, leapt from some bushes and plunged a huge banoffee pie right into the middle of my face.

Then a Liberal Democrat MP called Tom Brake, who has the silliest teeth in politics, said he was going to table an early-day motion and drag me to London to watch him doing it. Now look. I don't want to see anyone's early-day motion, least of all a Liberal Democrat's, which would be full of leaf mulch. And I especially don't want to see it on a table.

Why can't these people write me a letter saying, 'I don't agree with you'? Why do they have to pie me and make me stand around watching a Liberal with mad teeth doing his number twos? It's beyond comprehension.

But last week the environmental protest about my way of life took an altogether more sinister turn when a Labour MP called Colin Challen made a speech in which he said he wanted me to be killed. No more pies. No more early-day motions.

Executed. Maybe he was joking, maybe he wasn't.

Strangely, he's on record as saying he doesn't believe in capital punishment, so he doesn't want Peter Sutcliffe dead. He doesn't want Ian Huntley dead. And he thinks

Gary Glitter should evade the firing squad. But he does want to see me swinging from the rafters in Wormwood Scrubs. He wants to see the faces of my distraught children on the television news and laugh at my wife as they cut me down and feed my limp, lifeless body to the prison pigs.

Now, presumably before calling for my death he'd have done some research, in which case he'd have noted the way I use sheep to keep the grass down on my land rather than driving around in a lawnmower, which uses fuel and minces all the beasties that so amaze us in David Attenborough's new programme.

What's more, a man who charges the taxpayer £64,000 a year to pay for staff would surely have had the human resources to find out that this year I grew some totally organic, fertiliser-free barley. It didn't go well. Come autumn, I had six acres of what looked like soggy grey drinking straws, which I sold for exactly £325 less than it cost to buy the seed and rent a combine harvester.

But no matter. I didn't do this out of the goodness of my heart, and nor did I do it to save the world or the whale. I did it because barley attracts lots of interesting birds that I like to look at. Selfish, I know, but, ecologically speaking, I like to think I achieved a little bit more than Colin Challen, who stomps round the Yorkshire Dales in a hideous purple cagoule, dreaming up new and interesting people he'd like to kill.

So is he mad? Well, he can't be a complete window-licker because he managed to convince 20,570 people in the last election that he should be a member of the governing party. But then again, he does have a beard, he is called Colin, and he is a member of something called the Socialist Environment Resources Association.

This is the key. On the face of it, SERA sounds like a fairly benign organisation – it raises sponsorship, for instance, for people to host low-carbon-transport dinners. Mmmm. They sound like fun.

But nothing with the word 'socialist' in its name can ever be truly benign. You may remember the Union of Soviet Socialist Republics, for example, where people were sentenced to death for arguing with the leadership. That's what Beardy is doing here. Like that fellow member of the face-hair owners' club, Stalin, he wants me dead for disagreeing with him.

I love arguing. I love filling my dining room with social workers and foxhunters so everyone can roll up their sleeves and have a damn good row. That's because I believe in freedom of speech.

Plainly, the honourable member for Morley & Roth-well does not. And nor does Tom Brake from the Liberal Democrats, and nor does that girl with the big bum who pushed a pie in my face. In fact, no one from the environmental bandwagon has even half an inkling about the concept of debate.

I do not believe that man is responsible for global warming. There are many eminent scientists who would agree. And I believe that western governments are in the process of spending billions of pounds trying to stem something over which we have no control. I believe that this money could be used to make the world a fairer, more peaceful place.

I would much rather bring clean drinking water to an

impoverished village in Sudan than bring a wind farm to the shores of Scotland. You might not agree, but surely you can see it is a reasonable argument.

Tom Brake can't. That bird with the pie can't. And certainly Colin Challen can't.

Plainly, he doesn't mind if all the Africans die of disease and hunger because, like all socialists, he wants to help the poor only about half as much as he wants to hurt the rich.

I respect that argument. I respect the people of Leeds who listened to it and voted him into office. And I'd love to chat to him about it. But that's hard when you've got a face full of banana pie, you're faced with a pile of Mr Brake's veggie droppings and you're dead.

Sunday 11 December 2005

What happened? I'm not grumpy

For the past five years I've come into your world on a Sunday morning and moaned about pretty well everything. I've complained about the wings on an Airbus and the way foxes keep eating my chickens. I've whined about people who turn up late to parties and the stickers they put on spectacle lenses so you can't see what you look like in the shop. I've looked under every conceivable stone and been grumpy about everything I've found.

Well, not today. As I write, the sky is a vivid blue and it's so beautifully warm, all the leaves are still on the trees. In my house a big log fire is roaring and the Christmas decorations are shiny and bright.

My book is still at number one in the charts, my annual DVD is selling well, the children are healthy, my wife is happy and tonight I'm going to a dear old friend's birthday party, which will be fun.

So, as a result of all this, I'm in something quite unusual. I'm in a good mood.

I looked at the huge explosion that took out half of Hertfordshire last week and didn't think, 'Oh no, what about the pollution and the effect on people with breathing difficulties.' I just thought, 'Wow. That's fantastic.'

Normally, of course, I could have filled my little corner of the page with lots of grumpiness about why the police reacted by shutting all roads in the area; but hey, they are paid to protect and serve. And they wouldn't be fulfilling their remit if they let people drive near some smoke.

I can't even get my knickers in much of a twist about the *Space Cadets* show on Channel 4, either. Good luck to all concerned is what I say.

Good luck, too, to David Cameron as he marches into the spotlight and announces that he'll be pursuing a range of green policies with lots of sustainable, wholemeal growth. Why not? He's not going to get elected if he comes out saying he's going to bring back flogging and national service.

It's the same story with Tony Blair. It must be hard running the country while trying not to laugh at your son's new face-hair. I think he's done a pretty good job these past few years. Certainly, I doubt if I could have done any better, chiefly because when I say I'm going to do something I usually do it. It can't be easy saying every day you're going to do something and then doing the exact opposite.

Usually I can whip up some ire about his wife, but not today. How would you like to go through life with that mouth? How long would it be before you were taking a big fat fee that left peanuts for a kids' charity? How else can you be expected to pay for your new house?

Even the news on the state of the planet is cheery this week. It seems the magnetic north pole is moving away from Canada so fast it could be off the coast of Russia within 50 years. So, within our lifetime, the people of northern England will get regular views of the aurora borealis. Unless, of course, they've all been killed by bird flu in the meantime, which, to be honest, seems unlikely.

There's more good news from the top of the world, too. Scientists have found that killer whales in the Arctic Ocean have overtaken polar bears to become the most contaminated creatures on earth. Analysis of their blubber has shown an extraordinarily high concentration of man-made chemicals, including pesticides, PCBs and flame retardants. This means they'll never get a headache and they'll never catch fire. And isn't that a heart-warming tale in this festive season.

It's nearly as cheery, in fact, as the conversation I had just last week with Britain's leading expert on face transplants. Apparently it would be very easy to transplant a whole head, which means I could have mine sewn on to Kate Moss's body, and how much fun would that be.

Obviously, it wouldn't move about, so I wouldn't be able to play with the more interesting parts, which is a bit of a shame, but it would keep me alive. Better still, it would even be possible to take the head off a diseased body and keep it for a while on your mantelpiece. Imagine that – being able to chat with a loved one's head if there's nothing on television.

You think I'm joking, don't you? Well, I'm not. We live in an age when surgeons can remove a head and keep it alive. Doesn't that make you feel proud and happy to be a human in the early part of the best century there's ever been?

Of course, musically it's not so good. The battle for the Christmas number one is being fought out by a boy band, the England cricket team and some chap who's written a truly woeful song about a boy getting a ride in his dad's JCB digger.

Van Halen it isn't. But, since I don't really listen to Radio 1, I don't really care.

In fact, I'm so cheerful I would like to wish even the world's most lunatic environmentalists a happy Christmas. I'd extend season's greetings also to the Health and Safety Executive, cyclists, the woman who's trying to write a biography about me, American politicians, Piers Morgan and even people who put the stickers on the lenses of spectacles in shops.

Not lawyers, though. You lot sit over the land like a pall of smoke, bringing doom and gloom to even the brightest, sunniest day. You lot can go fooey.

Sunday 18 December 2005